Narrative and Fantasy in the Post-War German Novel

A STUDY OF NOVELS BY JOHNSON, FRISCH, WOLF, BECKER, AND GRASS

CHLOE E. M. PAVER

CLARENDON PRESS · OXFORD
1999

Oxford University Press, Great Clarendon Street, Oxford OX2 6DP

Oxford New York

Athens Auckland Bangkok Bogotá Buenos Aires Calcutta
Cape Town Chennai Dar es Salaam Delhi Florence Hong Kong Istanbul
Karachi Kuala Lumpur Madrid Melbourne Mexico City Mumbai
Nairobi Paris São Paulo Singapore Taipei Tokyo Toronto Warsaw

and associated companies in Berlin Ibadan

Oxford is a registered trade mark of Oxford University Press

Published in the United States
by Oxford University Press Inc., New York

British Library Cataloguing in Publication Data
Data available

Library of Congress Cataloging in Publication Data
Paver, Chloe E. M.
Narrative and fantasy in the post-war German novel: a study of
novels by Johnson, Frisch, Wolf, Becker, and Grass / Chloe E. M.
Paver.
(Oxford modern languages and literature monographs)
Includes bibliographical references.
1. German fiction—20th century—History and criticism.
2. Fantasy in literature. I. Title. II. Series.
PT772.P37 1999 833'.0876609—dc21 98-37706
ISBN 0-19-815965-X

1 3 5 7 9 10 8 6 4 2

Typeset in New Baskerville
by Vera A. Keep, Cheltenham
Printed in Great Britain
on acid-free paper by
Bookcraft Ltd,
Midsomer Norton, Somerset

ACKNOWLEDGEMENTS

Thanks are due to all those who gave me help and support during my work on this book, which is based on a doctoral thesis submitted to the University of Oxford in 1995. I owe a great debt of gratitude to my supervisor, Professor Richard Sheppard, for his invaluable advice and constructive criticism over five years. Jim Reed, Ray Ockenden, and Katrin Kohl all took an interest in my work in its early stages. A grant from the Gerrans Fund allowed me to make an initial visit to the Deutsches Literaturarchiv at Marbach in 1991, and another grant from the British Academy funded a longer visit in 1992. Latterly I have received much-appreciated support and encouragement from my colleagues at Exeter, including Gar Yates, John McKenzie, and Gerald Opie, who read and advised on drafts of my work. I am also indebted to Bridget Deasy for her proof-reading skills.

I am grateful to Elm Bank Publications for permission to reproduce, in Chapter 4, a revised version of an article which first appeared in *The Short Story: Structure and Statement*, ed. William J. Hunter (Exeter: Elm Bank, 1996). Quotations from *Das dritte Buch über Achim*, *Mein Name sei Gantenbein*, and *Jakob der Lügner* are reproduced by kind permission of the Suhrkamp Verlag; quotations from *Nachdenken über Christa T.* by kind permission of the Mitteldeutscher Verlag; and quotations from *örtlich betäubt* by kind permission of the Steidl Verlag.

Finally, I would like to thank Oxfordshire artist Tanja Entwistle for permission to use a detail from one of her tree studies as a jacket illustration.

CONTENTS

ABBREVIATIONS

The following abbreviations are used throughout the book:

ABNG	*Amsterdamer Beiträge zur neueren Germanistik*
CG	*Colloquia Germanica*
DVLG	*Deutsche Vierteljahrsschrift für Literaturwissenschaft und Geistesgeschichte*
EG	*Etudes germaniques*
FAZ	*Frankfurter Allgemeine Zeitung*
FH	*Frankfurter Hefte*
FMLS	*Forum for Modern Language Studies*
GLL	*German Life and Letters*
GR	*Germanic Review*
LK	*Literatur und Kritik*
MDU	*Monatshefte für den deutschen Unterricht*
MFS	*Modern Fiction Studies*
MLR	*Modern Language Review*
ML	*Modern Languages*
NDH	*Neue deutsche Hefte*
NDL	*Neue deutsche Literatur*
NGC	*New German Critique*
NR	*Neue Rundschau*
OGS	*Oxford German Studies*
PMLAA	*Publications of the Modern Languages Association of America*
RLV	*Revue des langues vivantes*
SF	*Sinn und Form*
WB	*Weimarer Beiträge*
ZDP	*Zeitschrift für deutsche Philologie*

INTRODUCTION

This book investigates a trend in post-war German fiction through a comparative study of five novels: Uwe Johnson's *Das dritte Buch über Achim*, Max Frisch's *Mein Name sei Gantenbein*, Christa Wolf's *Nachdenken über Christa T.*, Jurek Becker's *Jakob der Lügner* and Günter Grass's *örtlich betäubt*.[1] What links the five texts (apart from their publication in the 1960s) is that each employs a first-person narrator who admits openly to inventing parts of the narrative.[2] In some instances, the narrators create fictional roles for themselves, inventing characters with whom they identify and imagining situations in which these characters might act; in others they freely invent scenes and conversations in an attempt to reconstruct the past. In both cases, having once projected these imaginary scenes the narrators usually retract or cancel them, either by reminding the reader that the scene is no more than hypothetical or provisional (using a phrase such as 'Denken ließe sich das' or 'So oder ähnlich'), or by rejecting the scene as unsatisfactory. At this point the narrator may substitute a new fiction, which contradicts the previous one. In this way, each narrator deliberately draws attention to the process of inventing fictions.

Although a number of critics have pointed to connections between the novels (particularly between *Gantenbein* and *Christa T.* and between *Gantenbein* and *örtlich betäubt*), these comparisons usually take the form of a passing allusion and no thorough analysis of the narrative strategies common to all five texts has been undertaken. One critic who *has*

---

[1] Uwe Johnson, *Das dritte Buch über Achim* (Frankfurt/Main: Suhrkamp, 1961); Max Frisch, *Mein Name sei Gantenbein* (Frankfurt/Main: Suhrkamp, 1964); Christa Wolf, *Nachdenken über Christa T.* (Halle (Saale): Mitteldeutscher Verlag, 1968); Jurek Becker, *Jakob der Lügner* (Berlin and Weimar: Aufbau Verlag, 1969); Günter Grass, *örtlich betäubt* (Darmstadt and Neuwied: Luchterhand, 1969). These are first editions; details of the editions from which I quote in this study can be found at the beginning of the relevant chapters.

[2] As I show in Chapter 2, Johnson's narrator disguises his identity by speaking of himself in the third person, but he can nevertheless be understood as a first-person narrator.

attempted to identify and define some of the narrative strategies which I outlined above is Jürgen Petersen, who argues
in his 1984 article, 'Die Preisgabe des Erzählten als Fiktion',[3]
that a new narrative technique emerges in German novels of
the 1960s whereby narrators draw attention to the fact that
they are inventing what we read. Instead of presenting the
fictional world as a 'reality', this new kind of novel offers the
reader mere possibilities, each of which could be replaced by
any number of variations ('Textontologisch dominiert nicht
die (fiktionale) Wirklichkeit, sondern die bloße Möglichkeit
des So-oder-auch-anders-Seins eines erzählten Vorfalls');[4]
and instead of relating actions which took place in the past,
the narrator engages in a game with future possibilities: 'ein
Spiel mit Möglichkeiten, mit potentiell Erzählbarem'.[5] Petersen also notes the role played by the subjunctive mood in
drawing attention to the hypothetical status of such scenes;
and he recognizes the importance of Frisch's *Mein Name sei
Gantenbein* in establishing this trend (although he makes no
mention of the other four novels which are examined in this
study).

While Petersen's article represents an important first step
towards a proper study of this trend, his argument has its
limitations: not only is much of the article concerned with
establishing a theoretical distinction between 'Fiktionalität'
and 'Fiktion' which is arguably of only limited use; he is also
unable, in the scope of a short article, to do justice to the
variety of devices by which narrators draw attention to the
fictional status of parts of their narrative. Most importantly,
Petersen restricts himself largely to registering the *existence* of
this technique within a selection of novels: he makes no
attempt to explore its *purpose* within individual texts. Accordingly, my own analysis (which follows in Chapters 2 to 6)
includes a detailed examination of the substance and purpose of each narrator's fictions and fantasies.

Finally, neither Petersen nor any other critic has found a

---

[3] Jürgen H. Petersen, 'Die Preisgabe des Erzählten als Fiktion. Zur Wesensbestimmung modernen Erzählens am Beispiel des deutschen Romans der sechziger und
siebziger Jahre', *Zeitschrift für Kulturaustausch*, 34 (1984), 112–19.

[4] Ibid. 113.

[5] Ibid. 114.

satisfactory label for this technique, certainly none which has gained common currency. In fact, the very absence of such a label supports my basic contention that this trend has yet to be properly investigated. In the absence of a generally recognized term for the devices which I outlined above, I call the technique 'overt fictionalization'.[6]

---

[6] It has been suggested to me that these narrators are simply liars, and it would certainly make my task easier if I could speak simply of the 'lying narrator'; but, as my analysis of the five novels will show, the negative connotations of 'liar' are not appropriate to these narrators, whose intention is not to deceive. The epithet 'der Lügner' in the title *Jakob der Lügner* refers not to the narrator but to the central character, and the moral condemnation it implies is in any case called into question in the narrative, in which Jakob's 'lies' are portrayed as positive actions. The title may have been inspired by the Hebrew etymology of the name Jakob, which means 'the deceiver'.

OVERT FICTIONALIZATION AND SOME THEORIES OF NARRATIVE

This first chapter is concerned with establishing a theoretical framework for the comparative analysis which follows, and poses the question: how far can theories of narrative help us to categorize and understand the technique of overt fictionalization? Three of the most influential narratologists writing in German since the War are Eberhard Lämmert, Käte Hamburger, and Franz Stanzel. There are few studies of the postwar German novel which do not cite at least two of this trio in their bibliography, and many such studies make explicit use of the narratological categories established by the three theorists. It seems appropriate, therefore, to begin with a look at their theories. I examine them in the order Lämmert —Hamburger—Stanzel, since this order corresponds to the increasing sophistication of the theories.

1. Eberhard Lämmert: The Realist Approach

Lämmert's *Bauformen des Erzählens*[1] seeks to categorize narratives by analysing both the relationship between the time-span of the action (the 'erzählte Zeit') and the time it takes to narrate it (the 'Erzählzeit'), and the relationship between what E. M. Forster called 'story' (a series of narrated events arranged in their chronological order) and 'plot' (the re-arrangement of these events by the narrator). Having established these terms, Lämmert constructs three 'Typenreihen': axes which set up an opposition between two formal types. The first focuses on the 'erzählte Zeit' of a narrative: at one end of the axis is the narrative which deals with a specific period in a character's life leading to a crisis, and at the other end is the narrative which follows a character from birth to

---

[1] Eberhard Lämmert, *Bauformen des Erzählens* (Stuttgart: Metzler, 1955).

death (or at least to adulthood). The second 'Typenreihe' is concerned with plot (as defined above) and sets up an opposition between the narrative which relates events in their chronological order and the narrative whose chronology is disturbed by the manipulations of the plot. Finally, the third axis is concerned with elements which are extraneous to the story, such as description and abstract ideas: at one pole is the action-packed novel in which everything has a bearing on the story, and at the opposite pole is the novel whose action is interrupted by extensive descriptions of milieu and society, or of the workings of characters' minds.

While some of Lämmert's terms, such as 'erzählte Zeit' and 'Erzählzeit', are tools which can usefully be applied to any text, his work does not allow us to categorize or understand 'overt fictionalization'. For example, if we place the five novels which I examine in this study on the first axis, we find that some (such as *Jakob der Lügner*) are closer to the first pole (since they deal with one phase in a character's life leading to a crisis), whereas others (such as *Nachdenken über Christa T.*) are closer to the second pole (since they deal with successive stages of a character's biography). Thus, while Lämmert's distinction may serve to illustrate important differences between nineteenth-century genres—it would, for instance, be of use in differentiating between the *Bildungsroman* and the majority of short stories (or between Goethe's *Wilhelm Meister* and *Werther*, to quote Lämmert's examples)[2]—it cannot be used to refine our definition of the more modern technique of overt fictionalization.

The same goes for Lämmert's third 'Typenreihe'. If we try to place our five novels on this axis, the result is inconclusive: most are a combination of action, descriptions of milieu, and psychological analysis, but no clear pattern emerges. Moreover, it is difficult to know how one should classify those novels or parts of novels in which there is plenty of action, but all of it is imagined. The protagonists of both *Mein Name sei Gantenbein* and *örtlich betäubt*, for instance, are great men of action *in their minds*. On the one hand these novels focus on the workings of the mind; but on the other hand the

---

[2] Lämmert, 37.

reader's impression is of external action. While this third axis could usefully serve to pinpoint the difference between a Kleist *Novelle* and a Balzac novel (Lämmert's examples again, though he refers also to twentieth-century stream-of-consciousness novels),[3] it is of little help in understanding the narrative devices which interest us here.

There is a different problem with the second axis (which sets up an opposition between narratives told in chronological order and narratives whose chronology is disturbed). Lämmert's argument here rests on the assumption that any work of fiction contains a 'story', a series of narrative events occurring over time, whose chronology is manipulated to form a 'plot', and whose true order can therefore be reconstructed by analysing the plot. Although this may be a reasonable assumption to make of narratives constructed according to the mimetic conventions of Realism, and even of those modernist texts in which the reader is forced to reconstruct the chronology of events from a fragmented narrative, many modern novels are characterized by the absence, or the deliberate blurring of such a 'story'. In each of the five novels examined here the narrator makes use of fictional fantasies whose action has no real temporal status, and this can make it difficult, or even irrelevant, to establish a comprehensive chronology of events.

Lämmert's bibliography hints at a possible explanation for the limitations of his theory: more than 50 per cent of the works from which he quotes or to which he refers were written in the late eighteenth or the nineteenth century. He refers to Goethe, Raabe, Keller, Stifter, Jean-Paul, and Kleist more often than he does to any single twentieth-century author, while the twentieth-century author he cites most frequently is Thomas Mann, of all modern German writers the one who might be considered the principal heir to the nineteenth-century tradition. On the other hand only four post-1945 works are mentioned. This gives the impression that Lämmert's main interest lies in nineteenth-century Realism. Notwithstanding his claim that his typology 'nivelliert von sich aus historische Besonderheiten',[4] Lämmert's theory

---

[3] Ibid. 40–1.   [4] Ibid. 251.

deals in categories which are demonstrably empirically derived and therefore historical.

2. Käte Hamburger: Logical and Illogical Literature

In her 1957 work, *Die Logik der Dichtung,* Hamburger set out to define epic, drama, and poetry in terms of the logical laws which govern them.[5] Since the present study is concerned exclusively with prose fiction, we need only consider her definitions of first- and third-person narrative here.[6] Hamburger bases her theory on what she terms the 'Aussage-system', which she explains as follows: when a statement is made in real life, there is a speaker or subject and a genuine temporal relationship between the time at which the speaker makes the statement and the time at which the event or events described took place. What is described belongs to the speaker's field of experience and exists or existed independently of whether (s)he makes a statement about it.

In a third-person narrative, however, what is described is not part of the field of experience of the narrator, but part of the field of experience of the characters, and the 'narrator' (a term she rejects as nonsensical in this context) is no more than a literary device by which the experiences of the characters are recorded. In other words, Hamburger argues, it would be wrong to suggest that the 'narrator' makes a statement *about* an object, because that object does not exist independently of the narration. Rather, the object is created through the act of narration: 'Das Erzählen, so kann man auch sagen, ist eine Funktion, durch die das Erzählte erzeugt wird, die *Erzählfunktion* [. . .]. Das heißt, der erzählende Dichter ist kein Aussagesubjekt, er erzählt nicht von Personen und Dingen, sondern er erzählt die Personen und Dinge; die Romanpersonen sind erzählte Personen.'[7] Hamburger goes on to demonstrate that once the past tense (together with the so-called 'historic present') is placed in a

---

[5] Käte Hamburger, *Die Logik der Dichtung* (Munich: dtv, 1987).
[6] Ibid. 15–170, 272–97.
[7] Ibid. 123.

third-person narrative, it loses its grammatical function of designating the past, since it cannot refer to a real past (the narrator's or the reader's), and refers not to the characters' past but to their present. Hamburger also notes the import-ant role played in third-person narrative by descriptions of the workings of the characters' minds (often transcribed using *erlebte Rede*).[8]

In contrast, Hamburger argues, first-person narrative is to all intents and purposes a 'Wirklichkeitsaussage' or real state-ment. The subject 'Ich' describes events which belong to its own field of experience and therefore exist independently of their narration, and there is a real temporal relationship between the events narrated and the narrator's present moment, such that any past tense refers to a grammatical past, and any historic present is 'historic'. Moreover, accord-ing to Hamburger, the first-person narrator describes third persons as objects, having no access to their thoughts.[9]

As we can see, Hamburger's theory rests on an absolute distinction between first- and third-person fiction. Yet the five novels which I examine in this study all tend to blur this distinction. Not only is the perspective of one novel (*Das dritte Buch über Achim*) indeterminate throughout (because the first-person narrator appears to speak of himself in the third person throughout); wherever the narrators fictionalize in the manner described in the Introduction they appear to

[8] Whereas *direkte Rede* uses a tag such as 'dachte er' together with speech marks to indicate that thoughts are being reported (and *indirekte Rede* uses a similar tag followed by a subordinate clause), *erlebte Rede* (English: free indirect speech) dispenses with such overt textual markers and indicates instead by grammatical means that the thoughts are reported, transferring thoughts which were originally in the first person and present tense into the third person and past tense (with equivalent transitions for other tenses). In addition, the following devices often signal the presence of *erlebte Rede*: questions and exclamations; the use of particles ('doch', 'nun', etc.) which are a feature of the character's colloquial speech rather than of the narrator's more literary, written discourse; and the use of temporal and spatial phrases which indicate that the thoughts emanate from the consciousness of a character within the fictional world. The following quotation from the opening page of *Tonio Kröger* illustrates the technique: 'Tonio verstummte und seine Augen trübten sich. Hatte Hans es vergessen, fiel es ihm erst jetzt wieder ein, daß sie heute mittag ein wenig zusammen spazieren gehen wollten? Und er selbst hatte sich seit der Verabredung fast unaufgesetzt darauf gefreut!' What Tonio actually thinks (though no doubt less coherently) is: 'Hat Hans es vergessen, fällt es ihm erst jetzt wieder ein', etc.

[9] *Die Logik der Dichtung* (1987), 272–8.

cross the boundary from first-person to third-person fiction, as defined by Hamburger. These violations of Hamburger's rules occur in two distinct ways (though they may be used in conjunction):

First, some of the narrators invent third-person roles which they subsequently 'adopt', at which point they begin to refer to the figure as 'ich'. However, the statements which the narrator makes in the guise of this 'ich' do not conform to Hamburger's definition of a first-person statement, for the narrator invents his persona as he narrates it, so that the events experienced by the persona do not exist independently of their narration. As a result, no real temporal relationship exists between the narrator's present moment and these experiences (so that any past tenses which are used refer not to the narrator's past, but to the invented figure's present).

Secondly, some of the narrators invent scenes and conversations involving other characters in the novel. In doing so, their statements also take on the characteristics of Hamburger's third-person narrative, since the narrators allow themselves privileged access to the minds of other characters, whose thoughts they record using *erlebte Rede* and interior monologue. Once again, the events which they narrate do not exist independently of their narration.

Of course, these deviations do not necessarily explode Hamburger's theory, but the fact that the theory forces us to see these narratives as 'deviants' or 'rule-breakers' (without offering any criteria which would allow us to understand better the *function* of the technique) is not particularly helpful. Although the five novels appeared after the first edition of *Die Logik der Dichtung*, Hamburger had a chance to modify her theories in the light of new trends in post-war fiction when, in 1968, she revised her work for a new edition. While these revisions amount mainly to a strengthening of her original argument through the clarification of her terms, she does acknowledge a trend among modern novelists for combining first- and third-person perspectives, which are sometimes interwoven to such an extent that the exact structure of the narrative becomes difficult to determine (and she cites Robbe-Grillet's *La Jalousie* and Grass's *Hundejahre* as examples). No further discussion follows, however: Hamburger simply notes that this phenomenon may affect the tenses of a narrative and concludes that the new technique is a deviation from the true laws of third-person fiction: '[eine] Abweichung von der Struktur der "echten Fiktion", der eigentlichen Er-Erzählung'.[10] In Hamburger's terms, overt fictionalization is simply illogical.

One might suppose that like Lämmert, Hamburger comes to these conclusions because her work is based largely on nineteenth-century fiction; but the range of her reading is, as far as can be ascertained from the references in her work, far less selective than Lämmert's. Clearly it is possible to be well read in twentieth-century works and still to exclude the narratological principles on which many major post-war works are based.

3. Franz K. Stanzel: The 'Circular' Argument

Like Hamburger's *Die Logik der Dichtung*, Stanzel's *Typische Formen des Romans* and *Theorie des Erzählens* are concerned largely with distinguishing between narrative points of view,[11] but where Hamburger identifies two narrative perspectives (first-person and third-person) Stanzel identifies three, which he calls 'Erzählsituationen' (abbreviated to 'ES'). Apart from the first-person narrator, Stanzel identifies an 'authorial' (or in more traditional terms omniscient) narrator, who has some substance as a character but stands outside the world of those whose lives he describes; and a 'personal' narrator, who effaces himself so thoroughly that the reader is barely conscious of his presence and has the impression of seeing events through the eyes of one or more of the characters. Stanzel does not argue that all narratives can be reduced to one of these three categories, but rather that there is a continuum of forms between these three types, so that they can be pictured as equidistant points on the circumference of a circle.

---

[10] Ibid. 113–14.
[11] Franz K. Stanzel, *Typische Formen des Romans* (Göttingen: Vandenhoeck & Ruprecht, 1964) and *Theorie des Erzählens*, 4th edn. (Göttingen: Vandenhoeck & Ruprecht, 1989, originally 1979).

There is little difference between the theories set out in *Typische Formen des Romans* (1964) and the later *Theorie des Erzählens* (1979). Having confidently asserted in 1964 that there could be no types of narrative situation other than those which he had posited, Stanzel was in no position to argue for new types of narrative when he came to update and expand his theory. Moreover, while Stanzel conceded that *Typische Formen des Romans* needed updating, he implied that this was because narratology, rather than fiction itself, had moved on since the publication of his earlier work.[12] Consequently, in *Theorie des Erzählens* he reiterates his theory of the three 'Erzählsituationen', but examines in more detail the intermediate forms between the three main types on his circle, and provides a pictorial representation of the 'Typenkreis', around which he places a number of representative works.

Nevertheless, Stanzel's theory is undoubtedly the most convincing of the three examined so far. Not only does he display by far the widest range of reading, and refer to almost twice as many twentieth- as nineteenth-century authors and works (including examples of the *nouveau roman* and other post-war experimental prose); he is also aware of the limitations of his theory (insisting that it can only be used to categorize the predominant narrative situation of a work of fiction); and he is flexible, recognizing that works can occupy an arc rather than a single point on his circle's circumference. Moreover, Stanzel takes an interest not just in existing narrative forms, but also in potential but as yet unrealized forms, anticipating the possible development of new types of narrative which would occupy those sections of his circle which have yet to be 'colonized' ('besiedelt'). He suggests, for instance, that should the technique of interior monologue continue to develop, this mode of writing would then occupy the rather sparsely populated 'Innenperspektive' axis on his circle and might lead to the development of a fourth 'ES'. This may seem a bold claim, but by suggesting that his theory allows for an abundance of as yet unfulfilled narrative possibilities, Stanzel is able to pre-empt any accusations that

---

[12] *Theorie des Erzählens*, 9–10, 68–9.

his typology represents nothing more than 'normative Vor-schreibungen'.[13]

One of the chief merits of Stanzel's *Theorie des Erzählens*, as far as the present study is concerned, is that it gives a much more detailed account than Hamburger's *Logik der Dichtung* of narratives (not all of them modern) which combine third- and first-person perspectives.[14] Firstly, Stanzel argues (using *Mein Name sei Gantenbein* as an example) that the switch between first and third person need not necessarily involve a switch in pronouns (from 'ich' to 'er'): whenever first-person narrators tell fictitious stories or adopt fictitious roles which they can alter at will, they take on the role of an authorial narrator, for 'Verfügungsgewalt über die dargestellte Welt der Charaktere ist ein Privileg, das eigentlich nur dem auk-torialen Erzähler über Er-Figuren vorbehalten ist'.[15] Like Hamburger, then, Stanzel classes the kinds of narratorial fan-tasies and imaginings with which this study is concerned as examples of third-person narrative within first-person texts. Stanzel goes on to argue that a switch between first-person and third-person reference often occurs when the 'erzähl-endes Ich' (the narrator at the time of writing) is trying to keep his past self (or 'erlebendes Ich') at arm's length: 'das *er* ist ein auf Distanz gehaltenes *ich*.'[16] This seems to me to be a useful principle, and although the narrators of *örtlich betäubt* and *Mein Name sei Gantenbein* may appear to be doing the reverse (for they invent third-person roles which they then adopt as an 'ich') their motivation is ultimately the same: in inventing new identities for themselves they are indeed attempting to escape their past lives. Stanzel also links the increasing frequency with which such switches in point of view occur in the modern novel with the tendency of con-temporary writers to problematize identity (an idea which is equally relevant to *Gantenbein* and *örtlich betäubt*). However, Stanzel's comments are less helpful in explaining the role of the narrator's imaginings in the other three novels examined in this study. For while these narrators invent scenes involving third persons (and in doing so demonstrate the 'Verfügungs-gewalt über die dargestellte Welt der Charaktere' which is,

---

[13] Ibid. 87.   [14] Ibid. 135–48.   [15] Ibid. 142.   [16] Ibid. 135.

for Stanzel, typical of the authorial narrator), they are not primarily concerned with 'Bewußtseinsspaltung' or with problems of identity.

My main objection to Stanzel's theory is that little is gained by trying to situate the type of fiction with which I am concerned on his 'Typenkreis'. To begin with, the five novels examined in this study would certainly not all occupy exactly the same position within the 'Ich-ES' sector, since they devote varying amounts of narrative time to the 'erzählendes Ich' and the 'erlebendes Ich' (a key factor governing a first-person novel's place on the circle). Moreover, it is a moot point whether one should place these novels in the 'Ich-ES' sector at all, as this would not account for the combination of first- and third-person perspectives which is, if one judges them by Stanzel's own criteria, one of their chief characteristics. Stanzel argues that the modulations of the 'ES' within a narrative can be seen in terms of a fluctuation within an arc of the circle: 'die ES des einzelnen Werkes ist nicht ein statischer Zustand, sondern ein dynamischer Vorgang der ständigen Modulation oder des Oszillierens innerhalb eines bestimmten Bogenabschnittes des Typenkreises.'[17] However, I want to account for the fact that the ostensibly first-person novels which will be examined in later chapters make use, to a greater or lesser extent, of the narrative situations which belong in the *opposite* half of Stanzel's circle. This phenomenon can be described using the metaphor of 'oscillation' only if it is possible to oscillate through an arc of 180 degrees, whereas Stanzel's notion of 'Oszillieren innerhalb eines bestimmten Bogenabschnittes des Typenkreises' suggests a far more restricted movement. Indeed, because the first- and third-person perspectives are diagrammatically opposed on Stanzel's circle, his theory encourages the view that these modes of narrative are mutually exclusive and that to combine them is an infringement of unwritten narratological law.

It is interesting that having discussed *Mein Name sei Gantenbein* in detail, Stanzel makes no attempt to locate it on his circle. He does, however, place Thackeray's *Henry Esmond* on

---

[17] *Theorie des Erzählens*, 240.

the circle, having demonstrated that the narrator freely combines third-person (authorial) and first-person perspectives
in his description of his life. Stanzel's decision to place the
novel at the mid-point of the 'Ich-ES' sector would seem to
do little justice to a work which is written almost entirely in
the third person. Another work which shows up the limitations of Stanzel's 'Typenkreis' is Robbe-Grillet's *La Jalousie*,
which Stanzel locates at two points on his circle, one in
the first-person sector and one in the personal sector, each
accompanied by a question mark. This reflects the absolute
ambiguity of the text, for it is impossible to gauge whether
the 'onlooker' in the novel is a first-person narrator, or
whether a third-person narrator is depicting the fictional
world through the onlooker's eyes. However, precisely because it can be located at two distinct points on the circle
without occupying the middle ground between them—i.e.
without any 'oscillation'—*La Jalousie* calls into question Stanzel's theory.

Thus, while Stanzel claims that his theory can accom-
modate all imaginable forms of narrative, it cannot really
cope with works which do not respect his categorization. As
with Hamburger's theory, the result is that these narrative
forms have to be seen as 'rule-breakers', although, unlike
Hamburger, Stanzel does at least attempt to provide more
positive criteria for understanding the techniques involved.
Finally, while there can be little objection to Stanzel's prediction that in the future, currently vacant points on his circle
may be 'colonized' (just as the personal sector came to be
colonized at least a century after the authorial sector), he
might also have considered the possibility that narrative
might develop by exploding the circle, by breaking in practice the barriers between theoretically different narrative
situations.

While this analysis of the work of Lämmert, Hamburger,
and Stanzel may seem to confirm my contention that we are
dealing here with a technique which has yet to be accounted
for adequately, it leaves us with a rather negative definition of
what the novels to be examined have in common: they are
a series of works which do not have a 'story' in Lämmert's
sense; which transgress the boundary between first- and

third-person perspectives laid down by Hamburger; and which call into question the validity of Stanzel's 'Typenkreis'. The only positive statements which can be made on the basis of my discussion so far is that the five narrators use alternating narrative perspectives and that this alternation may be connected with the theme of the fragmentation of identity. We can arrive at a more positive definition with the help of Brian McHale's *Postmodernist Fiction*.

4. Brian McHale: Textual Worlds

The argument of McHale's *Postmodernist Fiction*[18] rests on a distinction between modernist and postmodernist fiction which he establishes with the help of the Russian Formalist notion of 'the dominant'. The Formalists saw literary evolution in terms of a rearrangement of the hierarchy of elements which make up a literary work. When one constituent element comes to determine all the others it is known as 'the dominant', and developments in literature can thus be explained in terms of shifts in the 'dominant'. For McHale, the 'dominant' of modernist fiction is *epistemological,* while the 'dominant' of postmodernist fiction is *ontological.* Naturally, any text is likely to have both epistemological and ontological concerns, since epistemology and ontology are two key areas of philosophical enquiry. Nevertheless, the 'dominant' determines which is the more important or more urgent concern. In other words, it determines which set of questions a reader should ask about a text first.

McHale has a specific set of questions in mind. He prefaces Part One of his book with a quotation from Dick Higgins, who distinguishes between 'the Cognitive Questions (asked by most artists of the 20th century, Platonic or Aristotelian, till around 1958)' and 'the Postcognitive Questions (asked by most artists since then)'.[19] McHale sees Higgins's Cognitive Questions: 'how can I interpret this world of which I am a part? And what am I in it?' as typically modernist, since

---

[18] Brian McHale, *Postmodernist Fiction* (London: Routledge, 1989).
[19] Ibid. 1.

they relate to epistemological concerns, and he adds to them his own list of questions posed by modernist writers:

What is there to be known?; Who knows it?; How do they know it, and with what degree of certainty?; How is knowledge transmitted from one knower to another, and with what degree of reliability?; How does the object of knowledge change as it passes from knower to knower?; What are the limits of the knowable?[20]

Narrative strategies which can be used to foreground these questions include: the use of multiple perspectives, the use of a single 'centre of consciousness' or limited point of view, variants on interior monologue, the deliberate dislocation of chronology, and the deliberate withholding of information. Each of these techniques helps to pass on to the reader the epistemological difficulties which are the modernist novel's central concern. For McHale, the detective story, with its characteristic quest for knowledge, is the epistemological genre *par excellence* and the low-art counterpart to the modernist text.

In contrast, postmodernist fiction—as McHale defines it —poses questions concerning different modes of being, or 'worlds', including Higgins's 'Postcognitive Questions': 'Which world is this? What is to be done in it? Which of my selves is to do it?', as well as the following questions listed by McHale:

What is a world?; What kinds of worlds are there, how are they constituted, and how do they differ?; What happens when different kinds of world are placed in confrontation, or when boundaries between worlds are violated?; What is the mode of existence of a text, and what is the mode of existence of the world (or worlds) it projects?; How is a projected world structured?[21]

Like the modernist text, the postmodernist text has a low-art equivalent, science fiction, and McHale shows that postmodernist writers borrow plot-lines and motifs from science fiction as a convenient way or foregrounding questions about worlds.

However, McHale's main interest is in the *formal* strategies which can be used to foreground ontological questions. His argument here is based on the assumption that the world

[20] Ibid. 9.   [21] Ibid. 10.

projected within a literary text has its own ontological structure or mode of being. From the beginnings of poetics,
McHale argues, one finds references to the 'otherness' of
the fictional world, which presupposes that an ontological
boundary separates the real world in which the reader exists
from the world in which the characters of a fiction exist.
Another strand of poetics recognizes that there is a relationship of similarity (but not identity) between the fictional
world and the real world. Benjamin Hrushovski, for example,
conceives the notion of a 'double-decker' effect: the narrative text both projects a coherent 'world' and refers outside
itself to the real world. However, the theory which is most
valuable to McHale's argument is that of Roman Ingarden,
who sees the literary work as stratified, with the material book
and its typography forming a kind of foundation upon which
all the other layers of the literary text rest.[22] For our present
purposes, we need concern ourselves only with Ingarden's
third stratum, the stratum of presented objects. According
to McHale, Ingarden's most valuable insight is that, taken
together, the objects presented in the text constitute a 'world'
or 'ontic sphere'.

Having established this theoretical basis, McHale translates
these ideas into an examination of actual narrative strategies.
Whereas Ingarden sees his strata as belonging firmly to the
background of the literary work ('the skeleton of the layers
and the structural order of sequence in a literary work of art
are of neutral artistic value')[23] many of the postmodernist
devices for foregrounding ontological concerns which are
catalogued by McHale deliberately draw attention to this
textual skeleton. Again, for our present purposes, we need
only concern ourselves with the ways in which, according to
McHale, authors draw attention to the third of Ingarden's
strata, the stratum of presented objects. This can happen in
two ways:

(*a*) The postmodernist text may foreground the 'projection'
of a fictional world. In this connection, McHale quotes
Oedipa in Thomas Pynchon's *The Crying of Lot 49*, who asks:
'Shall I project a world?'[24] and cites Faulkner's *Absalom, Absa-*

---

[22] McHale, 30–3.   [23] Ibid. 39.   [24] Ibid. 10.

lom!, in which two characters, having reached an epistemological dead end in their investigation of a mystery, are forced
to resort to imagining what must have happened: 'Abandoning the intractable problems of attaining to reliable knowledge of *our* world, they improvise a *possible world*; they
fictionalize.'[25] In this way, McHale suggests that when doubt
about the possibility of attaining reliable knowledge (a typical
modernist concern) is pushed to its limits, epistemological
concerns 'tip over' into ontological ones, and lead to the
projection of fictional worlds.

(*b*) Speaking of the common literary device of ambiguity,
Ingarden argues that where ambiguity is sustained over a
length of text this may lead to 'opalescence' or 'iridescence'.[26]
McHale argues that many postmodernist writers depict this
'opalescence' in slow motion, so that projected objects or
events 'flicker' in and out of existence. In this way, scenes are
brought into being (by narration) and then cancelled by the
narrator, their existence denied or negated. The theorist and
novelist Christine Brooke-Rose also touches on this
phenomenon in a discussion of postmodernism, and uses
David Lodge's term 'self-cancelling discourse'.[27] And indeed,
Brooke-Rose appears to be well qualified to discuss self-
cancelling discourse, since McHale quotes from one of her
own novels, *Thru*, in which she describes a locale, and then
cancels it out with the words: 'Scrub that.'[28] McHale's own
terms for this device, 'narrative under erasure' and 'self-
erasure', are inspired by Jacques Derrida's practice of placing
words 'sous rature', that is, of crossing words out while en-
suring that they still remain visible. McHale explains: 'Physically canceled, yet still legible beneath the cancelation, these
signs *sous rature* continue to function in the discourse even
while they are excluded from it.'[29] In the case of self-
cancelling narrative, McHale argues, the reader concretizes
or visualizes part of the textual world, which is subsequently
withdrawn or cancelled out, but the event or object continues

[25] Ibid.   [26] Ingarden, quoted in ibid., 32.
[27] Christine Brooke-Rose, *A Rhetoric of the Unreal: Studies in Narrative and Structure, Especially of the Fantastic* (Cambridge: Cambridge University Press, 1981), 356.
[28] McHale, 106.   [29] Ibid. 100.

to 'function' in the sense that the reader cannot simply erase it from his or her memory. McHale distinguishes between two methods of 'self-erasure' in postmodernist texts. On the one hand, a narrator may project a scene, object, or character and then withdraw it using a phrase such as 'Scrub that', 'Retake!' or 'I erase him', often replacing it with a more suitable or satisfactory version. On the other hand, a narrator may simply place mutually exclusive scenes or events side by side. In this case each version cancels out the others, though here the cancellation tends to be implicit rather than explicit. McHale explains this second form of erasure with reference to Jorge Luis Borges's text 'The Garden of Forking Paths', in which Borges suggests that any text is a series of 'branchings': at each 'fork' the narrator is faced with one of two possible outcomes and must make a choice. In most narratives these choices are made 'silently' (that is, they are made before the narrative is set down on paper, so that the reader is unaware that such choices existed). But Borges's narrator has heard of a Chinese novel in which *all* the possibilities are realized at once.[30] What we find in postmodernist texts, McHale argues, is a watered-down version of this apocryphal Chinese text: at certain points in the text, the narrator declines to make a choice and instead realizes two, three, or more possibilities simultaneously. Like many of the devices which McHale discusses, the device of erasure—in both its forms—violates the 'law of the excluded middle', according to which two propositions may both be false but not both be true. In this case, two mutually exclusive states of affairs, actions, or 'worlds' exist simultaneously. These devices correspond closely to what I have called overt fictionalization.

McHale's work may also help to explain why so little is gained by applying the theories of Hamburger and Stanzel to the texts examined in this study. When McHale expresses dissatisfaction with Tzvetan Todorov's theory of the fantastic, he blames Todorov's 'epistemological approach'. Todorov, he says, looks at texts which show a superficial level of epistemological hesitation (posing the question: are the events

---

[30] McHale, 106–7.

naturally or supernaturally motivated?), but fails to see that the underlying structure involves a dual ontology, a frontier zone between this world and another one. In a similar way, Hamburger and Stanzel both base their theories on distinctions between 'points of view' and establish their categories by asking questions similar to Higgins's Cognitive Questions, namely: 'Who is narrating?; What are the limits of the narrator's knowledge?; How does the narrator's perspective affect the objects or events which he or she describes?' In order to interrogate a postmodernist text it would be necessary, at least in theory, to pose the equivalent of Higgins's Postcognitive Questions, and these would include some of the questions listed by McHale: 'What is the mode of existence of a text, and what is the mode of existence of the world (or worlds) it projects?; How is a projected world structured?'

In practice, as my analysis in the chapters which follow will show, these are not necessarily the questions which present themselves most pressingly to the reader of the five novels examined here (although they do play a part in my analysis). Nevertheless, McHale's approach is clearly useful to the present study. Whereas Hamburger's and Stanzel's theories tend to classify the five novels as rule-breakers, without giving us a vocabulary with which to talk about them, McHale's theory not only provides a useful vocabulary ('erasure', 'forking paths', etc.), but also allows us to understand overt fictionalization as a method by which writers foreground the construction and constitution of the fictional text and the constitution of the self. From a literary-historical point of view, McHale's work suggests reasons for the popularity of the technique in the post-war years, in particular that it grows out of techniques which had their heyday in the early part of century (for example, the use of limited or conflicting perspectives and of the so-called 'unreliable narrator'), and whose use had therefore become somewhat clichéd by the post-war period. As we shall see, some of the authors whose work is examined in this study employed such techniques in their early works before moving on to the more innovative technique of overt fictionalization. Moreover, whereas Hamburger and Stanzel's approaches tend to isolate this technique, offering us nothing with which to compare it,

McHale's approach invites us to see it as just one of a repertoire of related narrative techniques which are employed by
a large number of post-war writers in Europe and the Amer-
icas.[31]

Finally, to accept McHale's theoretical framework is not
necessarily to accept that the five novels to be examined here
are *postmodernist* texts. This is certainly not a term which is
commonly used of the five authors concerned (except, perhaps, in connection with Grass's apocalyptic novel *Die Rättin*).
On the rare occasions when the term 'Postmoderne' is used
by German-speaking critics, it tends to be associated with
writers such as Botho Strauß, Patrick Süskind, and Peter
Handke. And inasmuch as Postmodernism is associated with
the undermining of key post-Enlightenment beliefs (a belief
in linear progress; in man's capacity to intervene rationally
in social affairs; in the value of the unified, integrated personality; and in absolute truths and universal values) and with
a corresponding suspicion of those discourses which purport
to be able to interpret the world in its totality—including
religions, political theory, mythology, history, and psychology—it is, I think, an inappropriate term to use of Johnson,
Frisch, Wolf, Becker, and Grass.[32] While all five writers are

---

[31] In placing the technique in an international context I do not, however, mean
to neglect the German context. The technique of overt fictionalization can be
linked to the German picaresque tradition, with its fabulating narrators (e.g. Felix
Krull and Oskar Matzerath); to Schlegel's Romantic Irony, with its aim of destroying
the illusion of reality; and to Brecht's similarly anti-illusionary *Verfremdungseffekt*,
which Frisch proposed to adapt to prose fiction (Max Frisch, *Gesammelte Werke in
zeitlicher Folge*, ed. Hans Mayer in collaboration with Walter Schmitz, 6 vols. (Frank-
furt/Main: Suhrkamp, 1976), II. 600–1).

[32] In offering this extremely condensed account of postmodernist concerns, I
acknowledge that the debate surrounding postmodernism is both extremely complex and still evolving. A broader view of postmodernist debates in the German-
speaking world can be gleaned from the following: Axel Honneth, 'Der Affekt
gegen das Allgemeine. Zu Lyotards Konzept der Postmoderne', *Merkur*, 38 (1984),
893–902; Hans Egon Holthusen, 'Heimweh nach Geschichte'. Postmoderne und
Posthistoire in der Literatur der Gegenwart', *Merkur*, 38 (1984), 902–17; Heinz-
Günter Vester, 'Konjunktur der Konjekturen. Postmodernität bei Pynchon, Eco,
Strauß', *L80* (1985), 11–28; Theo D'haen, 'Postmodern Fiction: Form and Function', *Neophilologus*, 71 (1987), 144–53; Gudrun Klatt, 'Moderne und Postmoderne
im Streit zwischen Jean-François Lyotard und Jürgen Habermas', *WB* 35 (1989),
271–92; and Ferdinand Fellmann, 'Poetische Existentialien der Postmoderne',
DVLG 63 (1989), 751–63. I also recommend David Harvey, *The Condition of Postmodernity: An Enquiry into the Origins of Cultural Change* (Oxford: Blackwell, 1989).

aware of the fragmentation and loss of values which characterize our experience of the modern world (and while all are suspicious of religion, and some of political theory), all five remain committed, to a greater or lesser extent, to a humanist tradition which strives for growth and development (personal or social), and which presupposes the existence of such universal values as justice, humanity, and morality.

2

UWE JOHNSON: *DAS DRITTE BUCH ÜBER ACHIM*

1. Introduction

When his first novel, *Ingrid Babendererde* (published post-humously in 1985), was rejected by East German publishers, Uwe Johnson moved to West Berlin to secure the publication of his second novel, *Mutmaßungen über Jakob* (1959). In this novel the reader is invited to unravel the mystery of the central character's death with the help of statements from witnesses, whose evidence sometimes conflicts. McHale would classify it as a typical modernist text because it employs both multiple perspectives (which are juxtaposed in such a way as to highlight the limitations of each character's knowledge) and elements borrowed from detective fiction. Moreover, the complex form of *Mutmaßungen* ensures that problems associated with the accessibility and reliability of knowledge are passed on to the reader. In fact, these modernist strategies were taken to such an extreme in *Mutmaßungen* that it is difficult to see how Johnson could have pursued them further in his next novel, *Das dritte Buch über Achim*.[1] While this novel retains some elements of the detective's quest for truth (a journalist seeks to piece together the life of the East German racing cyclist Achim T. with the help of 'witnesses', chief among them Achim himself), a single perspective, that of Karsch, dominates the narrative, and— apart from some initial preconceptions about the GDR— this perspective is not noticeably biased or blinkered (on the contrary, it is often frustratingly neutral, making it difficult to determine his opinion of the characters or action). Most

[1] Uwe Johnson, *Das dritte Buch über Achim* (Frankfurt/Main: Suhrkamp, 1961). All further references to the novel are included in the main text. Johnson wrote an alternative (and greatly condensed) version of Karsch's visit to the GDR entitled 'Eine Reise wegwohin, 1960' (in Uwe Johnson, *Karsch, und andere Prosa* (Frankfurt/Main: Suhrkamp, 1964)).

importantly, Karsch is not constrained by the limits of his own knowledge, for he freely and openly invents scenes and conversations as he composes his account of Achim's life, often adopting an omniscient perspective which allows him to see into the minds of the other characters.

The action of the novel is considerably more straight-forward than that of *Mutmaßungen über Jakob*: in 1960 the West German journalist Karsch travels from Hamburg to a town in the GDR at the invitation of a former girlfriend, Karin, now a well-known actress and partner of the top East German racing cyclist Achim T. Karsch's decision to prolong his visit to the East and to attempt a biography of the cyclist (the third such biography to be written) appears to be motiv-ated as much by his desire to fathom Karin and Achim's relationship as by his fascination with the differences be-tween East and West German culture.[2] The novel chronicles Karsch's work on the biography, which falls roughly into three phases. At first, he freely invents scenes and conver-sations from Achim's youth to supplement the information which has been supplied by Karin, Achim, and Achim's father. Subsequently, Karsch meets with Frau Ammann, the *Lektorin* assigned to him by the publishing house which has commissioned the biography, and she asks him to improvise a series of (equally fictional) variations on his account of Achim's childhood. And finally, Achim begins to intervene in the writing process and obliges Karsch to erase a whole series of passages from the biography.

Despite this relatively accessible plot, the novel is highly

[2] The reader's suspicion that Karsch hopes to revive his relationship with Karin is never confirmed, but there are undertones of sexual tension throughout the novel. Karsch decides to extend his stay only after reading a newspaper interview in which Achim claims that he has not yet found the woman he wants to marry (which implies that Karin may be 'available') (39). Moreover, the narrator tells us that Karsch is intrigued by 'Achims ausgelieferter Blick auf Karins harten haarigen Nacken bei jedem Abschied' (47–8). On other occasions, too, he is particularly aware of physical contact between Karin and Achim (105, 106). Karsch even imagines two spectators at a cycle race discussing Karin, who—they say—has now left Achim and is having an affair with Karsch (164). While the narrator does not deny this rumour, he seems to enjoy playing with the reader's expectations, for when his interlocutor asks 'Wird es nun doch die Geschichte von der Dame mit den beiden Herren?' (133), the narrator reproaches him for reading too much between the lines.

complex. It is structured as a dialogue between the narrator and an unidentified interlocutor, whose questions, comments, and objections propel the narrative forward. As Johnson explained in his *Frankfurter Vorlesungen*, this unnamed figure grew out of one of Karsch's Hamburg friends who telephones him on his return to the West.[3] Hence the friend's question 'Wie war es denn?', with which the novel ends (337), is also the first question posed by the unnamed voice (10). The interlocutor also asks after Karin ('Wie geht es ihr?' (27)), implying that he (or she) has either met Karin in the past or has heard about her from Karsch. However, although initially inspired by Karsch's curious friends, the interlocutor figures in the text primarily as an 'implied reader', the imaginary recipient whom an author envisages reading the text as he writes.[4] In an interview with Horst Bienek, Johnson speaks of both the interlocutor's functions —as friend and as reader—without making any distinction between them:

Karsch wird nach seiner Rückkehr aus Ostdeutschland in Hamburg *von den anderen Leuten, die dageblieben sind*, gefragt, wie es denn war und ob man da leben könne, und wie es dem und jenem geht. Und nachdem Karsch dies eine Weile beschrieben hat, wird er [. . .] zurechtgewiesen *von dem zwischenfragenden Leser*: es ist so gar nicht spannend![5]

Johnson's comments also suggest that he conceived of the text as a dialogue between *Karsch* and an interlocutor, not between a *narrator* and an interlocutor. He therefore invites us to identify the third-person narrative voice (which, at first

---

[3] Uwe Johnson, *Begleitumstände. Frankfurter Vorlesungen* (Frankfurt/Main: Suhrkamp, 1980), 191–3.

[4] For instance, the narrator discusses with the interlocutor the constraints placed on him by 'der Verlag, der dies verkaufen soll' (26), indicating that the imagined dialogue takes place while the book is in the process of being written. Later, the narrator tells him that an article written by Karsch is 'der Text, den du jetzt als Antwort auf die Frage "wer ist Achim" gelesen hast' (45). The narrative is inconsistent, however, and at one point the interlocutor protests that Karsch cannot be about to return to the West because they are only half-way through the book: 'Und wieso sind es dann noch so eine Masse Seiten?' (129). This suggests that the interlocutor has the completed text in front of him (a logical impossibility, since he has not yet asked the questions which drive the narrative forward to the end of the text).

[5] Horst Bienek, *Werkstattgespräche mit Schriftstellern* (Munich: Hanser, 1962), 85–98 (90; my italics).

sight, appears to set this text apart from the other four novels examined in this study) with Karsch, who evidently uses the third person as a mask of objectivity to write about his experiences in the East.[6] Several clues in the text itself invite this reading: not only does the narrator speak of *remembering* things which Karsch wrote or heard during his time in the East, suggesting that Karsch and the narrator are one and the same (104, 143); the interlocutor also makes a telling slip of the tongue when he asks 'Deswegen bliebst du da? Blieb Karsch da?' (37). Nevertheless, I sometimes use the term 'narrator' in the analysis which follows as a convenient way of distinguishing between Karsch the narrator of the novel we are reading (writing in Hamburg after his return from the East) and Karsch the biographer (working in the GDR on his account of Achim's life).

Critical opinion is divided on this question, however, and not all critics accept that the narrator and Karsch are identical. Confusion arises partly because the narrator knows certain things which Karsch cannot: he is able, for instance, to see into the minds of various characters. For this reason, critics tend to argue either that the narrator *is* Karsch, writing about himself in the third person, and that he is therefore not an omniscient (Stanzel's authorial) narrator, but a non-omniscient first-person narrator, *or* that the narrator is omniscient (because he frequently knows things which Karsch cannot know) and therefore *cannot* be Karsch.[7] Such

---

[6] Not only does Johnson speak in the above quotation of a dialogue between Karsch and the implied reader; he is also asked explicitly by Bienek: 'Das, was Sie aufgeschrieben haben (wollen wir das einmal genau festhalten), sind also nichts anderes als Karschens Erzählungen?' Johnson replies: 'Es sind seine Erzählungen' (Bienek, 91).

[7] Carolyn Wellauer, for instance, argues that 'The story the first-person narrator tells [. . .] is told from Karsch's perspective because he *is* Karsch', and the proof she puts forward in support of this theory is that he is not omniscient: 'The first-person narrator, contrary to Migner's statement about his being omniscient, never knows more or less than Karsch actually experienced, observed or felt' (Carolyn Ann Wellauer, 'The Postwar German Novel of Speculations' (unpublished doctoral diss., University of Wisconsin, 1976), 100–1). Wolfgang Schober, on the other hand, sees the narrator and Karsch as two distinct individuals, because, he argues, the narrator is omniscient: 'Das Erzählmedium [. . .] läßt sich [. . .] keine Einschränkungen auferlegen. Es weiß genau, wo Karsch sich nur auf Vermutungen stützen kann' (Wolfgang Heinz Schober, *Erzähltechniken in Romanen. Eine Untersuchung erzähltechnischer Probleme in zeitgenössischen deutschen Romanen* (Wiesbaden: Athenaion, 1975), 119–23 (121)).

critics apply the 'logical' criteria established by theorists such as Hamburger and Stanzel, according to which a narrator cannot be both first-person and omniscient. Yet authors are under no obligation to make their works logically coherent and Johnson is particularly fond of this kind of illogicality, so that it may be a fruitless task to try to resolve the contradictions inherent in his texts.[8] However, if we accept that Karsch and the narrator are identical, then it is possible to interpret the narrator's apparent omniscience as another example of Karsch's tendency to fictionalize: just as Karsch the biographer, when inventing scenes for his biography, adopts temporarily the position of an omniscient narrator, allowing himself to see into the minds of Achim (79–81) or Achim's father (140–2), so Karsch the narrator permits himself to see through the eyes of Karin (11–12) or of a sales assistant in a typewriter shop (114–15).

2. 'Denken ließe sich das': Karsch's Fictions

Throughout this study I have taken the view that the technique of overt fictionalization has to be viewed within the broader context of a novel's narrative technique, since it

---

[8] In a much-quoted passage from his essay 'Berliner Stadtbahn', for instance, Johnson writes: 'Der Verfasser sollte zugeben, daß er erfunden hat, was er vorbringt, er sollte nicht verschweigen, daß seine Informationen lückenhaft sind und ungenau. Denn er verlangt Geld für was er anbietet. Dies eingestehen kann er, indem er etwa die schwierige Suche nach der Wahrheit ausdrücklich vorführt, indem er seine Auffassung des Geschehens mit der seiner Person vergleicht und relativiert, indem er ausläßt was er nicht wissen kann' (Uwe Johnson, 'Berliner Stadtbahn', in Eberhard Lämmert et al. (eds.), Romantheorie. Dokumentation ihrer Geschichte in Deutschland seit 1880 (Königstein/Ts.: Athenäum, 1984), 334–7 (337)). This statement cannot be understood literally, for since the object of a fictional narrative does not exist independently of the narrative, but only comes into being as it is narrated, there is nothing which the author/narrator cannot know about the characters and events which he has invented. Johnson appears to be treating his characters as real people, a habit which manifests itself elsewhere. In his Frankfurter Vorlesungen, for instance, he suggests that a critic write to the character Karsch, and gives him Karsch's address in Milan (Begleitumstände, 181). Elsewhere, he says of Gesine Cresspahl (whom he admits is 'eine erfundene Person'): 'Ich erzähle das, was diese Mrs. Cresspahl für wichtig hält in ihrem Leben, ich bin also begrenzt durch die Aufgabe, die sie mir gestellt oder vielmehr erlaubt hat' (Ree Post-Adams, 'Antworten von Uwe Johnson. Ein Gespräch mit dem Autor', German Quarterly, 50 (1977), 241–7 (244)). See also n. 4 above.

makes little sense to analyse it in isolation. In the case of *Das dritte Buch über Achim*, the scenes and conversations which Karsch invents form part of a repertoire of devices used by Johnson to foreground aspects of the text which normally remain invisible. In fact, Johnson draws attention to the invisible aspects of *two* texts (a duality reflected in Johnson's original title for the work, 'Beschreibung einer Beschreibung'): the account of Karsch's exploits in the GDR which we read under the title *Das dritte Buch über Achim*, and the unfinished biography which would have become the third book about Achim, and from which long extracts are reproduced in the novel. For instance, Karsch foregrounds the process of revision and redrafting which the biography undergoes while it is still in the making (a process which belongs to the pre-history of a text, and of which we are not normally aware when we read the final version). He describes a draft version of the biography's opening pages (a conversation between strangers at a railway station) and his decision to discard it (49–57); and he later describes a whole series of possible approaches to the description of Achim's life, each indicated by a letter of the alphabet, and ending 'G. Oder noch anders. H. Oder gar nicht. I. Wieviel Buchstaben hat das Alphabet?' (282). It is not only Karsch the biographer who has problems knowing how to begin, however. Instead of simply beginning the novel with an expository scene or conversation, the narrator describes a *possible* beginning which he has rejected as unsatisfactory: 'da dachte ich schlicht und streng anzufangen so: sie rief ihn an, innezuhalten mit einem Satzzeichen, und dann wie selbstverständlich hinzuzufügen: über die Grenze, damit du überrascht wirst und glaubst zu verstehen' (7). In this way, the narrator foregrounds the decisions which faced him during the process of composition (and of which the reader is normally unaware). The lower-case letter with which the novel begins contributes to the impression that this is no more than a tentative, provisional beginning. The opening also draws attention to the relationship between the narrator and his implied reader, that is, the imaginary recipient of the book whose opinions and reactions the narrator anticipates as he writes. Of course, it is not uncommon for the narrator of a novel to address this implied reader directly (particularly in novels of the eighteenth and nineteenth centuries), but Johnson takes this convention to the extreme by conducting a full-scale conversation with the implied reader, allowing him to interject and answer back throughout the novel.

Karsch's imaginings can be seen as part of the broader strategy illustrated above, for another way in which Karsch draws attention to the process of composition of the biography is by foregrounding the projection, revision, and retraction (or 'erasure') of the fictions he invents about Achim. In most cases, the reader is told in advance that the scene which follows is a fabrication. In the following example, for instance, Karsch admits to conjuring up scenes which might have happened in Achim's childhood. 'Die Mitgliedschaft' refers to membership of the Hitler Youth:

> Karsch nahm die Mitgliedschaft einfach für wahrscheinlich. Ich gebe zu: als er irgend wo auf die frühere Zugehörigkeit des Vaters zur (inzwischen verbotenen) sozialdemokratischen Partei gestoßen war, fing er an mit zu spielen mit dem leeren Raum, der zwischen dieser Angabe und einer Wahrscheinlichkeit gelegen Möglichkeiten ansog: wenn Achim sich darum nicht kümmert, muß er es später richtigstellen. Selber schuld. (81–2)

Since this is a typical example of Johnson's idiosyncratic and highly demanding prose style, I will begin by pointing out three stylistic features which appear again and again in the passages which I quote in my analysis. First, the orthography is unorthodox ('irgend wo' is written as two words); second, the punctuation is irregular (he omits the commas which should separate off the participial clause—'zwischen dieser Angabe und einer Wahrscheinlichkeit gelegen'—from the relative clause which contains it); and third, he switches mid-sentence, without making the transition explicit, into interior monologue (so that from the words 'wenn Achim' onwards we are inside Karsch's mind). While 'Angabe' refers to the revelation that Achim's father was a social democrat, 'eine Wahrscheinlichkeit' refers to the likelihood that Achim was a member of the Hitler Youth, as were all boys of his age. When he speaks of envisaging a 'leerer Raum', a realm of possibilities, lying between these two details, Karsch implies that he is so fascinated by the potential for tension between a social democrat father and his conformist son during the Nazi era that he begins to dream up scenarios which would express this tension, even though he knows that these may later have to be discarded if Achim's own testimony reveals them to be untruthful. We are therefore aware, when we read the passage which follows (82–6), that the scene is no more than a possible and provisional version of events.

On one or two occasions, however, we are alerted to the fictional status of a scene only *after* it has been projected. We assume, for instance, that a scene describing Achim as a young boy pleading with his father to give him a bicycle (78–9) has been related to Karsch by Achim, until Karsch suddenly relegates it to the realms of possibility and conjecture: 'Etwa so. So ungefähr. Achim konnte zur Not auch später sagen was anders vorgekommen war als Karsch sich dachte. Karsch ergänzte nun bedenkenlos was er wußte aus dieser Zeit und was er für Achim wahrscheinlich glaubte' (79). Once again we are made aware, but this time only in retrospect, that the scene must be regarded as a provisional version of events, which may have to be corrected and re-placed at some point in the future. Other phrases which are used to cancel out or erase Karsch's imaginings include: 'Nein. Das kann ich mir nicht recht vorstellen' (139); 'möglich ist die Sabotage' (146); 'Denken ließe sich das' (146); 'Ungefähr so?' (147); 'Vielleicht so?' (233); and 'Ich kann es mir nicht vorstellen' (331). All of these statements remind us that the scene which we have just read is just one of many possibilities.

Other devices which serve to draw attention to Karsch's fictions include lists of possible alternatives from which he has not yet made a choice (and which indicate that the narrative future remains open);[9] and the use of *Konjunktiv II*, which indicates that a scene is mere conjecture.[10] The

---

[9] For instance, the narrator imagines possible settings and scenarios for a story in which Achim's father is a resistance fighter: 'Harmlose Straßenecken oder das Bild von zwei zufälligen Männern beim Bier bieten sich an. Auch das Abgeben eines vollständigen Herrenanzugs in der Gepäckaufbewahrung des Hauptbahnhofs oder Flugblätter in der Jackentasche, der plötzlich unterkellerte Alltag, vorsichtiger Spateneinstich im nächtlichen Garten. Und warum nicht eine Übernachtung' (146).

[10] One fictional passage begins: 'Sehr aufregend könnte an Frau Liebenreuths

interlocutor also plays a part in reminding us of the fictional
status of these passages. After one description of Achim's
childhood he asks: 'Und wenn es nun doch ganz anders
war?' (86), indicating that other possible versions of Achim's
childhood exist. Similarly, when Frau Ammann suggests that
Karsch write an account of Achim's father's involvement in
an act of sabotage, the interlocutor protests 'Das ist doch da
nicht drin' (139). Karsch, however, asserts his right to play
with fictional possibilities: 'Nein warte mal. Laß mal ver-
suchen' (139).[11]

   While devices similar to those described above are employed in all five of the novels examined in this book, one
device is peculiar to Johnson's novel. This involves using
typographical means to foreground the shift from reality to
fantasy ('reality' meaning, in this context, the *fictional* reality
of the characters) and is used primarily when Karsch is
discussing drafts of his biography with Frau Ammann. The
following example records Karsch's response to Frau Ammann's suggestion that he revise his account of Achim's
childhood to show that Achim's commitment to socialist
values had begun to manifest itself even before the end of
the War:

— Sie meinen demnach: sagte Karsch: daß wer heute ganz anders lebt
und nützlich für eine neue Regierung besser damals schon hätte sollen
würgen am Krampf der Magennerven, du Günter
— Ja ja ich kann alles gut sehn. Ob sie ihm wohl ein Schild zwischen die
Finger binden wie bei Hermann Löns?
— Du, Günter. (138)[12]

Up to the words 'schon hätte sollen' Karsch is addressing
Frau Ammann, but with the words 'würgen am Krampf der

Klingelknopf eine sauber um den Nagel gerundete Fingerspitze erschienen sein'
(157). Similarly, Achim's response to one of the passages invented by Karsch to
describe events from his childhood is: 'So könnte [ich] auch gewesen sein' (87).

   [11] Normally the interlocutor converses with Karsch the narrator, but Johnson
does not aim at consistency (see n. 4 above), and here the interlocutor appears to
be talking to Karsch the biographer.
   [12] In this and the following few quotations I have followed exactly the typography
of the Suhrkamp edition (in which new paragraphs are not indented) in order to
show more clearly the visual effect of Johnson's unorthodox syntax and orthography (although it is, of course, impossible to know whether Johnson specified
this typographical scheme or simply followed Suhrkamp's house style).

Magennerven' we move into Karsch's imagination (and, simultaneously, into Achim's consciousness, because Karsch gives himself the powers of an omniscient narrator). Karsch then conjures up a scene in which Achim fights against feelings of nausea as he and his friend Günter watch a man being hanged by Nazi soldiers. Where another author might use punctuation (a colon, for instance, or a dash) to mark this transition from reality into fantasy, Johnson uses the conspicuous *absence* of punctuation (lack of a full stop after 'sollen', lack of a capital letter for 'würgen', despite its position at the beginning of a new paragraph) to draw attention to the shift. This scene is developed over the next page until it is erased in the same way:

[Achim] lief weg über den leergebombten Platz, die Schultasche schlug ihm gegen die Beine das Herz in die Kehle: wenn er jetzt Feigling sagt Schlappschwanz der kann nicht mal zusehen wie sie einen aufhängen: ein Deutscher Junge hat keine Nein. Das kann ich mir nicht recht vorstellen. Er hat es mir anders erzählt. (139)

Here again, the simple expedient of omitting a full stop and starting a new sentence (indicated on this occasion by a capital letter) foregrounds the shift from the imagined scene back to Karsch's reality, although the shift is further highlighted in this case because the last sentence of the imagined scene is cut short after 'keine' (the word 'Angst' would complete the Nazi slogan, as we know from p. 96). Karsch's explicit rejection of the scene as unsatisfactory, because implausible, further draws attention to its fictional status.

   The same principle is at work in the following examples, both of which introduce fictional scenes concerning Achim's father:

— Ach so: sagte Karsch: Sie denken daran daß Achims Vater gelernt haben könnte und mit ihm ein vorstellbarer Leser
aus der Parade ordentlich gereihter Leichen im sommerlichen Park vor dem qualmenden Hauptbahnhof [. . .]. (140)

and:

Sie meinen also:
der Verein für große Verschlechterung des Lebens in Deutschland
— warum sagen Sie nicht: die deutschen Faschisten, die mit den Geldern des Kapitals in seinem Dienst

der (die: such dir aus) verlangte die Billigung für was er tat begeistert und bekam sie nicht durchaus widerwillig; man sollte sich entsinnen der drängenden Trauben deutscher Frauen auf dem Bahnhof der sächsischen Kleinstadt in der verewigten Mittagstunde, als der Sonderzug des Hausanzünders sie durchfuhr. (143)[13]

In the first example, the shift from (fictional) reality to Karsch's imagination falls in the paragraph break between 'Leser' and the lower-case 'aus der Parade'; in the second case, between Frau Ammann's objection to Karsch's circumlocution, which is cut short after 'in seinem Dienst', and the lower-case 'der (die: such dir aus)'.

In an analysis of *Mutmaßungen über Jakob*, Colin Good makes the following comments on the speculations of two of the characters (using the term 'narrative' in the restricted sense of passages of text attributable to the narrator, as opposed to passages of characters' monologue or dialogue):

> In a conversation between Rohlfs and Gesine as the two speculate together after Jakob's death as to why the latter was visited by Jonas in Dresden, the contributions to the conversation of each in turn become longer and longer. Their individual speculations thus begin to take on, as we lose sight of the context (i.e. within a speculative conversation) a reality and validity of their own, so that the 'imagined' descriptive detail about the meeting begins in itself to look and sound like narrative.[14]

As soon as the speculative 'frame' recedes into the background, the reader begins to experience the imagined scene as real, that is, as a piece of authoritative narrative. This process seems to me to be at work in *Das dritte Buch über Achim*, too: even when we are told in advance that the scene we are about to read is merely a product of the narrator's imagination, we soon become immersed in the projected

---

[13] Periphrasis, of which there are two examples here ('der Verein für große Verschlechterung des Lebens in Deutschland' for the Nazis, and 'der Hausanzünder' for Adolf Hitler), is a feature of Johnson's style in the novel. Other examples include 'der vormilitärische Kinderverband der Führerjugend' for the Hitler Youth organization (81); 'der Sachwalter' for Walter Ulbricht; and 'die Öfen zur Verbrennung der Opfer und Besserwisser' for the gas chambers (144). This device testifies to Johnson's desire (expressed in 'Berliner Stadtbahn') to find a language beyond the ideologically coloured languages of East and West (illustrated here by Frau Ammann's tendentious phrase 'die deutschen Faschisten, die mit den Geldern des Kapitals in seinem Dienst') ('Berliner Stadtbahn', 335).

[14] Colin H. Good, 'Uwe Johnson's Treatment of the Narrative in *Mutmaßungen über Jakob*', GLL 24 (1971), 358–70 (368).

scene and experience it as real, such is the power of fiction. Indeed, the process by which the conjectural frame recedes is sometimes encoded in the grammar of the text, when *Konjunktiv II* (indicating possibility) gives way to past indicative (indicating reality), as in the following example:

Sehr aufregend könnte an Frau Liebenreuths Klingelknopf eine sauber um den Nagel gerundete Fingerspitze erschienen sein, die mit Druck und Senkung den offenen Stromkreis schließt und auf der anderen Seite regelmäßige Schläge der Hammerfeder gegen eine isoliert aufgehängte Glockenscheibe auslöst: das bekannte Klingelrasseln dröhnt durch den düsteren Flur. (157)

Here the imaginary scene gradually 'begins to look and sound like narrative', to use Good's phrase, and at about the point where the grammatical switch takes place (with the verb 'schließt' or at the very latest with the verb 'dröhnt', which is no longer dependent on 'könnte') the reader, too, begins to treat the narrated events as though they belonged to Karsch's personal experience (until, that is, the narrator returns the whole scene to the subjunctive: 'Der an der Tür könnte ihm durch beredte Enttäuschung oder etwa Bedauern im Ausdruck des Gesichts beipflichten' (160) and then retracts the scene altogether). The reader's experience confirms McHale's theory that just as words which are placed under erasure 'continue to function in the discourse even while they are excluded from the discourse', so scenes which are erased from a narrative continue to function in the reader's understanding of a text because we cannot simply erase a scene from our memory once it has been projected.[15]

3. Karsch's Fictions and the Historical Process

For the most part, critics have restricted themselves to acknowledging the presence of the imagined scenes described above.[16] However, the fictions are more than just a clever

---

[15] McHale, 100.

[16] Colin Riordan, for instance, speaks of Karsch's use of 'unashamedly fictional reconstruction which uses the criterion of probability' (Colin Riordan, *The Ethics of Narration. Uwe Johnson's Novels from 'Ingrid Babendererde' to 'Jahrestage'* (London: Modern Humanities Research Association, 1989), 26). Carolyn Wellauer notes an

formal device: they give us an insight into Karsch's understanding of the relationship between historical events and
the individual. Karsch is particularly fascinated by the way in
which actions motivated by purely private concerns can have
historical implications and by the way in which historical
processes (which may appear to be supra-personal) are
driven by individual actions and desires. Consequently, what
interests him most in Achim's childhood and adolescence
are the points of contact between Achim's private world and
key historical events of the times (the Nazis' rise to power,
the Second World War, the advance of the Red Army into
German territory, the division of Germany, and the founding of the GDR). A few examples will illustrate this point.

In Karsch's imaginings, one of Achim's most salient characteristics as a child is his desire to be accepted by his peer
group. He wants a bike, for instance, because 'die anderen
haben auch alle eins' (78). Karsch shows that this childish
desire to fit in, while harmless in itself, can take on a more
menacing aspect when political forces act upon it. For the
Nazi authorities are able to recruit individuals to their own
projects by manipulating this desire to belong: not only does
Achim feel ashamed when he is reprimanded in front of his
classmates because he has not collected as many recyclable
materials (for the Nazi war effort) as others have (80); he is
also desperate to join the Hitler Youth, not from political
motives, but because his friend Eckhart and other classmates
have been called up (82). When at last Achim does join,
Karsch imagines his relief that his isolation is at an end: 'er
mochte nicht allein an der Straße stehen und zusehen wie
die Fähnlein in die Stadt zurückmarschiert kamen müde
und zerkratzt und zerschunden, er wollte sich nicht immer
nur erzählen lassen von dem was sie Dienst nannten' (87).
In a similar way, a perfectly innocent children's game, *Völker-
ball*, can become a propaganda instrument: in a scene set at
some time during the War, none of Achim's classmates wants
to play on the 'American' team because 'die müssen ja ver-
lieren' (80).

'interesting interplay between fact and invention' (Wellauer, 99). Neither explores
the technique further.

Karsch does not appear to condemn Achim for his childish need to belong, but Johnson implies that since our private emotional needs can be manipulated in the service of political movements, we must learn to take responsibility for our actions, at least when we are old enough to understand the connection. In this sense, Achim provides a negative example, for even as a young adult, when he commits himself to the new East German state, he is still giving in to his desire for 'die Empfindung der Zugehörigkeit' (196).

For a while, then, Karsch is able to indulge freely his view of the historical process and of the individual's place in it; but in his meetings with Frau Ammann he comes up against a very different view of history. Frau Ammann subordinates the personal to the historical: in her view, individuals should act out of a historical consciousness (not from private motives) and individual actions should point forward to historical goals (specifically, to the historical goals of Socialism). Moreover, in order to make Achim's biography conform to this model, she is prepared to reinvent aspects of his past (thereby further submerging his individuality). Karsch is at first willing to adopt Frau Ammann's approach (although the reasons for his compliant attitude remain opaque), but the experiment fails because his own habits of thought prove to be too deeply entrenched.

For instance, Frau Ammann advises Karsch to revise his description of Achim's childhood to show that Achim's commitment to socialist values had taken root well before the end of the War (136). Karsch consents, and conjures up a scene in which Achim witnesses the execution of a suspected traitor by Nazi soldiers in retaliation for the bombing of a local air-raid shelter. While his friend Günter takes a boyish delight in this dramatic spectacle, Achim is physically repulsed by the hanging and experiences it as a pointless revenge. Yet not only does Karsch feel obliged to cancel out this scene because it does not correspond to what Achim has told him about his past; his fiction also shows that he has not fully understood what Frau Ammann is asking of him ('sie hatte nicht das gemeint', as the narrator remarks (139)). For Achim—as Karsch portrays him in his fiction—has no historical understanding of the situation, only an instinctive sense that a revenge-killing is wrong. Moreover, he remains plagued by fears that his peers will reject him ('Wenn er jetzt Feigling sagt Schlappschwanz der kann nicht mal zusehen wie sie einen aufhängen' (139)). In other words, in Karsch's fiction Achim's private motivations still complicate the way in which he acts in historical situations. It seems that Karsch's (Western) mental habits are so deeply rooted that he finds it difficult to think in any other way.

Frau Ammann then asks Karsch to try out another possibility: he is to imagine a scene in which Achim's father, Herr T., commits an act of sabotage, building a design fault into a new German warplane which is of vital importance to the war effort (139). Once again, Karsch is happy to consent to her suggestion (even though there is no evidence that Achim's father was involved in such subversive activity). But although Karsch has no problems working with the subject-matter demanded by Frau Ammann (he duly shows Herr T. sabotaging the plane), he continues to treat this subject-matter in a distinctively Western manner, for he cannot help but present Herr T.'s motivation as an indissoluble mixture of political and private motives. Inasmuch as Karsch suggests that Achim's father is spurred on both by fear that his son is being corrupted by an inhuman ideology ('Ich muß aus dem Jungen einen Menschen machen' (141)) and by a desire to bring the War to a swift end to avoid further pointless killings ('Macht ein Abschuß weniger etwas aus? Ist ein halbes Jahr etwas wert?' (141)), his story is in line with Frau Ammann's programme. But the interior monologue which Karsch invents for Achim's father suggests an additional motivation: 'Gestern nacht sollen sie im Norden alles hingemacht haben aber auch alles. Wie hätte sie tot ausgesehen' (141). Here Johnson uses a stream-of-consciousness technique which attempts to reproduce the way in which thought processes work, namely by association (without the connections necessarily crystallizing into words). Thus, although the connection between the sentence beginning 'Gestern nacht' and the question 'Wie hätte sie tot ausgesehen' is not articulated and although 'sie' has no clear referent in the immediate context, we can guess that when Herr T. calls to mind an Allied bombing raid in the north of Germany he is reminded immediately of the death of his wife ('sie') in a similar bombing raid, from which her body was never recovered. In other words, his grief at the death of his wife (a grief complicated and intensified by the fact that he has never seen her dead body) plays an important part in his desire to help speed the end of the War. Not surprisingly, Frau Ammann objects to this story: 'Und so ist es noch zu privat' (142), a comment which the narrator explains: 'Sie meinte: das sei immer noch nicht mehr als die Wahrheit für Achims Vater: mit seinen Augen gesehen, die sahen nicht genug. Immer noch nicht genug' (143). Frau Ammann would prefer Achim's father to see more clearly the wider historical implications of his actions. He should recognize that the iniquity of the Nazi regime and the need to replace it with a more just (socialist) society make the sabotage imperative.

Finally, in response to these objections, Karsch improvises another (even more implausible) fictional variation in which Achim's father listens to foreign radio stations and becomes actively involved with the resistance movement (harbouring subversives, obtaining forged papers, and so on). Karsch may appear to be making major concessions to Frau Ammann's viewpoint here, but these concessions remain at the level of the subject-matter, for while Karsch is inventive enough to dream up a whole host of possible scenarios involving anti-fascist resistance, he persists in imagining that Herr T. acts from personal motives.[17] If we suspect at this point that Karsch and Frau Ammann will never be able to find any common ground, despite Karsch's apparent goodwill, this becomes absolutely clear when Frau Ammann objects once more to Karsch's fiction: 'Verstehen Sie: sagte sie: in der Ausarbeitung dürfen Sie ihm [= Herr T.] nun nicht vorwerfen daß er sich als Sozialdemokrat verhielt zu einer Zeit, da die Kommunistische Partei schon die künftigen Bürgermeister heraussuchte; er lebt ja noch. Nicht seine Fehler

---

[17] 'Er soll es ja nicht für richtig gehalten haben, aber wenn überhaupt entschloß er sich erst nach dem Verschwinden von Frau und Tochter, ich laß mir nicht alles wegnehmen' (146); and: 'Aber dies und so erst im halben Jahr vor dem Einmarsch der amerikanischen Truppen und aus persönlichen (privaten) Gründen: um die Anständigkeit zurückzukommen für das Gefühl nützlichen Lebens' (147).

sind wichtig sondern was ihn mit unserer neuen Zeit ver-
bindet' (147). Karsch is nonplussed by Frau Ammann's reaction because he had not intended any such reproach to Herr
T., and her words are not immediately intelligible to the
reader, either, because Karsch has made no reference in his
invented scene to either Social Democracy or Communism.
As I understand it, the confusion arises from another ideo-
logical clash. For Frau Ammann, the fact that Achim's father
acts from private motives is proof that he is a prey to the kind
of bourgeois subjectivism which (in her orthodox socialist
view) was typical of social democrats during the Nazi era.
True communists, on the other hand, demonstrated class
consciousness and were less concerned with their own private troubles than with the historical struggle for a new social
order.

Johnson appears to be pessimistic about the possibility of
mutual understanding here. It is not simply that Karsch and
Frau Ammann each apply a different interpretative model to
the world. Each of them has internalized this model so
thoroughly that neither is even aware of it. As a result, it is
not even possible for them to see what causes their misunder-
standings. Yet in so far as Johnson's portrayal of this ideo-
logical impasse shows an insight into *both* positions, and in so
far as he passes on his insights to the reader, his novel can be
said to have promoted understanding between East and
West.

One imagined scene (on pp. 157–60) stands out from
those analysed so far because it serves a quite different
function. This scene is imagined, not by Karsch the
biographer, but by Karsch the narrator, in response to the
interlocutor's complaint that the narrative is not exciting
enough: 'Es ist so gar nicht spannend' (157). The previous
section of the narrative had described how Achim's father
comes into possession of a copy of Karsch's original
(unpublished) article about a race meeting at which Achim
is honoured in celebration of his thirtieth birthday. The
article appears to have been copied secretly, and has been
annotated, apparently by opponents of the East German
regime (since they suggest that the author of the article
should depict more clearly the mass hysteria at the race

meeting, whereas the orthodox publisher Herr Fleisg had objected to the article precisely because it gave the impression that the crowd was hysterical (54)). Yet the interlocutor is disappointed with the narrator's account of this event, presumably because he feels that the narrator has not made enough of the intrigue and political subversion.

The interlocutor's disappointment appears to arise from his own preconceptions about the GDR; and the narrator, who had mocked these prejudices at the beginning of the novel,[18] decides to poke fun at the interlocutor once again by improvising an exaggeratedly exciting scene which borrows clichéd elements from the popular thriller. First, we see a finger pressing the doorbell of Karsch's landlady's house, but the identity of the finger's owner is withheld. In this way, we are kept in suspense while the landlady shuffles along the corridor to the door. We are then invited to share her surprise and confusion when she finds that two unknown men are demanding to speak to Karsch. The tension continues to rise as Frau Liebenreuth rushes to Karsch's room and warns him that he is about to be arrested. Karsch, however, is sufficiently convinced of his own innocence to let the two men in. If Karsch recognizes the men when they enter his room, then the narrator does not allow him to show it, so that the reader remains in the dark as to their status and purpose. Moreover, one of the men stands by the door (in

---

[18] In the novel's opening passage, the narrator anticipates that the implied reader will misconstrue the statement 'Sie rief ihn an über die Grenze', taking it to mean that a woman calls to a fleeing man from the other side of the barbed-wire border which separates the two Germanies. He therefore chides him for his too vivid imagination: 'Nun erwarte von mir nicht den Namen und Lebensumstände für eine wild dahinstürzende Gestalt im kalten Morgennebel und kleine nasse Erdklumpen, die unter ihren Tritten auffliegen, wieder reißt der stille Waldrand unter menschlichen Sprüngen auf, eifriges dummes Hundegebell, amtliche Anrufe, keuchender Atem, ein Schuß, unversehens fällt jemand hin, das wollte ich ebenso wenig wie der Schütze es am besten behaupten sollte gegen Ende seines Lebens; ich hatte ja nichts im Sinn als einen telefonischen Anruf' (8). The implied reader has wrongly assumed that the narrator is about to serve up a thrilling tale of daring and danger, relating a desperate attempt to escape to the West. His expectation that Karsch, as a West German visitor to the GDR, will be followed by the East German secret police (26) is also disappointed. In this way, the interlocutor is characterized as someone for whom East Germany is a land of intrigue and subversion, and for whom all literary representations of East Germany must therefore be thrillers.

order to prevent Karsch leaving?) while the other demands
to see Karsch's manuscript (in order to destroy it?). Having
artificially built up the interlocutor's expectations in this way,
the narrator then deflates them, explaining that these two
men are probably editors from the publishing house (hardly
a likely profession for the villains of a thriller), who have
come to make sure that he is earning his advance fee. What
is more, the solicitude they show when Karsch admits to his
slow progress ('Also mein Lieber, woran liegt es denn? Vielleicht hilft es dir, wenn du dich einmal darüber aussprichst?'
(160)) is the very opposite of the strong-arm tactics which
the interlocutor has been led to expect. Finally, the narrator
destroys the illusion altogether by erasing the scene, pointing out that it never took place. In this particular fictional
scene, then, the interlocutor is duped in order to expose
and mock his prejudices. In an interview with Wilhelm Johannes Schwarz, Johnson admitted that this was one of his
aims in the novel: 'In meinen beiden ersten Büchern habe
ich [. . .] gegen das Bild von der DDR gearbeitet, das man
so oft im Westen antrifft: Man sieht dort die DDR als einen
Staat, in dem die Geheimpolizei das Frühstück des einzelnen
Bürgers überwacht.' [19] As readers, we may enjoy a feeling of
superiority over the ignorant interlocutor, but, to the extent
that we are also taken in by the invented scene (and I suggested above that this is inevitable), we are invited to question our own prejudices about the GDR (although clearly
the effect which the passage has in the 1990s—when it has
emerged that the GDR's secret police did quite literally keep
its citizens under surveillance while they ate their breakfast
(witness Wolf's *Was bleibt*)—will be quite different from the
effect which Johnson intended for his contemporary readership in the 1960s).

4. 'Das streichen Sie mal': Erasing the Past

So far in this chapter, 'erasure' has been used as a metaphor
for Karsch's practice of projecting and then retracting or

---

[19] Wilhelm Johannes Schwarz, 'Gespräche mit Uwe Johnson', in Schwarz, *Der
Erzähler Uwe Johnson* (Berne and Munich: Francke, 1970), 86–98 (87).

negating scenes, and of placing side by side mutually exclusive versions of Achim's life which cancel one another
out. But a more literal form of erasure begins to take over in
the latter part of the novel. For Achim, having initially sup-
ported Karsch's work on his biography, begins to censor
Karsch's accounts of his life and requires him to delete
passages which conflict with his public image of an exem-
plary socialist.

The first passage which Achim insists on deleting depicts
him as an apprentice bricklayer shortly after the War. Karsch
imagines a conversation in which Achim resists his boss's
attempts to persuade him to join the newly established FDJ,
saying: 'Ich hab die Nase noch voll von dem einen Mal.
[. . .] Ich kann die Sorte Lärm einfach nicht mehr hören'
(190). By inventing this short exchange between Achim and
his boss, Karsch creates the impression that Achim is unwilling to join the FDJ because the ceremony and rhetoric
associated with it are too similar to the ceremony and rhetoric of the Hitler Youth. In other words, having made a
substantial emotional investment in the Hitler Youth, and
having suffered a grave emotional shock when the organization is disbanded and its activities and ideals condemned,
Achim is reluctant to risk disappointment again. As always,
then, Karsch is interested in the personal motivations which
lie behind an individual's involvement (or in this case non-
involvement) in key historical movements. Achim, however,
is unwilling to let this version of events stand and Karsch is
obliged to delete the whole episode and to replace 'die
getilgte Stelle' (171) with Achim's own explanation of events
(the word 'Anstecknadel' presumably refers to the badge
worn by members of the FDJ):

Aber wenn Achim diese Einzelheiten lieber ersetzt haben möchte durch
den in langsamem Tempo zum Mitschreiben formulierten Satz: Nach
anfänglichem Zögern erkannte ich (also da müssen Sie schreiben: er)
daß man sich nicht mit dem eigenen Leben zufrieden geben darf sondern
sich beteiligen muß an der Gesellschaft, und bat um die Mitgliedschaft—
so mußte Karsch eben anerkennen daß Achims Erinnerung auf den Besitz
der Anstecknadel schneller hinauslief als das vollständige Jahr, das er
damals mit (anfänglichem) Zögern verbracht hatte. (190–1)

In this way, Achim attempts to obliterate the difficulties he experienced in making the transition from the fascist state to the new socialist state.

Achim goes on to insist that Karsch delete a passage which shows the invading Soviet Army in a bad light. 'Und dies hier streichen Sie mal' (192), he says of a passage in which Russian soldiers are shown stealing a bicycle from a young girl and raping local women. He even makes a gesture with his hand as if he were crossing out the unwanted passage: 'und statt mit dem Gestrichenen können Sie doch hiermit auf den Ersten Versuch kommen . . . er zog mit dem Finger einen schwingenden Strich über das Blatt, warf es um in einem Schlag, ließ den Finger mit zielsicherem Schlenker landen in der Mitte der nächsten Seite. Das war in seinem Leben drei Jahre später' (195). Achim explains the reason for this erasure: 'Es ist doch wichtiger, ja? von heute aus gesehen! daß die Rote Armee uns vom Faschismus befreit hat und geholfen beim neuen Leben, ja? und nicht daß sie ab und zu mal sich hingelegt haben mit einer Frau, oder Fahrräder, oder so' (195). Here, Achim shows the kind of historical consciousness which Frau Ammann advocates: past events must point forward to the historical goals of Socialism. Karsch agrees to describe the 'Erster Versuch', the name given to an open day at Achim's local cycling club at which youngsters are invited to test out their cycling abilities. On this particular day, Achim achieves eleventh place in a race against experienced club members, even without a professional racing bike. Having described this impressive achievement, Karsch asks ironically 'Ist da auch was zu streichen?', knowing that Achim is unlikely to want to erase such a flattering portrait (200).

On another occasion, Achim asks Karsch not to include in the biography an account of his illegal trip to West Berlin at the age of 19 to buy a three-speed gear. His motives for suppressing this episode seem to be twofold: on the one hand, the fact that he broke the law by using East German money to buy West German goods sits ill with his present role as a model of socialist achievement; and on the other hand his desire to buy superior West German equipment suggests a lack of faith in East German technology, which, though slower to develop than Western technology, was eventually able to rival it. From a socialist perspective, then, he was guilty of putting the present before the future. When the interlocutor objects that Achim's version of his life—which would exclude his foray into West Berlin—is not true, the narrator reflects:

Er wollte nicht der sein, der roh und gern war im alten und zerschlagenen Verband der staatlichen Jugend, das streichen Sie mal; nicht einer, den ängstigte die Rote Armee, der hätte seinen Vater verraten (für eine schlechte Sache verraten), den haben wir ja mit Gewalt hineinbringen müssen ins blaue Hemd und eingesehen hat er es doch nicht. Er wollte gelebt haben schon wie immer jetzt und seit fünf Jahren Mitglied in der Sachwalterpartei. (238–9)[20]

This passage is typical of many in the novel inasmuch as the narrator twice switches in mid-sentence, and without in any way signalling the switch, from his own perspective to the perspective of a third person: the words 'das streichen Sie mal' must be attributed to Achim, while the words 'den haben wir ja mit Gewalt hineinbringen müssen' etc. belong to an (unspecified) socialist voice. It is not clear whether Achim actually speaks the words 'das streichen Sie mal', or whether the narrator uses the words ironically to anticipate what has, by now, become a familiar response from Achim. In either case, it is clear that Achim would like to remove from the biography all reference to his membership of the Hitler Youth, his fear of the Red Army, and his reluctance to join the FDJ. On another occasion, when Achim explains what finally persuaded him to join the SED (the Party's gratitude when he endorsed the first racing bike to be constructed in East Germany), the narrator juxtaposes this story with the story of a cycling colleague of Achim's who also tests out the East German bike but subsequently flees to the West. This story ends: 'den streichen Sie mal' (246). Although the comment is unattributed, it appears, once more, to be a request from Achim (real or anticipated).

In the end, Karsch is reduced to presenting Achim's life in terms of absolute ambiguity, according to which Achim was

[20] The 'Sachwalterpartei' is the SED, 'der Sachwalter' being Johnson's name for Walter Ulbricht, its First Secretary. See also n. 13 above.

both eager to accept the new socialist regime, and reluctant
to accept it:

Und dann entweder mochte es Achim gewesen sein, der nicht feindselig
aber unerklärlich sich weigerte das ernst blickende Bild des Sachwalters
am Stock über die Köpfe der Marschierenden zu halten, und darunter
nicht sichtbar sein wollte als der Träger von so etwas; oder jedoch mochte
es Achim sein, der ein über Holzleisten gespanntes Spruchband festhielt
an einem schwankenden Stangenbein und schrie im engen Gang des
Bürogebäudes, während alle an ihm vorbeiliefen in deutlicher Eile: Nun
nimm das doch mal einer verdammte Drückeberger! [. . .]

Oder ein Achim, dem die Funktion des Gruppenvorsitzenden zu-
geschoben wird im staatlichen Jugendverband, keiner will sie, jetzt mit
einem Mal sitzt er allein an der Kopfseite des Tisches und soll reden über
die Pläne des Sachwalters so, daß die Umsitzenden ihn wieder aufnehmen
als einen der ihren und dennoch glauben was er noch nie zum Sagen
vorgedacht hat; also ein finster grübelndes Gesicht über Papier gehalten,
unwillig hervorgestoßene Satzreste, krampfige Lockerheit, wieder das
ausgesetzte Gefühl.

Oder ein Achim, der dem zusieht: froh daß er es nicht ist. (241–2)

Here, Achim is depicted both as a man reluctant to carry a
banner showing Walter Ulbricht and as a man attempting to
encourage his workmates to carry such a banner; both as a
man bravely taking on the job of Group Leader in the FDJ
and as a man happy not to have that responsibility. Each pair
of scenes clearly violates what McHale calls the 'law of the
excluded middle', since both versions cannot simultaneously
be true. Finally, Achim tries to erase the most incriminating
episode in his past: his participation in the uprising of
17 June 1953. This is revealed to Karin and Karsch when an
unknown person sends Karsch a photograph showing Achim
amongst the crowd at the demonstration. In desperation,
Achim tells Karsch: 'Am Ende bin ich es gar nicht' (305),
and claims to have been training outside the city that day.
But though Karsch attempts to imagine the scene at the
training ground, he is finally defeated: 'Ich kann es mir nicht
vorstellen. [. . .] Mir fällt nichts mehr ein' (331).

These examples have demonstrated that the erasure
of scenes is not just a narrative device used by the narrator
to highlight the process of composition of the biography;
Achim is also concerned to erase parts of his life from the

official record. Johnson had experienced difficulties similar to those of Karsch when trying to find a publisher for his first novel, *Ingrid Babendererde*. In his *Frankfurter Vorlesungen* he recalls his reaction when the publishers, the Aufbau Verlag, returned his manuscript with an invitation to rework it in accordance with orthodox socialist views: 'Eine solche, von der noch herrschenden Ideologie bestimmte Umschreibung wäre dem Verfasser an die Substanz dessen gegangen, was er als Wahrheit für vertretbar, für belegbar hielt. Sie wäre hinausgelaufen auf Streichungen in der Wirklichkeit. Es gab andere Verlage.'[21] This may explain Johnson's interest in Karsch's difficulties with his own manuscript, which also arise from the requirement to make 'Streichungen in der Wirklichkeit'.

McHale prefaces his discussion of 'worlds under erasure' with a quotation from Ronald Sukenick, who writes that the State of Israel is 'a state in which certain things that have happened have not'.[22] The GDR, as Johnson portrays it, is just such a state. Moreover, by making the reader witness the projection and erasure of scenes, which are replaced by contradictory scenes, Johnson contrives to make the reader experience something of the unstable reality which—in his view—characterized life in the GDR. Just as the people of the GDR experienced the way in which aspects of their own or the historical past flickered in and out of existence at the will of the State, so we experience the way in which parts of the narrative world flicker in and out of existence at the will of the narrator. Walter Jens makes a similar point when he writes in his discussion of *Das dritte Buch* that the more elusive and contradictory Achim's life becomes: 'desto deutlicher wird die Lage von Millionen, die in eben dieser Unsicherheit aller Verhältnisse, dieser Austauschbarkeit, Vieldeutigkeit und Anonymität, diesem Vagen und Labilen, diesem "ich war's und war's doch wieder nicht" besteht'.[23]

Finally, a brief comparison of two of Walter Ulbricht's early speeches shows that Achim's attitude to the past corresponds closely to the treatment of the historical record by

---

[21] Johnson, *Begleitumstände*, 89. [22] McHale, 100.
[23] Walter Jens, 'Johnson auf der Schwelle der Meisterschaft', in Reinhard Baumgart (ed.), *Über Uwe Johnson* (Frankfurt/Main: Suhrkamp, 1970), 108–14 (111).

public figures in the GDR. In a speech given to a Communist Party conference in Berlin shortly after the Allied victory over the Nazis in 1945,[24] Ulbricht expresses the view that much of the blame for the atrocities of the Hitler regime and for the outbreak of the war lies with the German people, who followed the Prussian instinct for blind obedience, believed propaganda about other nations, and applauded Hitler's victories. Ulbricht stresses repeatedly that only an honest appraisal of this burden of responsibility will allow the German nation to face the challenge of the future: 'Die Erkenntnis dieser Schuld ist die Voraussetzung dafür, daß unser Volk endgültig mit dem reaktionären Vergangenen bricht und entschlossen einen neuen Weg geht.'[25] He also rejects the idea that the submissiveness of the Germans can be attributed to Hitler's strength and thereby explained away:

Es wäre eine Selbsttäuschung zu glauben, daß Hitler seine barbarische Kriegspolitik nur mit Hilfe des grausamen Terrors gegen das eigene Volk durchführen konnte. Wer sich daran erinnert, mit welcher Begeisterung die Mehrheit des deutschen Volkes Hitler zujubelte, als die deutschen Armeen vor Moskau standen, der wird nicht bestreiten können, daß die imperialistische und militaristische Ideologie tief in unserem Volk sitzt und daß selbst diejenigen, die von banger Sorge um die Zukunft Deutschlands erfüllt waren, nicht die Kraft aufbrachten, gegen den Strom zu schwimmen.[26]

Finally, he reserves particular criticism for the working classes, who, in his view, had failed in their historical task by allowing the fascists to come to power.

While the message of this early speech—that the majority of Germans collaborated to some extent with the Nazis—would not seem out of place in the works of such West German writers as Günter Grass and Heinrich Böll, by the late 1950s Ulbricht had modified his views and offered a rather different version of events. In a speech to mark the

---

[24] Walter Ulbricht, 'Das Programm der antifaschistisch-demokratischen Ordnung. Rede auf der ersten Funktionärkonferenz der KPD Groß-Berlins, 25. Juni 1945', in Ulbricht, *Zur Geschichte der deutschen Arbeiterbewegung: Aus Reden und Aufsätzen*, 10 vols. (Berlin, GDR: Dietz, 1953–71), II. 425–48.
[25] Ibid. 428.
[26] Ibid. 435.

tenth anniversary of the founding of the GDR,[27] Ulbricht, now First Secretary of the SED and First Deputy of the GDR, no longer speaks of the War as an event which could not have happened without the co-operation of the vast majority of German people. Instead he speaks of it as something more abstract, referring to 'der faschistische Raubkrieg'.[28] Moreover, where he does apportion blame, Ulbricht no longer points the finger of guilt at the whole German nation, but only at the middle classes. The working classes, who in 1945 had been reproached for their ineffective resistance to the Hitler regime, are now seen as the victims of that regime: 'die Werktätigen, die jahrelang in den Konzentrationslagern, Zuchthäusern und Gefängnissen des faschistischen Staates gelitten hatten'.[29] He also suggests that they had no option but to submit to Nazi propaganda: 'die Arbeiterklasse und die Werktätigen, die die nazistische Hetze über sich ergehen lassen mußten'.[30] Whereas in his early speeches Ulbricht states that the KPD and SPD were jointly responsible for failing to unite under one banner to resist Hitler, by the late 1950s he suggests that middle-class forces actively prevented the working classes from presenting a unified front which could have halted Hitler's rise to power. Commenting on the role of the bourgeoisie during the economic crisis of 1929, he writes: 'So tief auch die Krise war, so vermochte doch die deutsche Bourgeoisie die Spaltung der Arbeiterklasse aufrechtzuerhalten und die Führer der Sozialdemokratie und der Gewerkschaften von der Teilnahme an der antifaschistischen Einheitsfront abzuhalten.'[31] Although Ulbricht does give credit to a minority of the middle classes for resistance activities, on the whole his anniversary speech conveys the impression that the German working classes actively resisted Hitler, while the middle classes collaborated. It may be that Ulbricht's change of heart was necessary in order to effect the difficult transition from the original post-war project (conceived in conjunction with middle-class

---

[27] Walter Ulbricht, 'Des deutschen Volkes Weg und Ziel', in Ulbricht, *Zur Geschichte der deutschen Arbeiterbewegung*, VIII. 368–469.
[28] Ibid. 395.
[29] Ibid. 386–7.
[30] Ibid. 382.
[31] Ibid. 374–5.

resistance leaders) of an anti-fascist-democratic state, to a communist workers' state on the Soviet model. In order to justify rule by the workers, it was necessary to demonstrate that the working class, and not the middle class, was the only class with a legitimate right to power. Whatever the reasons for Ulbricht's U-turn, however, certain aspects of the past had to be forgotten. As far as working-class collaboration with the Nazis was concerned, Ulbricht felt it necessary to wipe the slate clean, even if this meant quite literally wiping out aspects of the historical past. Under Ulbricht, then, History was subject to the same kind of revision and cancellation as the story of Achim's life in Johnson's *Das dritte Buch.*

In *Das dritte Buch über Achim,* Johnson offers us two models of how to recount the past and there is no doubt which model he finds preferable. The model represented by Achim and Frau Ammann involves subordinating the individual to the historical and the present moment to future goals. But since ordinary people rarely live their lives in full consciousness of the historical implications of their actions, or with their sights set firmly on the historical future, this method inevitably necessitates the erasure and retrospective revision of parts of the past. Moreover, this is shown to be damaging to the individual, not only because it leads to alienation and a loss of integrity, but also because it can have a detrimental effect on the individual's personal relationships (leading, in Achim's case, to the disintegration of his relationship with Karin). Karsch, on the other hand, offers a more constructive model, based on an understanding that our private experiences and our experience of historical events are often indissolubly linked. Clearly the first model corresponds to what we now know as Socialist Realism, while the second corresponds to the kind of narrative written in the West by such prominent members of the Gruppe 47 as Grass and Böll. From our standpoint at the millennium, Johnson's insights into the differences between these two modes of writing may seem unremarkable, but in 1961 *Das dritte Buch über Achim* must have represented a very early attempt to explore and understand what separated Western writers from Eastern writers.[32]

---

[32] Although Johnson appears to favour Karsch's (Western) model of biography,

After the complexity of *Das dritte Buch über Achim*, the structure of Johnson's next novel, *Zwei Ansichten* (1965), appears surprisingly simple. The narrative switches between the perspective of B. (representing the *B*RD) and that of his girlfriend D. (representing the *D*DR), from whom he becomes separated by the building of the Berlin Wall. Despite this rather contrived, parable-like structure, the novel offers a subtle exploration of the theme of the division of Germany, and the perspective of B. is particularly compelling (revealing that he resents the pressure put on him, both by the expectations of others—or what he takes to be their expectations—and by his own fear of appearing inadequate, to 'rescue' D. from the East, despite his increasing indifference towards her). Johnson returned to more complex narrative forms with his four-volume novel *Jahrestage. Aus dem Leben von Gesine Cresspahl* (1970–83), in which the story of a year in the adult life of Gesine is interwoven with the story of her father's life and her own childhood. In this way, world events of the late 1960s (including the Vietnam War, student protests, and the Prague Spring) are juxtaposed with events of the Nazi era and the immediate post-war years. Johnson employs a complex montage technique combining factual sources with personal memory, and dialogue and interior monologue with a more distanced third-person narrative. The novel shows Johnson's habitual disregard for logical consistency: he switches indiscriminately, for instance, between first- and third-person narrative, and a comment in the first volume—'Wer erzählt hier eigentlich, Gesine. / Wir beide. Das hörst du doch, Johnson'[33]—makes plain that we are to understand the narrative as a collaborative effort, in which the author and his fictional character have an equal input (however impossible that may be).

it would be wrong to assume that Johnson was a champion of the Federal Republic. Johnson is critical of the FRG, not only in *Das dritte Buch* (where he deplores in particular West Germans' ignorance of the GDR), but also (more strongly) in his alternative short-prose version of Karsch's trip to the East, 'Eine Reise wegwohin, 1960'. There, he criticizes the FRG's paranoid suspicion of West Germans with links to the GDR; the undemocratic methods of its police force; and its policy of refusing to recognize the GDR's statehood.

[33] Uwe Johnson, *Jahrestage. Aus dem Leben von Gesine Cresspahl*, 4 vols. (Frankfurt/Main: Suhrkamp, 1970–83), I. 256. In this and in subsequent quotations, a solidus (/) indicates a paragraph break in the original.

3
MAX FRISCH: *MEIN NAME SEI GANTENBEIN*

1. The *Buch-Ich* and his Roles

Frisch's early prose works, written and published in the 1930s and 1940s, made no great impact,[1] but he returned to prose fiction in the 1950s, having in the mean time established his reputation as a dramatist, and achieved considerable success with the novel *Stiller* (1954),[2] in which he shows a mature grasp of the possibilities of narrative: a number of perspectives, each of which is in some way restricted or biased, are juxtaposed in such a way that each serves to highlight the limitations of the others. As Halina Malinowska has pointed out, this 'Point-of-view-Technik', in which each character possesses 'ein genau bestimmtes Teil-Wissen', is characteristic of much modernist prose.[3] However, there is evidence in *Stiller* that Frisch is already moving beyond this well-worn technique: for Stiller is not just a narrator with a biased perspective; he also tells fictions, stories which are intended to prove that he is not Stiller, as his wife and friends insist, but the American Jim White. Though he attempts at first to conceal the fictitious nature of these stories, Stiller later admits openly to having invented them. In this way he anticipates the narrator of *Mein Name sei Gantenbein*.[4]

Mein Name sei Gantenbein consists largely of a series of fictions invented (with no attempt at concealment) by an

[1] These include *Jürg Reinhart—eine sommerliche Schicksalsfahrt* (1934) and *J'adore ce qui me brûle oder Die Schwierigen* (1943: revised and retitled *Die Schwierigen oder j'adore ce qui me brûle* in 1957).

[2] Max Frisch, *Stiller*, in Frisch, *Gesammelte Werke in zeitlicher Folge*, ed. Hans Mayer in collaboration with Walter Schmitz, 6 vols. (Frankfurt/Main: Suhrkamp, 1976), III. 359–780 (first published 1954). All works by Frisch are quoted in this edition, hereafter abbreviated to *Werke*.

[3] Halina Milanowska, 'Der Erzählstandpunkt als Mittel zur Bestimmung des Erzählers im Roman *Stiller* von Max Frisch', *Studia Germanica Posnaniensia*, 1 (1971), 91–103 (92).

[4] Max Frisch, *Mein Name sei Gantenbein*, in Frisch, *Werke*, V. 5–320. All further references to the novel appear in the main text.

anonymous narrator whom Frisch, in a mock interview which he wrote to accompany the novel, dubbed the *Buch-Ich*.[5] Since the 'plot' of the novel is not of a type which can be readily reduced to a synopsis, I offer instead the following key facts as a framework for my discussion of the text:

— The narrator or *Buch-Ich* invents three main characters: Enderlin, an academic; Gantenbein, a man pretending to be blind; and Svoboda, an architect. Each of these men has a relationship with the same woman, Lila: Enderlin as her lover, Gantenbein and Svoboda as her husband. A second female figure, the prostitute Camilla, is associated exclusively with Gantenbein.

— The *Buch-Ich* identifies with the three male characters to differing extents: whereas he sometimes uses the first person to describe the actions of Enderlin and Gantenbein, Svoboda is referred to exclusively in the third person.

— The narrator constructs a series of fictional scenarios around these characters, scattered among which are a number of unrelated, anecdotal stories (mostly told by Gantenbein to Camilla) and a small number of scenes from the narrator's real life.

— Opinions differ as to which passages are unequivocally 'real' (that is, part of the narrator's past),[6] but it seems certain that they include at least the following: (*a*) the narrator's visit to his deserted flat following the breakup of a relationship (repeated three times: 18–20, 198, 313–14); (*b*) the vision of a petrified horse's head (generally taken to symbolize an unsuccessful attempt to break out of social roles) (12, 153–4); (*c*) a near-fatal car accident (22–5) and a similar experience in which the narrator nearly drowns (247–8); (*d*) two trips abroad, to the Via Appia in Italy (137–9) and to Jerusalem (154–6); and (*e*) a scene in which the narrator sits in a bar awaiting the arrival of a business colleague (48 ff.).

— The novel has no chapter divisions, but triple blank

---

[5] Max Frisch, 'Ich schreibe für Leser: Antworten auf vorgestellte Fragen', in Frisch, *Werke*, V. 323–34.

[6] Alfred White provides a useful summary of critical opinions on this point (Alfred D. White, 'Reality and Imagination in *Mein Name sei Gantenbein*', *OGS* 18–19 (1989–90), 150–64 (152 n. 2)).

lines are used to divide the narrative into passages of varying length (about ninety in all), which I refer to as 'sections'.

   In the absence of a clear storyline, we can approach *Gantenbein* through an analysis of the mechanics of the narrative.
A series of reflective passages embedded in the text suggests
that two contrary intentions are at work in the novel. A short
section in the opening pages offers the first key to the narrator's intentions: 'Ein Mann hat eine Erfahrung gemacht,
jetzt sucht er die Geschichte dazu—man kann nicht leben
mit einer Erfahrung, die ohne Geschichte bleibt, scheint es,
und manchmal stellte ich mir vor, ein andrer habe genau die
Geschichte meiner Erfahrung' (11). This suggests that the
Buch-Ich is using the three main fictional characters (Enderlin, Gantenbein, and Svoboda) to find a story through which
he can express his own recent experiences (which seem to
involve the breakup of a relationship and the struggle to
break free of social roles). A second, contrasting aim can be
inferred from three much-quoted sections which occur a
little later in the text. The first is an extended metaphor and
begins: 'Ich werde mir neue Kleider kaufen, dabei weiß ich:
es hilft nichts, nur im Schaufenster erscheinen sie anders'
(20). The second opens with the hypothetical question, 'Ein
anderes Leben—?' (21), a question which the *Buch-Ich* pro-
ceeds to answer by creating the figure of Gantenbein; while
the third consists of a single line: 'Ich probiere Geschichten
an wie Kleider!' (22). Taken together, these remarks suggest
that the narrator is interested in 'trying on' stories which,
because they differ from the stories he has lived out in the
past, offer the possibility of 'ein anderes Leben'. In other
words, the *Buch-Ich*'s intention is not simply to express the
experiences of his past life, but also to explore *alternatives* to
his past behaviour, that is, to explore 'what might have
happened'. In this way he is able to envisage a possible future
in which he might break free of the constraints of habitual
behaviour.[7] As Michael Pulham writes:

---

[7] I have deliberately condensed the evidence in support of this point. A detailed
analysis of the narrator's desire to escape his past would have to take into account
the following: the narrator's remark that his life holds no fascination for him except
when he imagines what he could have done but did not do (his 'Nicht-Taten', 59);

On the one hand Ich sets out programmatically to *discover* himself by investing various figures with invented roles in order to see what is common to all these roles and to reveal the 'Erlebnismuster' which underlies them; on the other hand Ich's very facility in invention and his desire to found a new self mean that he uses his inventions as an attempt at *self-escape* as much as self-discovery.[8]

The most successful analyses of the novel, in my view, are those which, like Pulham's excellent but sadly unpublished doctoral thesis, acknowledge this double process.[9]

If we return for a moment to the 'Kleider' metaphor and follow through its implications, we can establish more exactly the relationship between the opposing aims of self-discovery and self-escape. The image is of a customer who admires a suit in a shop window and imagines that it will create a new image for him. Once inside the fitting-room, however, he is faced with the unwelcome realization that, no matter how stylish or well-made the clothes, he cannot change the physical characteristics of the body underneath ('während ich meinen Hinterkopf sehe, der nicht zu ändern ist' (21)), so that after a few months the same creases will inevitably appear in the same places. By implication, then, no matter how much the *Buch-Ich* tries to create 'ein anderes Leben' by 'trying on' the lives of his fictional characters, he will always end up telling the same story: the story of his past experience. And this is indeed what happens. For all the narrator's efforts to direct the different strands of narrative towards a conclusion which he finds satisfactory or gratifying, the stories of Enderlin, Gantenbein, and Svoboda (as well as many of the anecdotes about other, often unnamed figures) all return to the same few, recurrent scenarios: either a character is unable to escape from the habit of

his habit of following strangers to see where they lead (8–11); and his admission that he pursues people in his imagination because he is fascinated by the idea that they might act differently from him in any given situation (160).

[8] Michael J. L. Pulham, 'A Critical Study of Five Novels by Max Frisch' (unpublished doctoral thesis, University of Oxford, 1975), 219–97 (233–4).

[9] In contrast, I find Claus Reschke's recent study less convincing because he shows no awareness of the *Buch-Ich*'s desire for self-escape, seeing the three main characters simply as a means by which the narrator illuminates or reflects facets of his identity (Claus Reschke, *Life as a Man: Contemporary Male–Female Relationships in the Novels of Max Frisch* (New York: Peter Lang, 1990), 191–266).

routine or from roles imposed by society; or a relationship
stagnates once the initial passion subsides; or a relationship
breaks up as a direct result of the male partner's jealousy.
Again, the analyses of *Gantenbein* which I find most helpful
are those which, like Alfred White's article, acknowledge the
way in which the narrator's attempts to escape his past are
repeatedly frustrated.[10]

Similarly, while thematic studies of the novel tend to treat
the narrative as static,[11] I prefer to treat it as a dynamic
process, what White calls 'the teleological movement of a
personality', which entails 'progression from the first to the
last page'.[12] By this White means that because the narrator's
attempts to escape himself bring him progressively closer to
the core of his personality, the order in which the episodes
are narrated is of vital importance. Frisch encourages this
approach to the text when he writes in his mock interview,
'Ich schreibe für Leser', that it is of little or no consequence
what has happened to the *Buch-Ich* in the past, or what
happens to his invented personae in the fictions he creates:
what matters is *when* these episodes are narrated.[13] In this
way, Frisch invites us to focus our attention on the mental
process which is reflected in the successive projection, revision, and cancellation of fictions. In view of this, we must
beware of treating the characters invented by the *Buch-Ich* as
coherent fictional characters motivated by their own needs
and desires. Since the *Buch-Ich* is at all times the puppeteer
pulling the strings, the characters' actions and attributes
must be understood in terms of his intentions at that particular point in the narrative.[14]

---

[10] 'All X's playful self-projections lead to the conclusion adumbrated at the
outset: alterations of his circumstances, attempts to favour some parts of his character against others, will not do away with the torments of jealousy' (White, 163).

[11] Three such studies are: Martin Kraft, *Studien zur Thematik von Max Frischs
Roman 'Mein Name sei Gantenbein'* (Berne: Herbert Lang, 1969); Heinz Gockel, *Max
Frisch. Gantenbein: das offen-artistische Erzählen* (Bonn: Bouvier, 1976), in which
Gockel analyses '[das] kontrastive Spiel der Spiegelungen' in *Gantenbein* (the
'mirroring' or contrasting of themes or characters from one part of the novel with
those in another part); and F. A. Lubich, 'Todeserfahrung und Lebensentwurf in
Max Frischs *Mein Name sei Gantenbein*', *Seminar*, 25 (1989), 147–66.

[12] White, 151.   [13] Frisch, *Werke*, V. 330.

[14] Critics sometimes fall into the trap of treating the characters in *Gantenbein* as
coherent figures. Paul Konrad Kurz, for instance, misunderstands the author's

2. 'Ich stelle mir vor': The Projection and Cancellation of Fictions in the Text

Frisch draws attention to his narrator's fictions by using devices similar to those employed in the other four novels examined in this study. Critics tend to single out the refrain 'Ich stelle mir vor', which prefaces many of the invented scenes and signals clearly that what follows is a product of the narrator's imagination; but while this is certainly the most frequently used device, it is by no means the only one.

On a number of occasions the *Buch-Ich* presents us with a set of alternatives from which he has yet to make a final choice (whereas such choices are normally made by an author or narrator before a narrative is set down in writing). In the following example, the *Buch-Ich* ponders Lila's parentage: 'Gesetzt den Fall, Lila wäre die Tochter eines Bankiers [. . .]. Oder aber, Lila wäre die Tochter eines elsässischen Kurzwarenhändlers [. . .]. Ich liebe Lila, ob sie die Tochter eines Bankiers ist oder die Tochter eines Kurzwarenhändlers oder die Tochter eines puritanischen Pfarrers—was ebenfalls denkbar wäre' (93). In another example, the narrator imagines Enderlin facing a dilemma: either he catches his plane and never sees his new lover again, or he misses the plane and returns to her. This is what Borges calls a 'forking path', a point at which the narrative could go in more than one direction (see my comments on p. 16 above), but whereas most narrators choose which path to take 'silently' (suppressing the discarded alternative), the *Buch-Ich* realizes both alternatives simultaneously: 'So oder so: / Einer wird fliegen — / Einer wird bleiben—' (130).[15] By such means the nar-

---

intentions when he upbraids him for creating characters lacking 'innere Einheit' and 'psychologische Wahrscheinlichkeit': 'Wie kommt, beispielsweise, Gantenbein dazu, die anspruchsvolle Lila zu heiraten? [. . .] Das wird psychologisch nicht begründet, bleibt bloßer, überlegener Wille des Erzählers gegenüber der Figur. Ähnlich unmotiviert erscheint Enderlins beruflicher Erfolg' (Paul Konrad Kurz, '*Mein Name sei Gantenbein*', *Stimmen der Zeit*, 90 (1964–5), 57–61 (61)). Critics of Grass's *örtlich betäubt* face similar problems, as I show in Chapter 6.

[15] See also the following examples: the narrator offers three different descriptions of Enderlin's lover's house, but refuses to indicate which is the definitive version (131–2); in his description of a dinner party laid on by Gantenbein and Lila, he leaves it to us to decide what sort of dog the hosts own: 'Dackel oder

rator draws our attention to the fact that the narrative world is not a pre-existing 'real' world, but comes into existence only as he invents it, so that each detail is only one of many possible variants. In a similar way the adverb 'hoffentlich' signals that the *Buch-Ich*'s narrative has a 'future' which is still open (whereas most narrative at least adopts the pose of recounting events from an already determined past—even if, in truth, this fake 'past' also comes into being only as it is narrated): 'Hoffentlich gibt Gantenbein nie seine Rolle auf' (84), 'Hoffentlich falle ich nie aus der Rolle' (103), and 'Hoffentlich werde ich nie eifersüchtig' (110).

The narrator also draws attention to the provisional, fictional status of the stories by revising and reworking them. Towards the end of the novel, for instance, the narrator decides that he no longer wants Lila to be an actress:

Ich wechsle den Beruf von Lila.
(Das Theater ist mir verleidet).
Lila ist keine Schauspielerin von Beruf, sondern Wissenschaftlerin, Medizinerin [. . .].
Oder:
Lila ist eine Contessa, katholisch, eine venezianische Contessa, Morphinistin. (209–10)

When this new fiction also proves unsatisfactory, however, the narrator cancels out all the versions of Lila's life that he has so far tried out:

Ich ändere nochmals:
Lila ist keine Contessa, sowenig wie eine Schauspielerin. Ich verstehe nicht, wie ich auf diese Idee habe kommen können. Lila ist einfach eine Frau, eine verheiratete Frau, verheiratet mit einem Mann, den ich damals in einer Bar hätte treffen sollen. Einunddreißig. Keine Morphinistin; nicht katholisch; berufslos. (219)

The deliberate enumeration of her previous (and now discarded) attributes draws attention to the artifice.[16]

Dogge?' (86); he offers five different possibilities, each introduced by 'Oder', of how Svoboda might react to Lila's infidelity (236–8); and he describes a present which Lila promises her child, whose sex he has not yet decided on: 'eine Puppe mit schottischem Röcklein (wenn es ein Mädchen ist) oder ein Segelschiff (wenn es ein Bub ist)' (266).

[16] See also pp. 84, 188, and 199.

Another device which highlights the fictional status of the *Buch-Ich*'s imaginings is the alternation between the third and first person. This contrivance is particularly conspicuous when the narrator switches in mid-sentence from one grammatical person to the other. For instance, when the narrator describes Gantenbein surrounded by mirrors in a boutique where his wife Lila is choosing new clothes, we read:

> Wo ich hinschaue: Gantenbein mit dem schwarzen Stöcklein zwischen den Knien, die finstere Brille im Gesicht. Ich sehe: Gantenbein ist eleganter geworden, seit ich mich aushalten lasse; ich schulde es Lila [. . .]. Lila probiert jetzt das nächste Modell, das fünfte, das seinem Urteil unterworfen werden soll. Ich bin ja gespannt; nicht auf das Modell, aber auf das Urteil von Gantenbein. (92)

In such instances, the reader is made acutely aware of the fictional status of the passage because the narrative violates what McHale calls the 'law of the excluded middle', (see p. 16 above). In this case, the narrator cannot be both identical with and separate from his characters: he cannot be Lila's husband ('seit ich mich aushalten lasse') and yet not know what Gantenbein—Lila's husband—is thinking ('ich bin gespannt [. . .] auf das Urteil von Gantenbein').[17]

In a similar way, the narrator sometimes switches in midsentence between an omniscient perspective and the limited perspective of a character in his fictional world. This happens when the *Buch-Ich* visits Enderlin in hospital, shortly after Enderlin has learnt that he has only a year to live. 'Ich kann ja nicht wissen, daß Enderlin sich seit heute vormittag für einen Todgeweihten hält' (150), the narrator writes, and imagines asking Enderlin about the future: 'während Enderlin (das sehe ich ihm aber nicht an) nur an seine eigene Lebenserwartung zu denken vermag' (151). In both cases, the narrator can both see into Enderlin's mind and, at the same time, *not* see into it. In another example, the narrator momentarily exchanges the role of Gantenbein for that of Gantenbein's friend, and invents a scene in which Gantenbein visits him at his home. The *Buch-Ich* imagines being tormented by shame at the hollowness of his materialistic

---

[17] Compare Enderlin at the airport: 'sein Gepäck ist aufgegeben, und so bin ich frei und ledig, abgesehen von seiner Mappe, die ich auf die Theke stelle' (123).

lifestyle, but is relieved that Gantenbein cannot see his expensive possessions: 'Wo ich hinsehe, sehe ich Geschmack, nichts Protziges, nein, aber nichts ist so, daß es noch besser, schöner oder auch nur nützlicher werden könnte. Fast bin ich froh um das Loch, das Gantenbein, um den Blinden zu spielen, in unser weißes Hirschleder brennt' (206). Here the *Buch-Ich* knows (as omniscient narrator and inventor of the Gantenbein figure) that Gantenbein is merely playing the blind man, a fact which the 'ich' of the passage— the friend—cannot know. Like the examples in the paragraph above, these sentences violate the law of the excluded middle, for the narrator is both omniscient and nescient. They also combine two narrative viewpoints which, according to the theories of Hamburger and Stanzel, are incompatible.

Given the variety of these devices and the frequency with which they recur in the novel, one might suppose that it is impossible for the reader to identify with the story at all. However, the experience of *Das dritte Buch* applies here too: even when the reader knows in advance that a scene is a fiction, he or she is unable to sustain this awareness and soon becomes immersed in the story, which takes on a reality of its own. Moreover, as in *Das dritte Buch*, the process by which the conjectural frame retreats into the background is sometimes encoded in the grammar of the text, when the subjunctive (indicating possibility or supposition) gives way to the indicative (which is conventionally used to describe real events—'real', that is, within the context of the fictional world). In one instance, the *Buch-Ich* imagines himself in Svoboda's shoes: 'Wenn ich Svoboda wäre: / Ich würde mein Gewehr aus dem Schrank holen, Armeegewehr, und mich auf den Bauch legen, vielleicht nochmals aufstehen, um die Jacke auszuziehen, ferner nehme ich die Pfeife aus dem Mund, bevor ich mich neuerdings auf den Bauch lege und dann den ersten Lader in das Gewehr drücke mit dem Daumen' (259–60). Here, the speculative frame disappears mid-sentence when the infinitives governed by the subjunctive 'ich würde' ('holen', 'legen', 'aufstehen', 'ausziehen') give way to a present indicative 'ich nehme'. A page and a half of prose in the indicative follows; but the conjectural frame reasserts itself when the *Buch-Ich* rejects the scene as pointless speculation: 'Aber ich bin nicht Svoboda' (261).[18]

In his correspondence with the Germanist Walter Höllerer, Frisch confirmed that he found it difficult to destroy the illusion of reality altogether. Despite the many *Verfremdungseffekte* in his play *Biografie*, he told Höllerer, it was difficult to prevent the audience from identifying with the story unfolding on stage. One reason was that the audience were 'auf Erschütterung abonniert' (that is, they had paid to be moved and were determined to get their money's worth);[19] but Frisch also blamed the innate power of theatre (evoking here a different sense of 'erschüttern', namely 'to shake [somebody's belief]'): 'Das Varianten-Spiel zielt auf Reflexion, insofern schon auf Erschütterung, aber das wäre Erschütterung unsrer Gläubigkeit durch Reflexion. Und das ist fast nicht zu erzielen. Sobald gespielt wird, und sei die Varianten-Szene noch so kurz, gilt es als geschehen. Macht des Theaters.'[20] This substantiates my claim that even an overtly fictional scene acquires a certain validity as soon as the reader visualizes it. Moreover, it suggests that the reader is taken in not simply because of entrenched reading habits but also because of a certain willingness to conspire in his or her deception.

The rest of this chapter is concerned with exploring the purpose of the narrative devices described above. Critics have pointed to links between the narrative strategies employed in the novel and Frisch's ideas on identity. Some argue that Frisch turns his back on traditional literary

[18] In his detailed analysis of the reader's response to the narrative, Heinz Gockel confirms that the narrator's candid admissions that he is inventing his stories do not prevent the reader from experiencing the stories as real: 'Es präsentiert sich nämlich im *Gantenbein* ein Erzählen, das keineswegs eine mögliche Illusionierung des Lesers von vornherein ausschließt. Im Gegenteil, die Genauigkeit der Beschreibungen und die Dichte der Bilder können auch im *Gantenbein* gelegentlich einen Grad erreichen, der die Illusionierung geradezu herausfordert. Die ständigen Anläufe zu Geschichten [. . .] geben sich doch auch so, als ob sie zu einer 'wirklichen' Geschichte führten. Und noch die Revision der angefangenen Geschichte durch die andere Variante ist wiederum so vorgetragen, daß sie—wenn auch als Gegenentwurf—doch vorstellbar wird, ja zur Schaffung einer Illusion einlädt' (Gockel, 40).

[19] Frisch to Höllerer [undated], in Max Frisch, *Dramaturgisches: Ein Briefwechsel mit Walter Höllerer* (Berlin, FRG: Literarisches Colloquium, 1969), 32.

[20] Ibid. 32.

characters (who are distinguished chiefly by what they do),
because he believes that each of us comprises a set of possibilities which includes not only what we do, but also what
we omit to do, an idea expressed in 'Ich schreibe für Leser':
'die Person ist eine Summe von verschiedenen Möglichkeiten, meine ich, eine nicht unbeschränkte Summe, aber
eine Summe, die über die Biographie hinausgeht. Erst die
Varianten zeigen die Konstante.'[21] Critics also point to a link
between Frisch's handling of characterization in *Gantenbein*
and his well-known interpretation of the Second Command-
ment, 'Du sollst dir kein Bildnis machen',[22] arguing that
Frisch deliberately obstructs the reader's attempts to build a
coherent figure out of the details in the text in order to
prevent us from making a graven image of the *Buch-Ich*.[23]
However, Frisch himself admits that a pattern emerges from
the limited number of alternative lives available to an individual ('Erst die Varianten zeigen die Konstante') and critics
have found it easy to identify the 'constants' in the *Buch-Ich*'s
fantasies (a tendency towards jealousy, a fear of emotional
commitment, an inability to break out of roles etc.), proving
that it is not difficult to construct a fairly coherent image of
the *Buch-Ich*.

In the analysis which follows, I am not primarily interested
in problems of identity. I argue that the *Buch-Ich* uses the
projection, revision, and cancellation of fictions as instru-
ments of control, attempting both to exercise control over
his runaway imagination and to create reassuring *alter egos*
who are likewise characterized by their firm control over
others and over their own emotions. This plan fails, however,
and the narrator increasingly loses control of his stories
(becoming a 'Zauberlehrling der eigenen Fiktion',[24] faced
with the unintended consequences of his own experi-
mentation). As his attempts to maintain control become

[21] Frisch, *Werke*, V. 327.

[22] Max Frisch, *Tagebuch 1946–49*, in Frisch, *Werke*, II. 347–750 (374).

[23] See, for instance, Gerhard F. Probst, 'Three Levels of Image Making in Frisch's *Mein Name sei Gantenbein*', in Jay F. Bodine and Gerhard F. Probst (eds.), *Perspectives on Max Frisch* (Lexington, Ky.: University Press of Kentucky, 1982), 154–65.

[24] Heinz-Ludwig Arnold, 'Möglichkeiten nicht möglicher Existenzen: Max Frischs Roman *Mein Name sei Gantenbein*', in Arnold, *Brauchen wir noch die Literatur?: Zur literarischen Situation in der Bundesrepublik* (Düsseldorf: Bertelsmann, 1972), 138–42 (140).

increasingly desperate, so his manipulation of the narrative becomes increasingly blatant and artificial, building up to a climax in a kind of crescendo.

3. Narrative Control and Uncontrollable Emotions in the Gantenbein Story

This pattern of increasingly artificial narrative contrivance is most obvious in the dominant story of Gantenbein. Accordingly, and since critics have already discussed the Enderlin figure in considerable depth, the following analysis focuses on the story of Gantenbein, the false blind man.

When he first invents the figure of Gantenbein, the narrator appears to have a double objective (although both aims are related to his desire to escape himself). First, he envisages Gantenbein as a solution to the problem of being trapped in a socially imposed role, a torment which the *Buch-Ich* has evidently endured in the past. Since Gantenbein's blindness is only a charade, a role which he has chosen himself, he remains secure in the knowledge that he has the upper hand over society, and not the other way round. For this reason, the narrator initially emphasizes the positive aspects of Gantenbein's role: 'seine gesellschaftlichen Möglichkeiten, seine beruflichen Möglichkeiten . . . seine Freiheit kraft eines Geheimnisses' (21). Second, the narrator envisages that Gantenbein, being blind (or at least restricted in his actions by his role as a blind man) will resist the temptation of becoming involved with women and in this way be preserved from the unsuccessful relationships which have traumatized the *Buch-Ich* in the past. Accordingly, the first Gantenbein episode is a deliberately exaggerated scenario contrived to prove just how safe from sexual involvement Gantenbein is. Having accompanied a prostitute, Camilla, to her flat, Gantenbein is preserved from the temptation to avail himself of her sexual services because of his 'blindness', for when she tells him that she is a manicurist he is obliged to go along with her pretence (32–9). In this way, Gantenbein offers the narrator a reassuring model of self-control.

Having thus contrived a satisfactory beginning for the Gantenbein story (that is, one which is diametrically opposed to his own experience), the narrator returns to reality and describes himself waiting in a bar for a male business colleague. When the man's wife arrives to apologize for her husband's absence, the narrator starts up a flirtatious conversation with her. The outcome of this meeting is unclear, because at some point (probably at the top of p. 69) the narrator abandons the real story and begins to imagine what the outcome *might* be, using the figure of Enderlin to act out the possibilities. Even though he knows from previous experience how the relationship is likely to end (an adulterous affair followed by marriage, followed by more adultery and eventual separation), Enderlin sleeps with the woman and even contemplates continuing the affair.[25]

At this juncture, the narrator suddenly abandons Enderlin to return to the Gantenbein story, and gives Gantenbein a wife (having originally envisaged him without one). This rather abrupt change of focus appears to be motivated by the *Buch-Ich*'s very evident distaste for Enderlin's actions (which, rather than allowing him to escape himself, have merely confronted him with his past behaviour). Having failed to prove through the figure of Enderlin that he is capable of avoiding long-term involvement with a woman to whom he is attracted, the *Buch-Ich* now tries a different tack: given that a long-term relationship leading to marriage seems inevitable for him, he tries to prove that he could make a success of such a marriage (since this would render redundant his obvious fear of long-term commitment).[26]

Accordingly, the *Buch-Ich* attempts to demonstrate that the false blind man's marriage to Lila would solve all the problems which he has encountered in past relationships, in particular his tendency to jealousy (reasoning, in his uniquely illogical way, that if Lila believes him to be blind

---

[25] See White, 155–8, for a more detailed analysis of this scene.

[26] Kürmann, the hero of Frisch's 1968 play *Biografie. Ein Spiel*, goes through a similar process when he is given the chance to live his life again: having first tried, and failed, to change the course of his life in such a way that he avoids becoming involved with, and subsequently marrying, his wife Antoinette, he attempts to change the course of their marriage to avert its eventual breakup. This too fails. (Max Frisch, *Biografie. Ein Spiel*, in Frisch, *Werke*, V. 481–578).

she will make no attempt to hide her adultery, thus sparing him the torment of uncertainty which is for him the most unbearable aspect of sexual jealousy).[27] However, the contrived nature of the Gantenbein marriage is obvious from the start, and this is of course Frisch's intention. The story opens as follows:

Mein Name sei Gantenbein.
    Ich stelle mir vor:
    mein Leben mit einer großen Schauspielerin, die ich liebe und daher glauben lasse, ich sei blind; unser Glück infolgedessen.
    Ihr Name sei Lila. (81)

While the narrator uses the words 'daher' and 'infolgedessen' to suggest a logical chain of cause and effect, the reader is clearly meant to feel that their use is inappropriate, that love is not a self-evident reason for deceiving one's partner and that marital contentment is not the logical outcome of such deception. The opening words of the next section work in the same way:

Wir sind glücklich wie kaum ein Paar.
    Ich stelle mir vor:
    Lila betrügt mich (um dieses sehr dumme Wort zu gebrauchen) von Anfang an, aber sie weiß nicht, daß ich es sehe. (82)

Once again, Frisch relies on the reader perceiving a contradiction between the confident statement of the couple's happiness and the description of a double deception (the wife's adultery and the husband's pretence of blindness).

As the scenario develops, the *Buch-Ich* attempts to idealize the marriage, contriving to make Gantenbein the perfect husband (to satisfy himself that he, too, could behave in such a way).[28] That Gantenbein's sympathetic attitude

---

[27] Imagining a woman who is *not* an adulteress seems to be beyond the narrator's capabilities and is symptomatic of his deeply negative view of women. See n. 29 below.

[28] For instance, Gantenbein refrains from saying reproachfully: 'Siehst du!' when, after half an hour of searching for Lila's car, it turns out to be parked a few yards from where they first started looking (84); he clears up after Lila without criticizing her untidiness (85); he puts things which she has lost in a place where she will find them so that she thinks she has found them herself (85); he allows her to be extravagant, but unselfishly reduces his own expenditure whenever she wants to save (89); and he gives her helpful advice when she shops for clothes or when she is rehearsing for a play (91–8).

towards his wife is no more than a contrivance is evident not only because the *Buch-Ich*'s misogyny remains thinly veiled,[29] but also because Gantenbein's behaviour is, on a number of occasions, improbable. Not only is Gantenbein immune to feelings of irritation during the long waits for Lila in the airport concourse ('Ich liebe das Warten auf Flugplätzen' (82)),[30] he is positively *pleased* when she arrives arm in arm with a man whom he supposes to be her lover, because she will be protected from the customs officials ('Ein Glück, daß jemand sich für meine Lila wehrt!' (83)):[31] there is no sign of the anger or jealousy one might expect from a cheated husband. Likewise he claims to enjoy listening to his wife regaling each new set of dinner party guests with the increasingly exaggerated story of their first meeting, finding it 'drolliger von Mal zu Mal' (87). In all these examples, Frisch works on the assumption that the reader has an expectation of what is 'normal' behaviour in such circumstances, and that Gantenbein's story will contradict these expectations (and therefore appear contrived).

However improbable his fictions may seem, thus far the narrator is firmly in control of them. What is more, his imaginary character Gantenbein is firmly in control of his life and his environment. Not only is he able to control

[29] Though he claims to love and admire Lila, the *Buch-Ich* finds it impossible to imagine a sympathetic character for her, and appears to enjoy his feeling of superiority over her: not only is she a liar and an adulteress, she is also untidy, unpunctual, and a hopeless hostess (85); she embellishes the truth about her past (87); she is ignorant of her husband's tastes (89); she has bad moods (105); and she takes the credit for Gantenbein's hard work in the kitchen (218–19). Frisch ironizes the narrator's view of women, but seems nevertheless to have been stung by accusations of misogyny, which are a recurring preoccupation of his autobiographical text, *Montauk*.

[30] This description seems particularly contrived in retrospect, once we have read the decidedly more realistic portrayal of the waiting husband in the closing pages of the novel, in which Gantenbein is overcome by feelings of intense boredom: 'Gantenbein weiß, das scheint ihm nur so, als stehe er zeitlebens, so wie jetzt, zeitlebens am Flugplatz und in dieser Halle und genau an dieser Stelle, um Lila abzuholen zeitlebens ... wie heute, wie immer' (309).

[31] Reschke, in common with other critics who comment on this scene, takes it at face value, as though Gantenbein were a 'real person', rather than a puppet in the narrator's hands: '[Gantenbein] remains divorced from the scene, stands outside it, and is thus free of its emotional content; hence he is able to remain unperturbed and relaxed' (Reschke, 237).

his relationship with Lila,[32] he also revels in the chance to control other people. His blind man's role allows him secretly to punish the owner of an expensive dress shop for her sycophantic attitude to his wife (91–5); and to force the director of a production of Macbeth in which Lila is starring to make changes to the play (95–8).

However, the narrator's feeling of control proves to be precarious, since Gantenbein soon begins to show signs of jealousy which undermine his alleged self-control at the airport: he has to stifle his anger at the sight of men he thinks are infatuated with his wife (100), and interprets possibly innocent gestures as indications that other men are trying to seduce Lila (101). At this point, seeing that the Gantenbein figure is heading into dangerous waters, the narrator carefully steers him away from them. To say this is of course to speak figuratively, as though Gantenbein were a semi-independent entity whom the narrator could 'watch' getting into trouble, rather than a character whom he creates as he writes. A more accurate (but less picturesque) way of putting it would be that when the Buch-Ich's imagination runs away with him, and he pictures Gantenbein becoming jealous (a thought which he would rather repress), he attempts to regain control of his fantasy by redirecting the narrative. He does this in two complementary ways: first, he offers another example of how Gantenbein's role allows him to control his environment (Gantenbein's apparent genius for playing chess without being able to see the board unsettles his chess partner so much that he loses the game); and secondly, he focuses on emotionally neutral matters (the technicalities of role-playing and the rational game of chess) (102–3). Although this represents a rather abrupt change of subject, it is nevertheless a minor and fairly unobtrusive contrivance, as it is simply a case of nudging the story in the right direction: there is nothing fundamentally implausible about Gantenbein's reflecting on his role or playing chess.

More obviously contrived is his statement: 'Ich bin glücklich wie noch nie mit einer Frau' (104): not only are we

---

[32] Gockel sees a desire to control Lila even in Gantenbein's supposed acts of kindness: 'Gerade das Vorbereiten der kleinen Unordentlichkeiten entlarvt die Fürsorge als geschickt getarnte Herrschaftsausübung' (Gockel, 90).

already aware of suggestions to the contrary, but the narrator further undermines the credibility of the statement by
imagining that Lila frequently lies to Gantenbein about
where she has been, and that she receives expensive presents
from male admirers (104–5). Gantenbein is allegedly unperturbed by both these facts, but his self-control appears improbable, given what we have already seen of his suspicious
mind. Then, once again—and here we can see a pattern
establishing itself—the narrative moves towards a more
plausible outcome, but one which is at the same time less
desirable from the narrator's point of view. First, the *Buch-
Ich* admits the possibility of Gantenbein becoming jealous
('Hoffentlich werde ich nie eifersüchtig!' (110)); and then,
having interrupted the narrative to tell the anecdote of the
Bäckermeister in O. who shoots his wife's lover in the loins out
of jealousy, the narrator has Gantenbein tell the prostitute
Camilla that he, too, would like to shoot his wife's lover
(identified for the first time as Enderlin) in the loins. This
admission of violent urges may resolve the disparity between
what the narrator is claiming about Gantenbein and his
marriage, and what the reader feels is plausible, but it also
represents the failure of the narrator's attempts to steer his
narrative away from the subject of jealousy. Accordingly, the
Buch-Ich resorts to even more blatant tactics, abandoning
Gantenbein's story without explanation and returning to
Enderlin.

Although the series of passages which follow form the
longest continuous portion of text to deal with Enderlin, I
do not intend to discuss it in any detail, because, as I suggested above, other critics have analysed Enderlin's story in
some depth.[33] Suffice it to say that here too there is a pattern
of increasingly overt contrivance,[34] and that this contrivance

[33] For an excellent analysis, see Pulham, 255–61.

[34] This can be summarized as follows. As Enderlin drives to the airport, the *Buch-
Ich* makes no effort to conceal how he would like the story to develop, for he tries
to 'persuade' Enderlin not to continue his affair with the woman from the bar.
When this fails and the narrator finds himself confronted instead with his own past
mistakes, he abruptly changes the subject, countering Enderlin's story with a real
story which proves that he is capable of resisting involvement with a woman (137).
He then places Enderlin in a situation in which he is more likely to 'succeed': he
gives him a year to live, in the (barely concealed) hope that his character will be

reaches a peak when the narrator unceremoniously abandons the character of Enderlin, who, having simply replic-
ated the narrator's past behaviour, no longer offers the
possibility of self-escape. In Ulrich Weisstein's words: 'Enderlin is thrown overboard, mainly because he is so uncomfort-
ably close to the narrator that he leaves little room for
expectation [. . .] whereas Gantenbein fascinates him
because, placed in the narrator's circumstances, he would
think and act differently.'[35]

Since Enderlin has proved an unsuitable vehicle for escaping the past, the narrator feels ready to return to Gantenbein's relationship with Lila. This time, however, he tries a
different tack: Gantenbein admits to his wife that he can see,
and that he knows of her adultery (163). The reader may
not immediately experience this new twist in the story as
contrived, because it does not directly contradict what has
gone before (Gantenbein simply changes his mind) and the
narrator is careful to motivate it, by pointing out the incon-
venience of the blind-man role (163); but in view of the
narrator's proven manipulative attitude to his narrative, it is
clear that his professed understanding for Gantenbein's dis-
enchantment with his role is disingenuous.

In any case the new strategy misfires, largely because Gantenbein assumes (with his usual skewed logic) that Lila must
be hiding her adultery from him now that she knows that he
can see her. As a result, he is soon reduced to the very
state of jealous speculation which the *Buch-Ich* had hoped to

able to start a completely new life in the face of death. When Enderlin is instead
reduced to a state of terror, the narrator once more intervenes and changes to an
emotionally neutral subject (the difficulty of experiencing Jerusalem in an authen-
tic way). Finally, the story reaches an impasse with Enderlin's stubborn refusal to
abandon his previous way of life, which prompts the narrator to abandon him
altogether (160).

[35] Ulrich Weisstein, *Max Frisch* (New York: Twayne, 1967), 78–89 (85). Reschke,
having argued that Enderlin was invented by the narrator as an *alter ego* to 'reflect
upon and illuminate the narrator's own attitude about himself and his relationships with women' (rather than as a possible means of self-escape), assumes that
'the narrator discards [Enderlin] as no longer a viable manifestation of that particular facet of himself. He can be of no further value in helping the narrator
understand his traumatic experience' (Reschke, 205). Yet the narrator makes quite
clear (160) that he gives up Enderlin not because Enderlin's behaviour has begun
to *deviate* from his own, but because his past life and Enderlin's present life have
begun to *converge*.

avoid. When Lila returns from a trip to Hamburg, he suspects her of sleeping either with her ex-husband (why else,
he 'reasons', would she mention him so casually, and then
insist, for the first time, that he is boring, if not to cover this
up?) or with an unknown lover (why else would she keep
mentioning mutual friends with whom she spent time, if not
to provide herself with an alibi?). When Lila mentions a
young admirer who walked her home from the ballet and
declared his desire to marry her, Gantenbein very nearly
resorts to violence, such is his certainty that Lila must be in
love with this young man (168). But just as a row is about to
begin, the narrator reasserts control and pulls Gantenbein
back from the brink: 'Was ging es diesen Kerl denn an, daß
Lila und Gantenbein, wie ich weiß, glücklich sind? Ich lege
die Platte auf, Lila hat recht, ich lege die Nadel auf die
laufende Platte . . . / So weit, so gut' (170).[36] Here again,
the change of direction is carefully motivated inasmuch as
Gantenbein realizes, of his own accord, that he is being
unreasonable, but the narrator tacitly admits that he is artificially shoring up the couple's crumbling relationship by
adding the comment, 'so weit, so gut', which will become a
kind of refrain over the pages which follow.

Despite this intervention, the situation immediately wor-
sens, for the very next thing which the narrator imagines is
the arrival of a telegram from the young admirer, 'Einhorn'
(the phallic name which Gantenbein invents for him in his
jealous rage), announcing his imminent arrival. With the
same lack of logic which made him assume that Lila must be
hiding her adulterous affairs from him because he could see
no evidence of them, Gantenbein takes the telegram as
proof that his wife has committed adultery and is about to
leave him. Again, a marital row threatens to break out, and
this time the *Buch-Ich* admits openly that he is worried about
where his imagination is leading him: 'Gantenbein, seit er
nicht mehr den Blinden spielt, ist unmöglich. Ich mache

[36] From the end of Gantenbein's confession to Lila (166), to the invention of
Gantenbein's *alter ego*, Philemon (174), the narrator speaks of Gantenbein in the
first person, but there are isolated references to him in the third person, as in this
quotation. 'Gantenbein' and 'ich' therefore refer to the same person in this context.

mir Sorgen . . . ' (172). Consequently, he attempts to steer the story clear of danger by contriving not only that the tension between husband and wife is quickly diffused, but also that the threat to their marriage brings Lila and Gantenbein closer together. This is, of course, within the bounds of possibility, but the narrator's comment 'So weit, so wunderbar' (172) leaves us in no doubt that he is manipulating events in an attempt to compensate for his (and Gantenbein's) disturbing loss of control. The narrative is now set to rights again: the next time Lila receives a telegram, she rips it up, and when Gantenbein takes her away on holiday the whole matter is forgotten and the couple make plans to build a house together. In fact, so idyllic is this picture of marital harmony that the narrator renames the couple Philemon and Baucis,[37] heightening further our sense of the artificiality of this new development.

Once back home, however, Gantenbein's new *alter ego* Philemon begins to take an unhealthy interest in a locked drawer in which he knows his wife keeps her correspondence, and when he finds it left open, he is tempted to pry inside. To prevent this, the narrator takes control of the story again, and this time the contrivance is more obvious than before, highlighted by the inappropriate use of the word 'natürlich':[38]

Er kann nicht vorbeigehen, ohne es zu sehen: eine Schublade voller Briefe. Er könnte sie lesen zwei Stunden lang. Briefe vom Einhorn? Nun

---

[37] The narrator continues to call Gantenbein 'Philemon' in the sections which follow (174–98). He is less consistent in the case of the woman, whom he calls both 'Baucis' and 'Lila' (no particular significance seems to attach to the alternation between these two names).

[38] This is one of three examples I can find of the inappropriate use of the word 'natürlich'. Gantenbein tells Camilla a story, 'von einem Mann, der immer wieder einmal entschlossen ist, seinen Lebenswandel zu ändern, und natürlich gelingt es ihm nie' (248). There is no objective reason why the endeavour should end in failure: it is 'natural' only to the narrator, who is dogged by a sense of his own inability to escape his habitual behaviour. In the other example, the *Buch-Ich* revises the story of Lila and Gantenbein's first meeting, to include a third man: 'Lila lebte damals natürlich nicht ohne einen Gefährten' (297). This is not 'natural' either, as there is no reason why she should not have been unattached, but it seems that the narrator is unable to imagine a relationship which does not begin by destroying a previous relationship (compare Enderlin's affair, which threatens to destroy Svoboda's marriage to Lila, and which the narrator imagines will, in turn, end with the arrival of '[der] Mann, der dazwischen kommt' (125)).

gibt es zweierlei: Er tut es oder er beherrscht sich. Natürlich tut er's nicht.
Aber es verstimmt ihn gegen Baucis, daß er sich beherrschen muß. Er
hat, wie gesagt, eigentlich andres zu tun. Und kurz und gut, er tut es
nicht.
    Ich bin erleichtert. (175)

From what we have seen of Gantenbein/Philemon's tendency to jealousy, such restraint is not at all 'natural', especially as the immediate justification for his action is so weak
(he 'has other things to do').[39] Moreover, the *Buch-Ich*'s sigh
of relief ('Ich bin erleichtert'), which reveals his fear that
Philemon *will* read the letters, betrays his strong vested interest in Philemon's self-restraint.

    However, even this intervention by the narrator cannot
prevent him from imagining Philemon keeping checks on
Lila's mail, which includes a suspiciously large number of
letters from Denmark. The *Buch-Ich* apparently recognizes in
this undignified behaviour the advanced stages of jealousy,
for he calls Philemon a 'Narr' and intervenes in the narrative in the most blatant way so far, by suggesting that a
more appropriate occupation than the present story would
be a discussion of world problems:

Natürlich schämt Philemon sich selber, daß er sie zählt [i.e. the Danish
letters], und ich brauche ihm nicht zu sagen, daß er, gelinde gesagt, ein
Narr ist.
    Kümmern wir uns um anderes!
    Zum Beispiel:
    das geteilte Deutschland, wobei man sich fragen muß, unter welchen
Voraussetzungen die wirklich oder scheinbar geforderte Wiederver-
einigung nicht eine Gefahr für Europa darstellte, eine Bedrohung des
Friedens; warum tun wir nicht alles, um Voraussetzungen zu schaffen—
    Oder:
    die Verhältnisse in Spanien—
    Oder:
    die Verschlammung unsrer Seen—
    Kümmern wir uns darum! (175–6)

---

[39] A similar situation had occurred a little earlier in the Gantenbein story, but on
that occasion no contrivance, and therefore no 'natürlich', was necessary, because
at that stage the narrative was not in danger of going in the wrong direction: 'Jetzt
ist es schon soweit, daß Lila sogar ihre Briefe herumliegen läßt, Briefe eines
fremden Herrn, die unsere Ehe sprengen würden, wenn Gantenbein sie lesen
würde. Er tut's nicht' (103).

The absurd artificiality of this passage, which bears no relation at all to the story of marital conflict which precedes it, is
an index of the narrator's fear of reliving his own jealous
tendencies through his characters.[40] Both the unnecessary
detail ('wobei man sich fragen muß' etc.) and the accom-
panying tone of earnest engagement serve to heighten our
sense of its inappropriateness in this context. Along with
similar passages (in which matters for rational debate are
likewise used as a means of repressing unwelcome emotions)[41] the passage can be read as a satire on liberal intel-
lectuals, whose social and political engagement is exposed as
a front behind which to hide the mire of their private lives.

Immediately following this strange outburst, the narrator
again intervenes in the story, albeit more subtly, allowing
Philemon/Gantenbein to let off some emotional steam by
committing adultery himself (prompting another narratorial 'So weit, so gut' (176)). Predictably, however, the counter-
adultery fails to cure Philemon's jealousy, and one morning
he steals some of the Danish letters. Having fought his urge
to read them, he finds himself in the ridiculous situation of

[40] It seems to me that Manfred Jurgensen misunderstands the passage when he
writes: 'Diese repräsentativen Probleme sollen der "klassischen Mär von Philemon
und Baucis" als dringlichere Realität entgegengestellt werden. Sie scheinen dem
Erzähler von größerer Bedeutung, weil diese Wirklichkeit verändert werden kann,
während das Verhältnis zwischen Mann und Frau seiner Meinung nach unverän-
derlich bleiben wird.' The passage is not so much a nod in the direction of social
engagement by the narrator as a knee-jerk reaction to the pain of the memory of
his own behaviour in a similar situation. (Manfred Jurgensen, *Max Frisch. Die
Romane* (Berne: Francke, 1972), 212.)

[41] For instance, the narrator tries to divert Enderlin's attention from thoughts of
his sexual encounter of the previous night: 'Ich versuche irgend etwas zu denken.
/ Zum Beispiel: / Was ich neulich in unserem Gespräch über Kommunismus und
Kapitalismus, über China, über Cuba, über Atomtod und über die Ernährungslage
der Menschheit, falls sie sich verzehnfacht, hätte sagen können' (122). Compare
Gantenbein's reaction when his wife receives a telegram from her 'lover': 'Nimmst
du noch Toast? fragt sie, und ich rede über Weltereignisse, bis Lila sich plötzlich
erhebt, um ein Taschentuch zu holen' (172); and his thoughts when Beatrice, who
he suspects may not be his own child, announces at a dinner party that she wants a
different father: 'das Kind hat so unrecht ja nicht: vielleicht ist dieser Mann, der da
blindlings seine Banane schält, wirklich nicht ihr Papi ... Aber wie dem auch sei:
Fernsehen, davon war die Rede, Fernsehen als Instrument der Bewußtseinsindus-
trie und überhaupt Kunst im technischen Zeitalter, insbesondere Fernsehen, dazu
kann jedermann etwas sagen' (296–7). Svoboda uses similar diversions, talking
about the 'Raumbühne' when his wife's lover comes round to his flat for drinks
(259).

trying to burn or bury them, and fails to do even that. Eventually, in a jealous rage (feeling that the lovers are conspiring against him), he opens the letters. The narrator interjects that Philemon does not need to read them because he (the narrator) has read such letters in the past, and knows what they contain. He even invents an example based on his experience. So painful is this reminder of a previous experience of betrayal that he attempts once more to regain control of the story in order to ensure that Philemon does not make the same mistake: 'Also: Philemon hat die Briefe nicht gelesen, er schiebt den ersten Gang hinein und löst die Bremse' (180). Not only is this the least probable option, given what we know of Philemon, but also, unlike some of the contrivances noted above, no motivation is given, an omission which nurtures our growing suspicion that the only motivation is the narrator's fear of reliving a painful experience through his character.

Despite making Philemon throw the letters down a drain (the cue for yet another 'So weit, so gut' (182)), the narrator is still not in complete control of his fiction, since he cannot make Philemon forget the Danish letters. He finds himself once more on the brink of a confrontation between Philemon and Lila, but this time he chooses not to hold his character back, suddenly seeing confrontation as the braver (and therefore more gratifying) option:

Warum stellt er sie nicht zur Rede?
    Keine Antwort.
    Angst?
    Ich stelle mir vor: Philemon stellt sie zur Rede, und Baucis hat etwas zu gestehen. (183)

It seems that because the *Buch-Ich* does not like to think of himself as a coward (even in his fictional role as Philemon), he is goaded by his own question—'Angst?'—into imagining Philemon bravely confronting Baucis. He is punished for his vanity, however, when the imagined scene takes him where he does not want to go, forcing him to relive his own experience of similar confrontations with unfaithful partners. Philemon asks Baucis questions as they sit drinking coffee, but they are 'lauter Fragen, die ich auch schon gestellt habe,

ich kann's nicht hindern, daß Philemon sie trotzdem stellt;
aber ohne meine Anteilnahme. Wozu muß ich immer wieder
dabei sein? [. . .] Nun wisse er's! sagt sie, während ich
Zucker nehme, einen Geschmack auf der Zunge, den ich
kenne' (183–4). This leads the narrator to talk more openly
than before about his past (184) but his memories are so
distressing that he feels compelled to guide the narrative in
an even more overtly contrived way than before, cancelling
out the passage we have just read, by deciding that the
confrontation does not take place: 'Also: / Philemon stellt
sie nicht zur Rede. / Ich gehe arbeiten.' (184).

The narrator continues to guide the narrative, by imagining that Philemon buys Baucis a sports car. It is clear from
the way in which he describes Lila's puzzled reaction to this
gesture that his specific intention in giving her the car is to
avoid the disastrous situation which threatened in the previous scene: 'Wie soll sie es fassen, sie, die keine Ahnung
haben kann von der Szene beim schwarzen Kaffee, die nicht
stattgefunden hat?' (184).[42] Finally, the narrator once more
expresses his satisfaction with this ploy: 'So weit, so gut. / Ich
bin erleichtert, daß Philemon sie nicht zur Rede gestellt hat'
(184).

Philemon now enters a new phase, becoming more self-
confident and entertaining, and, as a result, his wife finds
herself falling in love with him again. Inasmuch as this
change is at least possible, the narrator's redirection of the
story is at this point subtle rather than overt. However, while
the couple enjoy a romantic, moonlit dinner at the lake-side,
dangerous emotions appear to be threatening to surface
again, because the narrator makes Philemon return to one
of the intellectual concerns alluded to in the extract beginning 'Kümmern wir uns um was anderes':

Wie es wäre, wenn Baucis jetzt ein Kind bekäme, insbesondere die Frage,
wessen Kind es sein würde, scheint Philemon nicht zu beschäftigen;
jedenfalls raucht er seine Zigarre und spricht, Blick auf den nächtlichen

---

[42] Of course, the fact that the *Buch-Ich* thinks that he can solve his (fictional)
marital problems by buying his wife a sports car is just one more proof that he has a
negative image of women (here as shallow and materialistic), and that he is ill-
equipped to cope with the emotional challenges of a relationship.

See hinaus, von der Verschlammung unsrer Seen, was ein ernsthaftes
Problem ist. (186)

The only explanation for the narrator's rather absurdly
drawing attention to what Philemon is *not* thinking about
(the possibility that Lila is pregnant by another man) is that
the narrator knows that this is what *he* would think about if
he were in Philemon's situation. And as this is precisely what
he wants Philemon to avoid (the self-destructive speculations
of the jealous mind), he gives him something else to think
about, but at the same time draws attention to his own
manipulation of the scene.

　This passage prepares us for a new attack of jealous passion: Philemon picks up Baucis from a hotel in Munich and
convinces himself that a man who has just paid his hotel bill
is the dreaded Dane, Einhorn. To punish his wife, he drives
his car too fast, and when she threatens to get out if he does
not slow down, he slows down a little to make it easier for
her to execute her threat. Finally, he stops and actually
invites her to get out. So dissatisfied is the narrator with this
development ('Ich weiß, ich werde ungenießbar . . . ' (188)),
perhaps because he realizes that the attacks of jealousy are
becoming more frequent and more irrational, that he makes
even more blatant use of the technique which he had first
tried out a few pages earlier: whereas there he cancelled out
just one scene (the confrontation with Lila), he now erases
several scenes which he would prefer not to have happened:

Was ist eigentlich geschehen?
　Baucis hat jetzt einen eignen Austin-Sport, und alles andere ist nicht
geschehen: keine Aussprache beim schwarzen Kaffee, kein Hummeressen
mit Vollmond über dem See, kein albernes Gebaren auf offener Strecke.
Nichts von all dem! Als einziger Tatbestand bleibt: Baucis hat jetzt ihren
weißen Austin-Sport, der sie entzückt und tadellos läuft.
　So weit, so gut. (188)

Nor does this desperate intervention stop there, for the
narrator then tries once more to highlight Philemon's positive qualities, but this time in such a ludicrously artificial
manner that he basically re-invents him:

Und Philemon ist ein Mann, der sich wieder sehen lassen darf, Mann
unter Männern, ein Zeitgenosse zwischen Ost und West, ein Staatsbürger,

der sich gegen die Atomwaffen ausspricht, wenn auch erfolglos, ein Leser, ein Freund, der hilft, ein Schachspieler, ein Kopf, ein Glied der Gesellschaft, deren Veränderung ihm unerläßlich erscheint, ein Arbeiter von Morgen bis Abend, ein Tätiger, ein Teilnehmer und ein Widersacher, ein Mensch, den die Fragen der Welt beschäftigen, die Not der Völker, die Hoffnung der Völker, die Lügen der Machthaber, die Ideologien, die Technik, die Geschichte und die Zukunft, die Weltraumfahrt—ein Mensch . . . Was ihn fasziniert: der Gedanke, daß das menschliche Leben, wenn in Jahrmillionen unsere Erde erkaltet, während anderseits die Venus sich abkühlt und in Jahrmillionen ihrerseits eine Atmosphäre bekommt, in den Weltraum verpflanzt werden könnte (*Science and Future*).
Ich bin erleichtert. (188–9)

The passage stands out from the narrative around it in both content and style. It consists in the senseless enumeration of descriptive elements all connoting similar things (public and intellectual concerns). In particular it evokes the world of work ('ein Arbeiter von Morgen bis Abend') an area of activity used by the *Buch-Ich* throughout the novel to counterbalance or repress emotion.[43] Whereas earlier the mere mention of Gantenbein's hobby of playing chess was enough to reassure the narrator that his character was set on the right course, he is now obliged to pile one rational pursuit upon another in order to correct the impression that Philemon is jealous beyond help.

Once reassured, the narrator returns to the matter of the Danish letters, but jealousy quickly reasserts itself, and this time even more powerfully than before, for Philemon now breaks open the locked drawer in Lila's desk and reads a number of love letters (without recognizing that they are letters which he himself wrote to her before their marriage). His jealousy reaches a climax when a young man arrives at the flat asking for Lila. Assuming that he is the Dane, 'Einhorn', Philemon locks him in Lila's bedroom with her

---

[43] For instance, the *Buch-Ich* tries to distract Philemon from his jealous imaginings by drawing him back to work. When Philemon wonders what to do with the letters he has stolen, the *Buch-Ich* advises him: 'Ich bin für Verbrennen, aber rasch. Ich möchte an die Arbeit' (179). Compare pp. 183, 184, 193. Svoboda is on one occasion so 'gehetzt von beruflichen Dingen' (222) that he has no time to reflect on his crumbling marriage. Later, too, Svoboda uses work to distract himself from his marital troubles: 'Svoboda [. . .] blickt zum Fenster hinaus, indem er grad an etwas anderes denkt—an den gestrigen Abend mit Lila—aber nicht lang . . . Das hier, Projekt für einen öffentlichen Wettbewerb, ist dringender' (256).

and leaves the flat with the key, only to learn, on his return, that the young man is a student seeking advice about whether to take up a career in acting. Incensed, Lila tells Philemon that she is leaving him. As critics point out, this disastrous end to Philemon's story suggests to the reader that the narrator's recent relationship broke up for similar reasons.[44] Having thus failed to prevent the relationship from ending in the all-too-familiar disaster of a breakup, the narrator intervenes more blatantly than before by cancelling out the whole of the story in which Gantenbein admits to not being blind: 'Ich bleibe Gantenbein' (199).

I have shown that the narrator manipulates the story of Gantenbein in an increasingly obvious and drastic way, in an attempt to maintain control over his fictions. The contrivances begin as relatively unobtrusive features of the text, some of which may be recognized only in retrospect (such as Gantenbein's supposed immunity to jealous feelings), and become increasingly open, to the point where they become blatant. I am not suggesting that the reader consciously analyses this contrivance, but that he or she has a 'feel' for the relative artificiality of each successive passage of narrative and is aware that the Gantenbein story builds up gradually to a climax. Among the many disorienting narrative effects in *Mein Name sei Gantenbein*, this patterning provides a sense of orientation.

What happens in the remaining third of the novel is interesting. The contrivances continue, some subtle,[45] some blatant;[46] but there is not the same structure of increasingly

[44] See White: 'The invented Philemon story ends in a way which implicitly illuminates X's past: such attitudes as Philemon's led him to the *Ausgangsposition*' (White, 162).

[45] For instance, the narrator counteracts the disastrous passions of the Philemon story with a piece of unemotional social critique (Gantenbein exposing the hypocrisy and materialism of the rich man (201–8)). Also, when Burri tells Gantenbein that he is the only person who does not see Lila as she really is, the narrator responds with a passage in which Gantenbein, on the contrary, is the only person who *does* see her as she really is: a slovenly woman who puts on her apron as soon as her guests arrive, to disguise the fact that her husband has done all the work (218–19). In other words, the narrator refuses the implication that he is 'blind' in his relationship with women.

[46] The narrator decides to change Lila, tries her out in the role of Countess and finally cancels out all her previous roles, when the variations prove fruitless (219).

overt intervention by the *Buch-Ich* which has characterized the narrative up to this point. This explains why critics find Svoboda's story, and the final third of the narrative in general, less compelling than the rest of the novel.[47] This is due, at least in part, to the nature of the Svoboda story, which temporarily takes over from the Gantenbein story in this final third of the novel. It must be remembered that Svoboda grows out of the *Buch-Ich*'s rival (or potential rival): the husband of the woman whom he meets in the bar. This rivalry seems to enable the narrator to keep a distance from the Svoboda figure, because he clearly enjoys the spectacle of Svoboda making a fool of himself (like the traditional cuckold of farce) in his jealous reactions to Lila's affair.[48] Of course, Gantenbein/Philemon is a figure of fun too, but not for the narrator, only for Frisch and the reader: the narrator finds his absurd behaviour painful because he is unable to separate it from his own. Svoboda, on the other hand, is at the narrator's mercy. The Svoboda story is thus another example of the narrator's delight in controlling others, at least in his imagination, as well as illustrating the paradox that one can laugh at one's own faults in other people, but not in oneself. Only as he abandons the Svoboda story to return to Gantenbein does the narrator admit that he has more in common with Svoboda than he might like to think ('Bin ich Svoboda?', he asks (289)). The result of this

[47] Hans Mayer thinks that the later stories are 'künstlerisch unnotwendige Varianten' (Hans Mayer, 'Mögliche Ansichten über Herrn Gantenbein. Anmerkungen zu Max Frischs neuem Roman', in Walter Schmitz (ed.), *Über Max Frisch II* (Frankfurt/Main: Suhrkamp, 1976), 314–24 (321)); while Baumgart has the impression that beyond a certain point in the novel the narrator is simply trying out 'ein Perpetuum mobile von Kurzgeschichten, als sei er nichts weiter als ein Kleider—und Geschichtenständer' (Reinhard Baumgart, 'Othello als Hamlet', in Beckermann, Thomas (ed.), *Über Max Frisch* (Frankfurt/Main: Suhrkamp, 1971), 192–7 (194)).

[48] When the narrator imagines how Svoboda might react, were Lila to admit her affair with Enderlin, none of the alternatives is complimentary. The first makes him look particularly foolish: 'Svoboda saust mit seinem Wagen gegen einen Baum' (236), and the next three are equally self-defeating as they all end with his losing Lila anyway ('Natürlich verliert er sie auch so' (237)). He tries without success, for instance, to pick up women in nightclubs and at swimming pools (237); and he attempts to impress female hitchhikers with his expensive open-topped car, but finds that the women are always accompanied by men (237). Frisch speaks of the role of the cuckold in literature, and of the tendency of the jealous man towards ridiculous behaviour in his *Tagebuch 1946–1949* (*Werke*, II. 714).

distanced relationship to Svoboda is that there is no such urgent need to manipulate events as there was in the Gantenbein story (there is, for instance, no 'so weit, so gut', or 'Ich bin erleichtert'). Consequently, this part of the novel may hold the reader's interest less strongly.

4. Jealousy, Infidelity, and Fiction

So far my analysis has focused on the narrator's attempts to control his increasingly ungovernable narrative. I want now to draw out some correspondences between the form of the novel and its content, that is, between the narrative techniques discussed above and the novel's central thematic concerns (sexual jealousy and infidelity). First, *Gantenbein* seems to me to illustrate very well the workings of the jealous mind, not just at the level of plot (in Gantenbein/ Philemon's irrational behaviour), but also at the level of narration. For it is evident from the manner in which the *Buch-Ich* handles his fictions that his imagination is of the kind which is dangerously uncontrolled, which always finds it easiest to imagine the worst and, moreover, to imagine the worst in frighteningly realistic detail, to the extent that he begins to believe his own fictions (a point to which I will return presently). This tendency to imagine the worst possible outcome to a given scenario (and particularly to a scenario involving a female partner) is neatly summed up by the narrator's absurd proposition: 'Wo eine Liebe ist, da ist auch ein Flugzeug nach Uruguay' (meaning, in context, that if a stranger has fallen in love with his wife, it follows inevitably that this stranger intends to whisk his wife away to an exotic country in order to start a new and exciting life with her) (168). The same tendency is in evidence whenever the *Buch-Ich* invents fictions: having imagined his fictional wife mentioning a chance meeting with an admirer, the *Buch-Ich* cannot help but imagine her receiving frequent letters from this man; and having once posited the existence of these letters he cannot stop himself from imagining that his fictional persona tries to read them. By this I do not mean simply that the actions described by the *Buch-Ich* (such as opening his wife's mail) reflect actions which are typical of a jealous man (though they clearly do), but rather that the *Buch-Ich* demonstrates through his imaginings precisely the kind of rampant, runaway imagination which is most likely to be a prey to sexual jealousy.

Another correspondence between form and content in *Gantenbein* involves the confusion of fact and fantasy. At the level of plot, Frisch illustrates on more than one occasion the jealous man's tendency to confuse his imaginings with reality. In the episode concerning the 'Danish letters', which Philemon suspects have been sent by his wife's lover, the narrator invents, for Philemon's benefit, an example of such adulterous correspondence, only to find that once Philemon has 'heard' the fictional letter (the whole dialogue between narrator and character being, of course, another fabrication), he is unable to dismiss it from his mind and begins to act as though it were real, taking it as proof positive of Lila's infidelity (and remaining deaf to the narrator's protestations that his account of the letter's contents is nothing more than 'eine blinde Mutmaßung' (183)). Here, the narrator dissociates himself from this weakness by attributing it to his fictional character Philemon, but he later acknowledges it as his own problem. Explaining how he came to understand that jealousy is just one symptom of a more fundamental disorder (namely, paranoia), the *Buch-Ich* describes buying a tape recorder in an effort to discover what his friends say about him in his absence. This experience forces him to recognize that his tendency to imagine scenes and events is interfering with his behaviour in real life, because he is unable to keep reality and fantasy apart:

Indem ich Gespräche erfinde, die ohne mich stattfinden, laufe ich Gefahr, Menschen zu fürchten oder zu achten oder zu lieben, je nachdem wie sie in meiner Einbildung reden, wenn ich nicht zugegen bin. Mein fast blindes Vertrauen beispielsweise zu Burri, nur weil er in meinen erfundenen Gesprächen nicht anders redet und nicht anders schweigt und nicht anders lacht als in meiner Gegenwart, geht so weit, daß ich es einfach nicht glaube, wenn ich auf Umwegen erfahre, was Burri neulich gesagt haben soll. [. . .] Und genauso begründet oder unbegründet, nämlich ein Ergebnis meiner blinden Erfindung, die sich früher oder später um jeden Menschen bildet, ist mein jahrelanges Mißtrauen

gegenüber andern, beispielsweise meine schmerzliche Befangenheit gegenüber Dolf, nur weil er, sobald er nicht in meiner Gegenwart, sondern
in meiner Einbildung redet, plötzlich viel feiner und viel gescheiter redet.
[. . .] Denn in den Gesprächen, die ich auf dem Heimweg erfinde oder
wenn ich im Bad liege, in Gesprächen ohne mich ist dieser Dolf ein
wahrer Ausbund von Humor, ein Verschwender von Wissen, das er vor
mir stets verhehlt. (267–8)[49]

The words 'das er vor mir stets verhehlt', are of course
intended ironically. Dolf does not *hide* his wit and intel-
ligence from the *Buch-Ich*: he does not possess any; but because the narrator has credited him with these gifts in his
imagination, he must then invent further fictions to ration-
alize Dolf's manifestly unremarkable personality. In this way
the paranoid man (who is often also a jealous man) confuses
the real with the imaginary.

What is interesting about this aspect of jealousy, as
Frisch portrays it, is that it corresponds to our experience as
readers. We have already seen, in this and in the previous
chapter, that what begins as mere speculation or invention
in a novel may slowly break away from its speculative context
and take on a validity or reality to which it cannot lay claim.
In this way, Frisch contrives to make the reader experience a
similar confusion to that of the jealous man. Indeed, Frisch
himself recognized this correspondence between the form
of the novel and its content. In 'Ich schreibe für Leser' he
notes the way in which the imperfect tense gives a misleading
sense of reality, of 'what really happened'. While he found
this effect vexing at first, he realized later that it could be
used to good effect:

Aber das mit dem Imperfekt, das mich stört, ist etwas anderes: was ich für
eine Störung hielt, war das Thema selbst. Und drum kommt das Imperfekt immer streckenweise wieder vor. Um immer wieder einzustürzen.
Man beginnt ja an seine Fiktion zu glauben, aber was zu gelten scheint,

---

[49] In this passage, as in another just mentioned (where he refers to his speculation about the content of the Danish letters as 'eine blinde Mutmaßung'), Frisch
plays on figurative uses of the word 'blind', which we are clearly meant to connect
with Gantenbein's literal blindness. His comments in this particular passage seem
to suggest that blindness is not just a disability suffered by an unfortunate minority,
but something fundamental to the human condition, the result of our not being
able to see into other people's minds, a deficiency which forces us to rely on
unverifiable suppositions in our dealings with others.

erweist sich als Fiktion, und man weiß nicht, wo man sich befindet. Genau das wäre darzustellen.[50]

The disorientation experienced by the reader (as fictions which at first appear real are unmasked as unreal) therefore reproduces that experienced by the jealous man.

There is one final correspondence between form and content in *Gantenbein* which I would like to highlight, and this necessitates a short excursus into narrative theory. In *Story and Situation: Narrative Seduction and the Power of Fiction*,[51] Ross Chambers examines a series of nineteenth-century short stories which, in his view, use the motif of seduction as a metaphor for the narrative situation which underlies all modern story-telling. Chambers argues that modern fiction works on the basis of a 'contract' between the reader and the narrator, in which the narrator's desire to narrate is balanced by the reader's desire for narration. He attributes this phenomenon to the decline of a traditional form of story-telling which served to convey experience:

When narrative ceases to be (perceived as) a mode of direct communication of some preexisting knowledge and comes instead to figure as an oblique way of raising awkward, not to say unanswerable questions, it becomes necessary for it to trade in the manipulation of desire (that is, the desire to narrate must seek to arouse some corresponding desire for narration) to the precise extent that it can no longer depend, in its hearers or readers, on some sort of 'natural' thirst for information.[52]

Once literature becomes divorced from this traditional role of direct communication, it is invested with a value, but it also becomes subject to 'market forces': 'in order to realize this potential value, the alienated text must first be read, and its seductiveness appears, then, as the necessary means whereby such a text succeeds in acquiring a readership and inserting itself into the new interpretative contexts that will actualize its meaningfulness.'[53]

---

[50] Frisch, *Werke*, V. 326.
[51] Ross Chambers, *Story and Situation: Narrative Seduction and the Power of Fiction* (Minneapolis: University of Minnesota Press, 1984).
[52] Ibid. 11.
[53] Ibid. 12.

Chambers could be accused (*a*) of clothing a common-place ('a narrator must arouse the interest of the reader') in modern literary-critical jargon; and (*b*) of making a false distinction between the old and the new, since the devices employed by many medieval story-tellers to arouse interest in their listeners would seem to suggest that the problem of an inattentive audience/reader is not exclusive to the modern writer. However, Frisch, as we have seen, also speaks of a contract between writer and audience in his corres-pondence with Höllerer, describing the audience's dis-appointment when a scene which has just been acted out is discarded: 'der Zuschauer, auf Erschütterung abonniert, fühlt sich betrogen.'[54] The contract he speaks of is a literal, commercial one: the audience have paid for their tickets and expect 'value for money', but it is, at the same time, a more abstract, intellectual one: the audience agree to 'ac-tualize the meaningfulness' of the dramatic text in exchange for entertainment. Frisch's use of the word 'betrogen', is interesting, however. For if, as Chambers argues, narrative is by nature a kind of seduction, then the devices which I have grouped under the heading 'overt fictionalization' (and in particular the practice of cancelling out or erasing fictions) is a kind of 'narrative infidelity', in which the contract be-tween reader and writer, according to which it is understood that the writer will provide a story if the reader is willing to read it, is repeatedly broken by the writer. The reader may respond to the deception by nullifying the contract with the writer, i.e. by putting the book down, and this seems, from what I have heard, to be the response of many readers to *Gantenbein*. But my analysis has shown that the seductive power of fiction is stronger than one might suppose, since the reader may still be taken in by the promise of a story even after he or she has been deceived. Indeed, Chambers sees this as true of any difficult (he uses Barthes's term 'scriptible') modern text, which 'realizes itself as a seductive *object*, one very largely dependent, that is, on the willingness of its readership to be seduced, as opposed to the seduct-

[54] Frisch, *Dramaturgisches: Ein Briefwechsel mit Walter Höllerer*, 32.

iveness of the readerly text, which is much more strongly centered in a sense of its own power to take the initiative and to develop an *active* seductive maneuver'.[55] Far from leading us into abstract discussions about the nature of modern narrative, these insights direct us back to the content of *Gantenbein*, for infidelity and deception are at the heart of the story. There is Lila's infidelity, at times suspected but unproved, at times confirmed (that is, invented by the narrator); the counter-infidelity of each of the male characters; and Gantenbein's deception of Lila, when he tricks her into believing that he is blind. Thus, in making the reader feel 'cheated' (of the story to which (s)he feels (s)he has a right), Frisch is once more forcing the reader to enact the narrator's central problem.

One reason for emphasizing the connections between narrative technique and the content of the novel is to counter the suggestion (particularly prevalent in early reviews of the novel) that *Gantenbein* is a novel whose only subject is the creation of stories and which is, therefore, entirely self-absorbed. Hans Egon Holthusen, for instance, identifies the theme of the novel as 'ein Werkstattgespräch des Erzählers mit sich selbst über die Möglichkeit des Erzählens'.[56] This seems to me to be a distorted view of the novel: *Gantenbein* may not refer extensively to the social realities of modern Switzerland or to the political problems of the modern world (except, as I have shown, in order to satirize those who profess to take an interest in them), but it is grounded in real life, that is, it has a clear referent outside itself, namely sexual jealousy. The narrative technique plays an important role in the exploration of this theme.

Finally, it might be objected that my analysis takes too little account of the element of irony in *Gantenbein*. For there is a significant difference between having a runaway imagination and writing about one's runaway imagination. Behind the narrative voice which fails pitifully to control its wild

---

[55] Chambers, 14.

[56] Hans Egon Holthusen, 'Ein Mann von fünfzig Jahren', *Merkur*, 18 (1964), 1073–7 (1073). Cf. Rudolf Hartung, who claims that the novel is all about the problems of telling stories in the modern world: 'Die Problematik des Erzählens heute wurde zum Thema des Romans gemacht' (Rudolf Hartung, 'Max Frisch, *Mein Name sei Gantenbein*', *NR* 75 (1964), 682–6 (683)).

imaginings is a narrator giving a *written* account of this struggle who, we must suppose, is very much in control of what he writes (given that nothing prevents him from literally erasing those parts of the story with which he is dissatisfied, and suppressing what he has discarded). While the reader may derive added satisfaction from an awareness of this ironic dimension (from knowing that the narrator is consciously exhibiting his own impotence and ineptitude for our benefit), Frisch makes no particular attempt to draw attention to the irony, and the experience of a disturbing loss of control remains his primary focus.

Mein Name sei Gantenbein marks a highpoint in Frisch's treatment of narrative: none of his subsequent prose works matches its technical complexity. Indeed, in his next prose work, *Montauk* (1975), Frisch abandoned fictions (which, he now maintained, had falsified his life) in favour of a more direct and straightforward (though still unmistakably literary) autobiographical account. However, he returned to fiction with *Der Mensch erscheint im Holozän* (1979), in which a fairly conventional third-person narrative (related largely through the consciousness of the central figure, Herr Geiser) is enlivened and enriched by the skilful use of montage. Haunted by fear of an impending natural disaster, Herr Geiser seeks reassurance in factual knowledge. Photocopies of the texts which he reads (ranging from Bible extracts to entries in encyclopaedias) and of his handwritten notes on these texts are interspersed in the narrative. The montage technique invites the reader to find connections between the excerpts, and to consider, among other things, the way in which Man's understanding of Nature (and of the relationship between Nature and Civilization) has developed over time. Frisch's final prose work, the story *Blaubart* (1982), interweaves a series of courtroom dialogues with a monologue in which the acquitted man, Schaad, remembers and reflects on his trial for murder. The ending of this double-stranded narrative is given a subtle twist when Schaad (perhaps conditioned by his recent experiences to conceive of every encounter in terms of a cross-examination) begins to *imagine* dialogues between a prosecutor and various witnesses (including his dead parents and his alleged murder victim). Thus, even though *Gantenbein* seems temporarily to have dulled Frisch's appetite for fictions, it by no means exhausted his capacity for devising new and fruitful narrative strategies.

4

CHRISTA WOLF: *NACHDENKEN ÜBER CHRISTA T.*

1. Publication History

Even before it reached the GDR's bookshops early in 1969 *Nachdenken über Christa T.*,[1] Christa Wolf's second major novel, was already the subject of speculation in the German book world. Delays in the book's production and two luke-warm reviews which appeared in advance of the novel itself[2] led to the suspicion that *Christa T.* was being suppressed because it was unpalatable to the SED.[3] When it finally appeared, the novel became a *cause célèbre*, partly because of the undeservedly hostile reception which it received in the East, partly because of the equally undeserved tag of 'oppositional literature' which was attached to it in the West, and in no small part because its publisher took the extraordinary step of distancing himself publicly from the book, in the pages of *Neues Deutschland*.[4]

Just how unpopular Christa Wolf made herself with the GDR regime by writing *Christa T.* has become clear only since the *Wende*. *Stasi* files on Wolf, released to her in 1992 by the Gauck Commission (and leaked to the press), show that in 1968 *Stasi* surveillance of Wolf was stepped up to the

---

[1] Christa Wolf, *Nachdenken über Christa T.* (Halle (Saale): Mitteldeutscher Verlag, 1968). All further references to the novel are included in the text.

[2] Hermann Kähler, 'Christa Wolfs Elegie', *SF* 21 (1969), 251–61, and Horst Haase, 'Nachdenken über ein Buch', *NDL* 17/4 (April 1969), 174–85.

[3] Wolfgang Werth ('Nachricht aus einem stillen Deutschland', *Der Monat*, 21 (1969), 90–4) reported being unable to find the novel at the Leipzig book fair, and was told that a new edition was not being planned. He warned: 'Die Rechnung derer, die Bücher fürchten und sie deshalb unterdrücken, ist noch nie aufgegangen' (94). Günter Zehm, writing in *Die Welt* in March 1969, admitted to hearing rumours, 'daß viertausend Exemplare "nur zum Gebrauch für Funktionäre" gedruckt worden seien' (Günter Zehm, 'Nachdenken über Christa W.' (extracts), in Manfred Behn (ed.), *Wirkungsgeschichte von Christa Wolfs 'Nachdenken über Christa T.'* (Königstein/Ts.: Athenäum, 1978), 38–9 (38)).

[4] Heinz Sachs, 'Verleger sein heißt ideologisch kämpfen' (extracts), in Behn, 54–6.

most intensive level, the so-called 'Operativer Vorgang', probably as a result of the SED's displeasure at *Christa T.*[5] In fact, the fall of the Berlin Wall and the end of the GDR has opened up to Wolf scholars a rich new seam of archival material relating to the novel; the first to exploit it, Angela Drescher, has collated and edited previously confidential or inaccessible documents concerning the novel's publication, including extracts from the diary which Wolf kept in the late 1960s, in which she records her thoughts on the novel's composition and on the battle to publish it.[6] Drescher's work is important for several reasons: it renders redundant many of the previous, speculative accounts of the publication history of *Christa T.*; it gives a fascinating insight into GDR cultural policy; and in particular it reveals to what extent all parties in the debate over the novel used half-truths and false arguments to manipulate one another.

While the full implications of this material have yet to be assessed (not least because the editor makes little attempt to assess them herself), Drescher's *Dokumentation* seems unlikely to lead to radically new interpretations of the novel itself. Although Wolf's personal testimony (in her diary entries and in conversations with Drescher) contains a few points of interest to the critic of *Christa T.*,[7] none has had a significant bearing on my interpretation of the novel's narrative technique. This involves a reassessment of the relationship between the narrator and her central character and shows that the narrator invents fictions about Christa T. as a way of atoning for what she perceives to be failings in her own past life.

---

[5] [anonymous], 'Die ängstliche Margarete', *Der Spiegel*, 25 January 1993, 158–65.

[6] Angela Drescher (ed.), *Dokumentation zu Christa Wolf 'Nachdenken über Christa T.'* (Hamburg: Luchterhand, 1991).

[7] For instance, the *Dokumentation* shows that Chapter 19 of *Christa T.* was added some time after the original draft of the novel had been completed, as a 'Hochreißer' (196), in order to fill 'ein dramaturgisches Loch' (11); and that there was a real Christa T. whose papers came into the possession of Christa Wolf and who became the model for the novel's central character (196). This last revelation is certain to add further fuel to the long-running debate over the relationship between Christa Wolf, her narrator, and Christa T., which is summarized by Christa Thomassen in *Der lange Weg zu uns selbst. Christa Wolfs Roman 'Nachdenken über Christa T.' als Erfahrungs- und Handlungsmuster* (Kronberg/Ts.: Scriptor, 1977), 20–33.

2. 'Was man erfinden muß, um der Wahrheit willen': The Narrator and her Narrative Strategies

Nachdenken über Christa T. depicts the attempt of a grieving woman (the unnamed narrator) to come to terms with the death of a close friend by reflecting on the friend's life and by communicating this process of reflection to her readers. After a Preface in which the narrator sets out her aims, the novel's twenty short chapters relate key stages in Christa T.'s life: her childhood during the Nazi years, the trek westwards with other refugees in 1945, her job as a village school-teacher, her years as a student of German, a second teaching post, marriage to Justus and the birth of her children, her house-building plans, and finally her early death from leukaemia. The chronology of events, though clearly discernible, is disrupted by frequent flashbacks and 'flash-forwards', and by the narrator's reflections on the task of writing about Christa T.

The narrator is not merely concerned to reconstruct Christa T.'s biography: in the course of her reflections she also reassesses her own past life, and that of her generation of GDR citizens. Christa T.'s thoughts and actions—seen now from a more mature and informed viewpoint—challenge the narrator to acknowledge past mistakes and omissions. In a much-quoted passage from the 'Selbstinterview' which Christa Wolf wrote during composition of *Christa T.* in anticipation of the criticisms which would be levelled at it (and which stands in much the same relationship to *Christa T.* as Frisch's 'Ich schreibe für Leser' to *Gantenbein*), Wolf stated quite explicitly that the focus of the novel is not Christa T. herself, but this emotional process in which the first-person narrator is engaged;[8] and in an interview given in 1974, Wolf insisted that this was to be understood as an *ongoing* process. Asked why she shied away from calling *Christa T.* an 'Erzählung', Wolf invoked Anna Segher's maxim: 'Was

---

[8] Christa Wolf, 'Selbstinterview', in Wolf, *Die Dimension des Autors: Essays und Aufsätze. Reden und Gespräche. 1959–1985*, 2 vols. (Berlin: Aufbau Verlag, 1986), I. 31–5 (32). Wolf may well have borrowed the form of the fictional interview from Frisch, although his 'Selbstinterview' differs from hers inasmuch as the questions are not recorded, and must be deduced from his answers to them.

erzählbar geworden ist, ist überwunden.' She, on the other hand, 'hatte erlebt, daß der Erzähler [. . .] gezwungen sein kann, das strenge Nacheinander von Leben, "Überwinden" und Schreiben aufzugeben und um der inneren Authentizität willen, die er anstrebt, den Denk- und Lebensprozeß, in dem er steht [. . .] im Arbeitsprozeß mit zur Sprache zu bringen'.[9] Even as she writes, then, the narrator is still coming to terms with the raw material of her narrative, so that the reader is a witness to her continuing struggle to understand and give shape to her experience.

Like Johnson's *Mutmaßungen über Jakob* and *Das dritte Buch über Achim*, the novel contains elements of the classic modernist 'quest for truth' (and the title of the first English translation, *The Quest for Christa T.*, reflects this).[10] Like a detective searching for the truth, the narrator uses written evidence (Christa T.'s diaries and sketches, which her husband has made available to the narrator) and spoken evidence (the testimony of Christa's friends) to supplement her own, necessarily limited view. In this way, conflicting perspectives are juxtaposed with one another. In Chapter 7, for instance, which relates the story of two rivals in love, Kostja and Günter, she plays off three contradictory perspectives against one another: her own memory of events, Christa T.'s point of view as recorded in her diaries, and Kostja's point of view as revealed in a letter to Christa T. written many years later. Alongside these more conventional pieces of evidence, however, she sets a series of freely and openly invented passages. Reflecting on this peculiar combination of narrative strategies, the narrator writes:

Aber es wird auch schon schwerer, auseinanderzuhalten: was man mit Sicherheit weiß und seit wann; was sie selbst, was andere einem enthüllten; was ihre Hinterlassenschaft hinzufügt, was auch sie verbirgt; was man erfinden muß, um der Wahrheit willen [. . .].

Da überlagern sich schon die Wege, die wir wirklich gegangen sind, mit ungegangenen. Da höre ich schon Worte, die wir nie gesprochen haben. Schon sehe ich sie, Christa T., wenn sie ohne Zeugen war. (31–2)

---

[9] Hans Kaufmann, 'Gespräch mit Christa Wolf', *WB* 20/6 (1974), 90–112 (93–4).

[10] Christa Wolf, *The Quest for Christa T.*, trans. Christopher Middleton (London: Hutchinson, 1971).

The fact that in Chapter 5 the narrator considers 'calling witnesses' (58), in true detective-story fashion, but instead *invents* a witness also lends weight to my contention that it is a short step from the use of limited perspectives and unreliable narration to the use of such undisguised fictional invention.

On several occasions the narrator invents isolated remarks which she puts into the mouth (or mind) of one or other of the characters, and some of these will be analysed in what follows. More often, however, the narrator's inventions take the form of complete scenes and conversations. The most important of these are: an account of a summer romance between Christa T. and the young headmaster of a village school (48–54); an interview with Christa's university friend Gertrud Born-Dölling (58–65); parts of the account of Christa's encounter with a clairvoyant known as the 'Generool' (102–7); a conversation between Christa T. and the headmaster of a school in which she works after graduating from university (129–34); a fancy-dress party which Christa T. attends with her fiancé, Justus (148–52); and an alternative to this scene, in which Christa T. visits Justus in Mecklenburg (152–4).

These inventions follow a pattern seen in each of the five novels examined in this study. In most cases, Wolf's narrator indicates in advance that the scene is invented, by means of a comment such as: 'Ich nehme mir heraus, sie zu korrigieren, und erfinde mir meinen General selbst' (102); or: 'Dieser Mann, von dem sie mir erzählt hat—aber ich kenne ihn nicht—, muß hier erfunden werden' (130). And in most cases the narrator cancels out the completed scene by reminding us that it is only one of many fictional possibilities, or by rejecting it as unsatisfactory:

So oder anders. In diesem oder im folgenden Jahr. Dieser oder ein anderer. (53)

or:

So kann es gewesen sein, aber ich bestehe nicht darauf. [. . .] Vielleicht war der Mann, ihr Direktor, nicht so, aber er könnte so gewesen sein. (134)

or:

Nein.

Ich werde nicht zu ihr gehen, ich werde Gertrud Dölling nicht besuchen. Das Gespräch wird nicht stattfinden, diese Gemütsbewegungen
werden wir uns ersparen. [. . .] Der Umweg war überflüssig. (64–5)

In one case, however, the story of the fancy-dress ball, the
reader is initially led to believe that the scene is real, since
the narrator begins in a tone of certainty (indicated grammatically by the use of the past indicative): 'Bis zu dem
Kostümfest, da kam sie als Sophie la Roche' (148). Only in
retrospect do we learn that the scene was a product of the
narrator's imagination. 'Wir können noch einen Versuch
machen', she writes at the beginning of the next chapter:
'Nicht jenes Kostümfest soll es gewesen sein, das sowieso
erfunden ist, sondern eine einfache Ankunft' (152). Here
again, the scene is relegated to the realms of the possible
and provisional, as just one 'Versuch' among many.

Within the scenes themselves, we find other techniques
typical of what I call 'overt fictionalization'. Sometimes the
narrator foregrounds the 'forking paths' of the narrative,
that is, the choices with which a story-teller is faced in the
process of composition. These choices are conventionally
taken 'silently' (cf. p. 16 above), but Wolf's narrator deliberately draws them to our attention, writing, for instance:
'Ob ihre Freude gekünstelt wäre oder echt, das würde viel
entscheiden. Nehmen wir an, ihre Freude wäre echt. So
würde sie sich doch [. . .]' (59).[11] Other markers which
indicate that a scene represents an imaginative possibility rather than a lived experience include the use
of words such as 'womöglich' and 'vielleicht';[12] the use of

---

[11] Similarly, she draws attention to the way in which she modifies her narrative as
she goes along: 'Sie dachte vielleicht: Also kommt er doch, gerade heute. Oder sie
dachte es nicht, sondern fühlte es' (48–9); and: 'Jetzt ist die Sonne in die Hecken
gefallen. Fehlt bloß noch, daß sie quer über eine Wiese laufen und das ausge-
breitete Heu duftet. Also gut, sie laufen, und das Heu duftet, das haben wir ja alles
in der Hand' (51).

[12] 'So daß es womöglich ihr letzter Dorfsommer war' (48); 'Sie dachte vielleicht:
Also kommt er doch' (48–9); 'Was meinen Sie, wird er wohl fragen' (51); 'Durch
ihre Vorstellungskraft, wird sie dann vielleicht sagen' (61); 'Übrigens, sagt sie da
wahrscheinlich: Außer mir hat sie damals niemanden gehabt' (62).

Konjunktiv II;[13] and of the modal auxiliaries 'mögen' and 'können'.[14]

Some of the devices for foregrounding the fictional status of scenes are peculiar to Wolf's novel. In the interview with Gertrud Dölling, for instance, *Konjunktiv II* alternates with the future tense, which likewise serves to indicate the hypothetical status of the scene.[15] In the scene which describes Christa T.'s encounter with the clairvoyant, invented details are highlighted simply by the words 'mein General', which distinguish the narrator's imagined version of events from Christa T.'s own account (indicated by 'ihr General').

However, what I have said of Johnson and Frisch's novels holds true for *Christa T.*: that our sense of the fictional status of a scene gradually gives way to an impression of reality, so that its subsequent cancellation comes as a surprise. Sometimes this process is encoded in the grammar of the passage, a device already familiar to us from *Das dritte Buch über Achim* and *Gantenbein*.[16] Several critics have analysed this process with reference to the imaginary interview with Gertrud Dölling (although it is not clear why this particular invented scene should have received so much attention, while the others have been neglected). Heinrich Mohr comments: 'Es beginnt im Konjunktiv "ich würde", wechselt ins Futur und partienweise in den Indikativ Präsens. Zunächst als bloße Möglichkeit vorgestellt, wird es immer "wirklicher", bis der

---

[13] 'Wo sie also, wenn wir wollten [. . .]' (48); 'Im Innern des Gebäudes übrigens würde ich wenig verändert finden [. . .]. Die Studenten von heute würden, wie wir damals, gleichgültig an dem Schild und an mir, der Fremden, vorbeigehen, ich müßte mir einen Ruck geben und mir klarmachen, daß sie mich nicht als ihre Altersgenossin erkennen [. . .]. Ich würde auf der Treppe [. . .] einen von ihnen ansprechen, nach Frau Doktor Dölling fragen' etc. (58–9); 'Das würde ich, während ich mich ihr gegenüber setzte, zu respektieren haben' (60); 'Sie war merkwürdig, würde Gertrud Dölling sagen. Und ich müßte sie lange auffordernd ansehen, bis sie das Wort herausrückte' (60).

[14] 'So ist das alles, mag sie gedacht haben' (52); 'Ich könnte Zeugen aufsuchen [. . .]. Könnte in die Stadt fahren, in der wir gemeinsam studierten. Über den Platz vor der Universität gehen' (58).

[15] 'Ich werde lachen müssen' (58); 'Gertrud Dölling wird eine Abwehrhaltung einnehmen, und ich werde nicht wissen, warum, werde mich aber verwünschen, daß ich hierhergekommen bin. / Sie war, wird sie sagen, anders als andere' (60); 'Durch ihre Vorstellungskraft, wird sie dann vielleicht sagen' (61); 'Hier werde ich anfangen, Achtung vor ihr zu kriegen. Werde sie allerdings auch, auf Kosten der Wahrheit, beschwichtigen müssen' etc. (61–2).

[16] See Chapter 2, Section 2 and Chapter 3, Section 2 above.

Schluß mit einer Entscheidung der Erzählerin die Fiktion wieder sicherstellt.'[17] Birgitta Schuler argues that it is specifically the narrator's use of detailed description in the passage which tricks the reader into forgetting that the interview is imaginary.[18] Thomassen attributes the reader's reaction not just to the choice of tense and mood, but also to the use of direct speech and dialogue:

Vollzieht der Leser bei der Szene dieses Besuchs zunächst den Irrealis ('würde') mit, so verfällt er bald der Illusion, er nähme an einer 'echten' (innerhalb der Fiktion der Romanwelt) Szene teil. Die ab und zu verwendeten Zeitformen des Präsens und Präteritums sowie die direkte Rede und die gelegentliche unmittelbare szenische Wechselrede lassen ihn annehmen, der Besuch habe 'wirklich' stattgefunden. Dieser Eindruck wird mehrmals durch einen neuen Irrealis oder eine futurale Verbform verfremdet, dann aber durch den Indikativ wieder hergestellt.[19]

One could add that in most of the imagined scenes the narrator also makes extensive use of interior monologue, allowing herself, in the manner of an omniscient narrator, to see into the minds of Christa T. and other characters. This also lends the inventions a powerful sense of reality.

Thomassen calls the narrator's practice of inventing scenes 'die fiktive Fiktion';[20] Rolf Michaelis describes it as 'das Erzählen in der Möglichkeitsform';[21] Klemens Renoldner speaks of 'das Zurücknehmen, Zerstören und Neuschaffen von Chiffrierungen, Bildern',[22] and Anna K. Kuhn of 'das die Fiktionalität des Textes unterstreichende ständige

[17] Heinrich Mohr, 'Produktive Sehnsucht: Struktur, Thematik und politische Relevanz von Christa Wolfs *Nachdenken über Christa T.*', *Basis*, 2 (1971), 191–233 (199).
[18] 'So wird der Besuch bei Gertrud Born respektive Dölling zunächst als reine Möglichkeit von der Erzählerin entworfen und dann sprachlich bis in alle Einzelheiten realisiert, so daß seine Wirklichkeit "wahrscheinlich", also wahr zu sein scheint. Schließlich verfügt die Erzählerin, das Geschehen doch dem Bereich des Fiktiven zuzuordnen. Wirklichkeit wird konsequent entworfen, um ebenso konsequent durchbrochen zu werden' (Birgitta Schuler, *Phantastische Authentizität. Wirklichkeit im Werk Christa Wolfs* (Frankfurt/Main, Berne, New York and Paris: Peter Lang, 1988), 114).
[19] Thomassen, 82.
[20] Ibid. 80.
[21] Rolf Michaelis, 'Der doppelte Himmel. Christa Wolfs zweites Buch *Nachdenken über Christa T.* Der umstrittene Roman aus der DDR' (extracts), in Behn, 65–9 (69).
[22] Klemens Renoldner, *Utopie und Geschichtsbewußtsein: Versuche zur Poetik Christa Wolfs* (Stuttgart: Akademische Verlag, 1981), 83–104 (98).

Entwerfen und Verwerfen von Alternativen',[23] while Schuler refers to the narrator's 'faktische Alternativ-Entwürfe'.[24] Hans Mayer even uses the metaphor of 'erasure': 'Sobald eine Episode schärferen Umriß zu gewinnen droht, wird radiert und wieder ausgewischt.'[25] There has been little attempt, however, to explore the narrator's motives for inventing individual scenes, which is the main task of this chapter. Moreover, the fact that each critic calls the narrator's strategy by a different name confirms my view that the narrative technique which is the subject of the present study has been accorded insufficient recognition (certainly too little for it to have acquired a widely accepted name).

Critics often speak of *Christa T.* in the same breath as novels by Johnson and Frisch, although without examining the correspondences between them in any depth.[26] While a few draw parallels with *Mein Name sei Gantenbein*,[27] by far the most persistent comparison is between *Christa T.* and Johnson's *Mutmaßungen über Jakob*. In addition to the many critics who mention Johnson's novel by name,[28] there are several allusive references: Wolfgang Werth speaks of Wolf's indebtedness to 'Mutmaßungsliteratur',[29] Fritz Raddatz of Wolf's use of a 'Mutmaßstil'[30] and Thomassen of her 'Mutmaßungsstil'.[31] While there clearly are similarities between *Christa T.*

[23] Anna K. Kuhn, 'Ich-Erweiterung und Ich-Aufspaltung. Überlegungen zu Max Frischs *Mein Name sei Gantenbein* und Christa Wolfs *Nachdenken über Christa T.*', in Inge Stephan and Carl Pietzcker (eds.), *Frauensprache—Frauenliteratur? Für und Wider einer Psychoanalyse literarischer Werke. Akten des VII. internationalen Germanisten-Kongresses. Göttingen 1985*, Kontroversen, alte und neue, VI (Tübingen: Niemeyer, 1986), 87–91 (87).   [24] Schuler, 113.

[25] Hans Mayer, 'Christa Wolf. *Nachdenken über Christa T.*', *NR* 81 (1970), 180–6 (182).

[26] The single exception is Anna Kuhn's 'Ich-Erweiterung und Ich-Aufspaltung'.

[27] e.g. Marcel Reich-Ranicki, 'Christa Wolfs unruhige Elegie' (extracts), in Behn, 59–64: 'Dieser Roman könnte also auch heißen: [. . .] "Mein Name sei Christa T."' (64); and Carolyn Ann Wellauer, 'The Postwar German Novel of Speculations' (unpublished doctoral diss., University of Wisconsin, 1976), 262. The comparison is also implicit in the title of Fritz Raddatz's review 'Mein Name sei Tonio K.' (extracts), in Behn, 73–6.

[28] e.g. Roland Wiegenstein, 'Verweigerung der Zustimmung', in Behn, 77–80 (78); Manfred Durzak, *Der deutsche Roman der Gegenwart* (Stuttgart: Kohlhammer, 1971), 206; Wolfram and Helmtrud Mauser, *Christa Wolf: 'Nachdenken über Christa T.'* (Munich: Fink, 1987), 94; Mohr, 230 n. 45; and Mayer, 90.

[29] Werth, 93.

[30] Raddatz, 75.

[31] Thomassen, 36.

and *Mutmaßungen über Jakob*—both are concerned with a search for the truth about a person who has died—it seems to me nevertheless that Wolf moves beyond the kind of well-worn detective-story techniques employed in Johnson's *Mutmaßungen*, techniques which had evidently become so overused that they had spawned a whole genre: 'Mut-maßungsliteratur'.[32]

3. 'Damals' and 'heute': The Relationship between Past and Present in *Christa T.*

The invented scenes in *Christa T.* are an integral part of the narrator's re-evaluation of her past life and to understand them we must first understand the relationship between the past and the present, as the narrator presents it in the text. Christa Wolf has said that her own life is punctuated by crises and that after each she divides her experiences mentally into those which happened 'davor' and those which came 'danach'.[33] Her narrator in *Nachdenken über Christa T.* appears to be experiencing just such a crisis, and in her case the pivotal experience which separates 'davor' from 'danach' is her reading of Christa's papers and the process of reflection which this has set in motion. This results in two distinct textual 'levels': on the one hand what the narrator thought and felt about Christa T. in the past; and on the other hand what she has only come to understand or feel about Christa T. since she began to reflect on her life.

---

[32] In his review of the novel, Marcel Reich-Ranicki writes that *Christa T.* is 'glück-licherweise kein Puzzle-Spiel' (an expression which was used by several critics to describe the multiple perspectives of *Mutmaßungen über Jakob*): 'Man kennt das ja hinreichend: Eine Biographie soll rekonstruiert und somit ein mehr oder weniger dunkler Sachverhalt aufgedeckt werden. Der Beauftragte des Autors sammelt fleißig Material und findet auch allerlei, doch nie genug. Am Ende bekennt er sich zur Niederlage, denn, so hören wir mit schöner Regelmäßigkeit, eines Menschen Weg und Wesen lassen sich niemals gänzlich erfassen und darstellen. Christa Wolf erspart uns die Reprise dieses Spiels, das ihrige findet auf einer anderen Ebene statt' (Reich-Ranicki, 60). Reich-Ranicki's remarks indicate just how clichéd and overused the *Mutmaßungen*-formula was by the 1960s and therefore how necessary it was for authors to develop new techniques.

[33] 'Auf mir bestehen. Christa Wolf im Gespräch mit Günter Gaus', *NDL* 41/5 (May 1993), 20–40 (34).

Often, our attention is drawn to these two levels of consciousness when revelations contained in Christa's *Nachlaß*
force the narrator to view the past differently, as in the
following examples:

Ich fragte sie—erst heute begreife ich meine Ungeschicklichkeit—:
Kannst du dir denken, fragte ich, wer ausgerechnet der Metz, der Mathe-
matiklehrerin, die Blumen aufs Pult gelegt hat? [. . .] Jetzt weiß ich, daß
sie es war, Christa T., und daß sie mich belog, weil sie keinen Grund sah,
es mir zuzugeben. Die Metz nämlich, schrieb sie Jahre später in ihr
Tagebuch, sei die einzige gewesen, die sie nicht unfrei und unglücklich
machte. (17)

or:

Da stand der denn wie ein Feigling, und wir alle haben nichts anderes
gedacht. Ich würde es heute noch denken, wenn ich nicht seinen Brief
gelesen hätte. (87–8)

or:

Ich habe nämlich gar nicht gemerkt, als sie ziemlich lange vor den
Semesterferien auf einmal verschwand und nichts von sich hören ließ. In
dem Brief steht aber, daß sie sterben wollte und sonst zu nichts Lust hatte.
(89)

At other times the narrator's reflections have simply placed
their shared past in a new light:

Ich weiß heute, daß diese Art von Erbitterung nicht vergeht und daß wir
sie immer noch teilen würden. Damals schien sie uns zu trennen, wir
mißverstanden uns. (166)

or:

Was sie in Wirklichkeit meinte, geht heute so klar aus dem Satz hervor,
wie es sich damals darin versteckte. (173)

As these last two quotations show, the words 'damals' and
'heute' are often used to situate a passage of text in one of
the two levels of consciousness. However, the narrator does
not always signpost the contrast between 'then' and 'now'
so conspicuously, and Wolf demands of the reader a fairly
sophisticated sensitivity to the two levels. Often the narrator
merges the two time-levels, switching without any explan-
atory remark—and sometimes even mid-sentence—between

what she knew or thought then in the *erzählte Zeit* and what she knows or thinks now in the *Erzählzeit*. This fluidity of perspective is a distinctive feature of the novel,[34] and it represents a step forward in relation to Wolf's previous work, *Der geteilte Himmel*, in which a clear distinction was maintained throughout between 'damals' and 'heute'.

An example from Chapter 1 of *Christa T.*, which relates how Christa joins the narrator's primary school, will illustrate more precisely what I mean by 'fluidity'. Christa's new classmates, we are told, did not know what to make of her, for she appeared haughty, even though she lived in the local backwoods (and therefore, in their view, had no reason to feel superior). Having thus described the reaction of her class from a collective perspective (the perspective of 'wir dreißig Einheimische'), the narrator then focuses on her own feelings:

Was sollte man davon halten?

    Nichts. Nichts und gar nichts hielt ich davon, sondern ich sah gelangweilt aus dem Fenster, das sollte jeder merken, der von mir etwas wissen wollte. (11)

The childishly emphatic 'Nichts. Nichts und gar nichts' vividly recreates the narrator's reaction to Christa T. at the time (and represents the petulant answer she might have given had someone asked her: 'Was hältst du von der Neuen?'), but the narrator then retreats—in mid-sentence— to her more detached perspective at the time of narration and analyses objectively her behaviour ('das sollte jeder merken'). This implies that the narrator realizes now what she did not admit to herself at the time, namely that her boredom and disinterest were a pose intended to hide her envious fascination with the new girl. The reader must infer this, however, without the help of textual markers such as 'damals' and 'heute'.

Such switches between perspectives, whether openly signalled or not, allow the narrator to uncover what she had previously repressed or was too immature to understand and, more especially, to expose the conflict between her

---

[34] For a very thorough analysis of the novel's shifting perspectives and time-levels see Thomassen, 47–56.

former attitude to Christa T. (disapproving, discouraging, and dismissive) and her new-found appreciation of her dead friend's qualities and actions. The following passage is a typical expression of this conflict:

Sie sagt nämlich oder fragt: Denk mal nach. Lebst du eigentlich heute, jetzt, in diesem Augenblick? Ganz und gar?

Erbarm dich! sagte ich, worauf läuft das hinaus?

Heute möchte ich ihr die Frage zurückgeben können. Denn sie hat ja recht gehabt, wenn ich jetzt darüber nachdenke. Nichts hat uns ferner gelegen als der Gedanke, man würde eines Tages irgendwo ankommen und fertig. (126)

The narrator's response, 'Erbarm dich! [. . .] worauf läuft das hinaus?', shows that in the past she tended to dismiss Christa T.'s anxieties about self-fulfilment by gently mocking her earnest idealism. Today she recognizes the validity of those anxieties and would, if she could relive the past, take Christa's question seriously.

The narrator's preoccupation with her former critical attitude to Christa T. expresses itself forcefully in vivid evocations of the *gestures* associated with disapproval. When Christa T. is considering consulting a clairvoyant, the narrator writes: 'Wir aber, zusehend, *schieben die Unterlippe vor*, denn wir finden, was sie vorhat und also gewiß tun wird [. . .] bedenklich' (97: my emphasis in this and the following examples). She also imagines how her contemporaries would have reacted, had they subsequently learnt of the visit: 'Rückfall, hätten wir gesagt und *die Köpfe geschüttelt*' (108). This gesture would then have given way to another, with which the narrator is particularly familiar: '*dieses ungläubig-mitleidige Lächeln* [. . .]. Dafür verbürge ich mich, weil ich seinen Abdruck auf meinem eignenen Gesicht noch fühlen kann' (108). Finally, the narrator remembers the sceptical response to Christa T.'s plans to build her own house: 'Das Haus: Wir müssen unwillkürlich *die Hände gehoben* haben, da hat sie uns ganz geläufig die Zahlen erklärt [. . .] Aber wir hatten etwas gegen eigene Häuser. Hausbesitzer! sagten wir und *rümpften die Nase*. Ich sagte leise zu ihr: Und du wirst dich vergraben' (189–91). By repeatedly using the pronoun 'wir', the narrator implicates her whole generation—including her contemporary readership—in these disapproving gestures. However, in acknowledging this habit of criticizing Christa T., the narrator also distances herself from it, showing that she no longer considers it appropriate.

This pattern is repeated throughout the novel: having once discouraged or simply disregarded her friend's hopes and ambitions, the narrator now claims that Christa T.'s imagination, her sense of moral responsibility, and her desire to remain open to new possibilities were valuable qualities which could have been put to productive use within GDR society and which she and her generation would have done well to emulate. Thus, each revelation about Christa T. is for the narrator also a revelation about herself and what has been lacking from her life. The narrator's reflections are driven to a large extent by guilt (at her failure to recognize and value her friend) and by a desire to make amends (by demonstrating her new-found appreciation of her friend and by persuading her readership to share her appreciation). Schuler sums up this process succinctly:

Literatur wird der Erzählerin zur Methode, das Leiden an versäumten Gelegenheiten zu artikulieren. Schreibend versucht sie, Schuldgefühle angesichts des Versäumten zu lindern [. . .]. Etwas 'zu wiederholen' bedeutet nun es 'wieder zu holen', um ihm nun in der Gegenwart mit einem Verhalten zu entsprechen, das der Erzählerin in der Vergangenheit nicht möglich war.[35]

Moreover, as several critics have pointed out, in working on her *past* from her standpoint in the *present*, the narrator is also bringing into being a new *future* (in the sense that the process helps her develop as a human being).[36]

The passages which the narrator of *Christa T.* invents (and which I analyse in the next section) form an integral part of this process of reassessing her relationship with Christa T., for they cross the boundary between past and present: they are the product of the narrator's consciousness in the *Erzählzeit*, yet they recreate events which took place, or are imagined to have taken place, in the *erzählte Zeit*. In what follows I show that the narrator uses the fictions to project her present appreciation of Christa T.'s qualities back onto the past, even going so far as to transform Christa's past for the better, creating for her a fictional past in which she was appreciated and in which nobody stood in the way of her self-fulfilment, or at least in which she suffered less. This desire to rewrite Christa's past expresses itself particularly clearly in the narrator's description of a New Year's Eve party at Christa's house. The narrator describes the moment when it becomes clear to the assembled friends that one of their number, Günter, is still a little in love with Christa T. (hence the reference to 'ungeschickte Liebe oder altmodische Verehrung'):

Wir tranken alle auf sie—*oder ich wünsche mir doch sehr, wir hätten es getan* —, zu der jeder von uns feste und jeder andere Beziehungen hatte und die es fertigbrachte, alle diese Beziehungen geschickt und großzügig und vor allem ohne Berechnung zu handhaben.

Wenn alles so war, wie ich es mir jetzt wünsche, dann haben wir es ganz natürlich gefunden, daß unter diesen Beziehungen auch so etwas wie ungeschickte Liebe oder altmodische Verehrung war. *Wenn wir an jenem Abend so gewesen sind, wie ich es mir wünsche,* dann waren wir alle großmütig und wollten, daß uns kein Gefühl und keine Nuance eines Gefühls fehlen sollte, denn das alles, *mögen wir gedacht haben,* stand uns zu. Diesen einen Abend lang, die Silvesternacht von einundsechzig und zweiundsechzig, ihr vorletztes Silvester, *soll sie,* Christa T., uns das Beispiel abgegeben haben für die unendlichen Möglichkeiten, die noch in uns lagen. (210–11; my italics)

The narrator's admiration for Christa is unmistakable here, but she is not content with merely admiring her: she feels the need to reconstruct the past, to create—if only in imagination—a situation in which Christa T.'s contemporaries responded to her qualities with appreciation and respect, instead of their habitual incomprehension and censure; in which Christa's 'Großzügigkeit' was met with 'Großmut'; and in which her openness to change was seen as a quality worth emulating. However implausible the narrator's recreation of the scene may be (given what we know of her attitude to Christa at the time), the impulse to rewrite the past is typical of the text as a whole.

4. Expiating the Past through Narrative Invention

I shall begin with two examples of invention in the novel which might easily go unnoticed because the narrator imagines in each case a single remark, but which illustrate well the way in which she uses her fictions to transform, and make amends for, the past.

The following passage from Chapter 4 demonstrates the frustration felt by Christa T.'s fellow university students at her unconventional lack of ambition (once again, a collective perspective implicates the narrator's contemporaries in what happens):

Mir fällt ein, daß wir sie nie fragen konnten: Was willst du werden? Wie man andere doch fragt, ohne fürchten zu müssen, an Unaussprechliches zu rühren. [. . .]

Also?—Der bekannte Blick, dunkel, leicht spöttisch, ein wenig vorwurfsvoll. Ich? Lehrerin doch wohl? konnte sie fragen. Da gab man es auf, da schwieg man, ließ die Sache auf sich beruhen, bestand nicht darauf, sie festzulegen, da allzu deutlich war: Sie konnte es wirklich nicht wissen. Sie gab sich ja Mühe hineinzupassen, sie fiel nicht aus bloßem Übermut heraus. Sie hatte ja den guten Willen, sich einen der Namen zuzulegen, die auf andere so vorzüglich zutrafen, sie hat es sich als Mangel angekreidet, daß sie nicht fröhlich wie aus der Pistole geschossen erwidern konnte: Lehrerin, Aspirantin, Dozentin, Lektorin . . .

Ach, sie traute ja diesen Namen nicht. Sie traute sich ja nicht. Sie zweifelte ja, inmitten unseres Rauschs der Neubenennungen, sie zweifelte ja an der Wirklichkeit von Namen, mit denen sie doch umging; sie ahnte ja, daß die Benennung kaum je gelingt und daß sie dann nur für kurze Zeit mit dem Ding zusammenfällt, auf das sie gelegt wurde. Sie zuckte davor zurück, sich selbst einen Namen aufzudrücken, das Brandmal, mit welcher Herde in welchen Stall man zu gehen hat. *Leben, erleben, freies großes Leben! O herrliches Lebensgefühl, daß du mich nie verläßt! Nichts weiter als ein Mensch sein* . . .

Was willst du werden, Krischan? Ein Mensch? Nun weißt du . . . . (44–6)

This passage offers a further example of the fluid narrative perspective which I described earlier. While the second paragraph records the reaction of Christa's friends during their years at university (they tolerated her because she made an effort to fit in), the narrative subsequently shifts (with the

words: 'Ach, sie traute ja diesen Namen nicht') from what
the narrator knew at the time to what is clear to her today, at
the time of narration. The repeated use of the emphatic 'ja'
('sie traute ja' / 'sie zweifelte ja' / 'sie ahnte ja') confirms
that the paragraph expresses a *new* insight (since the particle
'ja' may be used to express surprise at something the speaker
has just noticed). It may also imply that the narrator is trying
to reassure herself of the validity of her insight by appealing
to the reader for agreement or by suggesting that she is
stating the obvious (another function of 'ja'). The quotation
from Christa's diary (in italics) reinforces the idea that this
insight is a recent one, since the narrator has read Christa's
papers only since her death. Whereas in the past Christa's
fellow students evidently approved of her guilt at not fitting
in (since they used it to excuse her errant behaviour), and
agreed with her judgement that her lack of ambition was a
'Mangel', the narrator now expresses a new sympathy and
understanding for Christa T.'s predicament. Although the
narrator is by no means sure of what she is trying to say (and
therefore draws no explicit conclusions), we can see her
groping towards the idea that Christa T. was right not to
conform, and therefore wrong to feel guilty about her nonconformism. The passage culminates in an imaginary question: 'Was willst du werden, Krischan?', to which Christa T.
gives the imaginary answer 'Ein Mensch'. By imagining
this brief exchange, the narrator superimposes her present
knowledge of Christa's diaries onto the past, and asks: what
would have happened had Christa T. given an honest answer
to our questions (instead of the evasive 'Lehrerin doch
wohl?') and told us that her secret desire—expressed only in
the privacy of her diary—was to be a human being (that is,
to fulfil her human potential)? The narrator's imagined
response, 'Nun weißt du . . . ', seems to express relief that
Christa has at last found a satisfactory answer to a question
which has long troubled her. Yet given what we know of
the dismissive and discouraging attitude which the narrator
showed to Christa T. at that time, it seems unlikely that she
would have greeted Christa's idealistic aspirations so sym-
pathetically. The narrator is therefore projecting her new-
found understanding for her friend's aspirations back onto

the past, and, in doing so, indicating that she no longer feels
driven to curb Christa's idealistic yearning for self-fulfilment.

In Chapter 8, which deals with Christa T.'s nervous breakdown following the end of a relationship with a fellow
student, Kostja, we find a second example of an invented
passage which, while extremely short, is nevertheless telling.
We learn in this chapter that the split with Kostja was merely
a trigger for Christa's breakdown, and in a letter to her
sister, from which the narrator quotes extracts, Christa
reveals its underlying cause: she despairs of finding a useful
role in society. The content of the letter—in which Christa
contemplates suicide—shocks the narrator, who knew nothing of the depth of her friend's despair, and she reproaches
herself for not having been in a position to offer support:
'Warum nur habe ich sie damals nicht vermißt? Womit waren
wir denn so sehr beschäftigt?' (92). Christa T., as the narrator now learns, was diagnosed as having a nervous illness
which, in the words of her doctor, resulted from her inability
to accept and adjust to reality ('Neurose als mangelnde
Anpassungsfähigkeit an gegebene Umstände'). Christa's
diary entries from this time reveal that as her condition
improved, she began to envisage the possibility that the
qualities which others rejected in her might have a positive
value: '*Mein Denken ist dunkler, merkwürdig mit Empfindungen
gemischt. Muß es deshalb falsch sein?*' (94–5). Shortly after
quoting this passage from Christa's diary, the narrator writes:
'Anpassen lernen! Und wenn nicht ich es wäre, die sich
anzupassen hätte?—Doch so weit ging sie nicht' (95). This
short paragraph makes the reader work hard. Although it is
not at first clear whether the exclamation 'Anpassen lernen!'
should be attributed to the narrator or to Christa T., the
question which follows establishes that the words are spoken,
or thought, by Christa T.—until the narrator cancels them
out with the words 'Doch so weit ging sie nicht', unmasking
them as a fiction. Why does the narrator put thoughts into
Christa T.'s mind in this way? It seems to me that this is
another expression of her instinct to transform Christa's past
for the better: she would like Christa to have had the confidence to question the values of her society, knowing that
she bears part of the blame for Christa's well-documented

lack of self-confidence. Moreover, the imagined question shows that the narrator has begun to question the GDR's values herself, and recognizes that her generation might have done well to adjust to Christa T.'s way of thinking, rather than the other way around.

The longer scenes and conversations invented by the narrator serve a similar purpose to the short passages examined above. The first of these passages (48–54) depicts a conversation between Christa T. and a young headmaster at the beginning of a brief relationship which comes to an end when Christa goes to university. Although the scene is based on Christa's allusion to a 'Sommerliebe', the details are the narrator's own invention.

The invented conversation depicts Christa T. and the young headmaster as like-minded in some ways, but incompatible in others. When Christa asks the headmaster whether he has ever robbed a magpie's nest and killed the chicks, he tells her that he has always found such cruelty impossible. We know already (from a passage narrated on pp. 41–2) that Christa has seen a boy from her class do just this, urged on by his schoolmates, and that the experience had deeply shocked her because she sees cruelty to animals as symptomatic of a brutality which, given the right circumstances, would be turned against human beings. In the light of Christa's previous reflections on this subject, then, the headmaster's answer (that such cruelty is alien to him) demonstrates his fundamental humanity. Yet although the headmaster claims to want to work for change (calling his school 'entwicklungsfähig'), he treats socialist ideals as abstract concepts which, while worthy and laudable in themselves, need not actively be striven for. Christa T., on the other hand, believes that reality must be continually measured against her ideals, in order to see where work still needs to be done. Moreover, while the headmaster would like to stay in the village 'für immer', Christa T. is afraid of stagnation and eager to move on to new experiences.

We might ask what the narrator has to gain by imposing on her dead friend a boyfriend she never had. But by imagining this scene, and using the boyfriend as a foil, the narrator attempts to demonstrate her appreciation of the qualities she most admires in Christa: her thirst for new experiences, her humanity, her desire to make her ideals a reality. There is also a hint that the narrator is again creating a more favourable past for Christa: 'Das soll sie gehabt haben, ich will es. Sie soll erfahren haben, was sie wissen mußte, und gegangen sein' (53–4). It appears that the narrator would like Christa to have realized the value of striving for one's ideals and of remaining open to new experiences, because she herself now values these qualities.

A rather different purpose is served by the imaginary interview with Christa's old university friend Gertrud Dölling (née Born), related in Chapter 5 (58–65). In this chapter the narrator continues to subject herself to an uncompromising self-scrutiny (a practice which is typical of Wolf's fictional characters—or at least of those which she holds up to us as a model), asking herself in particular why she was so blind to Christa's despair. This is such a sore point, however, that she suddenly claims the right, as the surviving partner in the friendship, to determine what is and what is not spoken about, invoking 'das Recht des Nichtwissenwollens oder des Nichtsagenmüssens' (58). Set in this context, the imagined interview with Gertrud Dölling which then follows seems to be an attempt to approach in a roundabout way the intensely distressing reasons for the narrator's neglect of Christa T.

In order to approach the subject obliquely, the narrator projects the painful process of 'confession' onto another person: Gertrud Born-Dölling. The imaginary Gertrud, now a university lecturer, is at first defensive and disinclined to reveal her true feelings, offering neutral or vaguely disapproving comments about Christa T.'s lack of discipline, until the narrator makes her say what she (Gertrud) is really thinking:

Sie [Christa T.] hat es nicht fertiggebracht, die Grenzen anzuerkennen, die jedem nun einmal gesetzt sind. Sie verlor sich in jede Sache, du konntest drauf warten. Manchmal konnte man denken, das ganze Studium, der ganze Bücherkram gingen sie eigentlich nichts an, sie war auf was andres aus. Und das, weißt du, war fast—verletzend.

Sie blickte mich schnell an. Das wird der Augenblick sein, da ich die Lider senke, nehme ich an, denn daß ich mein eigenes Empfinden ruhig von ihr ausgedrückt hören kann, ist nicht denkbar.

Gertrud Born ist immer schnell errötet, sie steht auf und tritt ans Fenster. Ich aber begreife endlich die Rolle, die Christa T. in ihrem Leben gespielt hat: Sie hat es in Frage gestellt. (61)

This fake 'confession' extracted from the imaginary Gertrud implies that she could not cope with Christa T.'s wayward attitudes because they suggested that her own, disciplined and conformist life was somehow inadequate. She experienced Christa's existence as a kind of reproach, as a subversion of the values by which she lived her life. But these feelings apply equally to the narrator, who admits as much momentarily ('mein eigenes Empfinden'), only to withdraw immediately to the morally superior position of the disinterested, analytical observer: 'Ich aber begreife endlich die Rolle, die Christa in ihrem Leben gespielt hat: Sie hat es in Frage gestellt.' In this way the narrator is able to approach the question of her own repressed fears and insecurity indirectly, and to acknowledge, without having to admit it openly, the reason why she ostracized Christa T. and ignored her unhappiness: her selfish desire to preserve intact her sense of purpose in life by excluding anything which might cause her to doubt herself and her role.

However, in the course of the interview with Gertrud, what had begun as a protective manœuvre (projecting her own painful feelings of guilt onto another person) backfires, and the narrator finds her imaginings taking her where she does not want to go: towards realizations with which she is not yet fully able to cope. Like the narrator of Frisch's *Gantenbein*, she becomes a sorcerer's apprentice in her own narrative.

The narrator's difficulties begin when the imaginary Gertrud claims to have been Christa's only friend: 'Außer mir hat sie damals niemanden gehabt' (62). When the narrator suggests that Kostja was also Christa's friend, Gertrud dismisses their relationship as a mere infatuation: 'Kann man dieses Umeinanderherumgehen ernst nehmen?' (62). This prompts the narrator to write: 'Ich, im Besitz der Tagebücher von Christa T., werde in Schweigen verfallen. Also hat sie wirklich niemanden gehabt, also ist mein Rechtfertigungsversuch—denn warum sonst wäre ich zu Gertrud Dölling gegangen?—gescheitert' (62–3). I take this to mean that since Gertrud Born was apparently unaware of the

strength of Christa's feelings for Kostja (described to us in
Chapter 7 of the novel), she was not the real friend the
narrator had thought her to be. The narrator is therefore
forced to acknowledge that Christa T. was entirely alone.
This is a painful insight: the narrator would prefer to believe
that Christa T. received sufficient emotional support from
her friends and that she alone was, in consequence, to blame
for her depressions. This would then exonerate the narrator
—hence the 'Rechtfertigungsversuch'. Instead, she has to
admit that Christa T. might have been saved from the
despondency recorded secretly in her diary had her peers
been more sympathetic.

A little later in their imaginary conversation, the narrator
senses that Gertrud Born holds some grudge against Christa
T. and is curious about its cause. After some hesitation
Gertrud tells her that she resents the fact that Christa T. had
given up the will to live: 'Immer konnte sie mit allem wieder
aufhören und ganz was anderes anfangen, wer kann das
schon? Und dann legt sie sich hin und stirbt in vollem Ernst
und kann damit nicht mehr aufhören.—Oder denkst du,
daß sie an dieser Krankheit gestorben ist?' (64). The narrator's next word 'Nein' (on a line of its own) appears at first
to be an answer to Gertrud's question, but its significance
changes as we read on, and it becomes part of the process by
which the narrator cancels out the scene:

Nein.
 Ich werde nicht zu ihr gehen, ich werde Gertrud Dölling nicht besuchen. Das Gespräch wird nicht stattfinden, diese Gemütsbewegungen
werden wir uns ersparen. Und die Frage, woran Christa T. gestorben ist,
werde ich selbst stellen, zu ihrer Zeit, ohne in Zweifel zu ziehen, daß es
die Krankheit war, Leukämie, mit der sie nicht fertig werden konnte.
 Ich werde zu Hause bleiben. Warum soll ich Gertrud Dölling traurig
machen? Sie ist, wie sie sein kann. Wer kann wie sie von sich sagen, daß er
bis an seine Grenzen geht? Und gewisse Fragen, die ich ihr stellen wollte,
kann ich ebensogut—oder besser—mir selbst stellen. Der Umweg war
überflüssig. (64–5)

My impression of this passage is that the narrator's thoughts
have taken her further than she had initially intended to go:
to the point of acknowledging that Christa T. died not of
leukemia, but because she could find no viable way to live in

her society (this being the initial implication of the 'Nein' she gives in response to Gertrud's question). Consequently, it seems to me, the narrator beats a hasty retreat. This explains the unnecessarily emphatic and repeated erasure of this scene: 'Ich werde *nicht* zu ihr gehen, ich werde Gertrud Dölling *nicht* besuchen. Das Gespräch wird *nicht* stattfinden, diese Gemütsbewegungen werden wir uns *ersparen*' (my italics). Moreover, she then reassures herself that Gertrud is mistaken and that Christa T. really did die of leukemia. And finally, the narrator invents unconvincing excuses for not having this conversation: it would sadden Gertrud unnecessarily, and besides, she can answer the questions herself. By reassuring herself that this visit would be pointless, the narrator tries to cancel out its implications for herself. For, if she admits that Christa T. wanted to die, she has to admit her own responsibility both for failing to offer the kind of support and sympathy which would have kept Christa from despair and for failing to build the kind of society in which her friend could have developed her full potential. In other words, she has to face both her own inadequacy as a friend and the inadequacy of the social order which she has helped to create, an admission for which she is evidently not yet ready. For this reason I am not convinced by Alexander Stephan's view that the narrator cancels out this scene because it is '[eine] die Wahrheit verzerrende Erfindung'.[37] While the narrator may wish to convince herself that this is the reason for the cancellation, it is clear to us that far from distorting the truth this scene approaches tentatively a truth which the narrator, at this stage, wishes to repress.

A remark in the following chapter of the novel (Chapter 6) lends support to my reading of the interview with Gertrud Dölling. Here, the narrator reflects on Christa T.'s ability to conceal things from herself, in particular her ability to repress the knowledge that she longs to be a writer, a psychological defence mechanism which seems to be motivated by a lack of self-confidence and fear of disappointment. The narrator then exclaims: 'Wie ich alle ihre Ausflüchte jetzt durchschaue! Wie ich ihre Versuche, sich zu entziehen, jetzt

---

[37] Alexander Stephan, *Christa Wolf*, 3rd rev. edn. (Munich: Beck, 1987), 82.

durchkreuzen würde! Da hat sie sich endgültig entzogen. Das war die Krankheit, die Krankheit war es, Gertrud' (70). Here again we see how the narrator's new-found sympathy for Christa awakens in her a desire to transform the past. For the narrator's sudden insight into Christa's capacity for self-deception inspires in her the wish to live her life again and to do what she had failed to do the first time round: to help Christa T. to fulfil her potential as a writer. However, this fantasy immediately comes up against the inescapable fact of Christa T.'s death: 'Da hat sie sich endgültig entzogen.' The use of the verb 'entziehen' to describe both Christa's self-deception and her eventual death implies that her death was just one more psychological manœuvre, one more attempt to avoid disappointment in a hostile world. And because this insight frightens the narrator, who knows that she shares responsibility for the environment in which Christa failed to thrive, she represses the idea again, reassuring herself— by refuting Gertrud's comments once more—that Christa's death was caused by leukemia.

The story headed 'Wat de Generool seggt hett' (Chapter 9), which relates Christa's visit to a clairvoyant, an ex-soldier known locally as the 'Generool', employs even more complicated narrative devices than those already examined. Part-way through this story the narrator claims both that Christa T. 'invented' the General and that she, as narrator, is also inventing him: 'Ich nehme mir heraus, sie zu korrigieren, und erfinde mir meinen General selbst' (102). What the narrator means by these remarks is clear from the context: Christa T. 'invented' the General inasmuch as she set down a subjective and selective view of him in her diaries: 'So ist sie gerecht, wie jedermann es ist: Holt heraus, was das Zeug hält und was aus ihrem Zeug ist, das andere aber, abstrus, falsch, mein Gott, ja: dumm bis zur Albernheit, wird gerade noch erwähnt' (102). The narrator's invention, on the other hand, is of a more literal kind: she invents details for which there is no evidence in Christa's papers. More specifically, she adopts the role of an omniscient narrator in order to imagine the thoughts which pass through the mind of the General as he tells Christa's fortune. Having explained that both she and Christa are involved in 'inventing' the General

in these different ways, the narrator then interweaves the
two accounts, indicating Christa T.'s version of events by the
words 'ihr General', and her own version by the words 'mein
General'.

In Christa's version of events, the General tells her that
her poor performance in exams has nothing to do with
intellectual mediocrity: she is simply someone who will reach
her peak later than most. He also foresees a nervous illness
in the near future, but reassures her that what she is going
through is only a temporary weakness. The reader knows
that these predictions will please Christa T., for she does
think of herself as someone with as yet unfulfilled potential,
and she is indeed going through a difficult time following
the breakup of her relationship with Kostja. At this point,
however, the narrator intervenes in Christa's account to add
an invented detail: 'Hier blickt mein General schnell in ihr
Gesicht, vergewissert sich, läßt sie nun endlich die Zügel
schießen, oder was? Da sieht er, daß er weitergehen kann'
(103). The 'narrator's General' is hesitant in his predictions,
looking at Christa T. for reassurance that he is on the right
track. In other words, the narrator suggests that the General
has no supernatural powers, relying only on his ability to
assess the personality of the woman before him and attempting, on this basis, to tell her what she wants to hear. When
'Christa's General' tells her that she will attend a funeral in
the near future, perhaps the funeral of an aunt, the narrator
again intervenes: 'Da sieht er: Schon entgleitet ihm diese
Dame. Es hilft nichts, er muß sich anstrengen, mein General'
(103). Christa T.'s face tells him that by making such specific
and implausible predictions he is losing her confidence.
Again the implication is that there is no authority in what
the General says, that his predictions are merely guesswork.

At one point, however, the narrator is tempted to believe
in the General's powers herself. 'Christa's General' advises
her to stop brooding and to have confidence in herself, for
in a couple of years' time, he predicts, she will outshine her
contemporaries. The narrator comments: 'Jetzt erst, seh'
ich, streicht sie die Segel, ich auch. Wenn er, trotz allem, ein
Menschensucher wäre, wenn er, in diesen Wochen nur
er, ein Wort gefunden hätte, das sie besänftigt, Milderung

bringt . . . ' (104). 'Die Segel streichen' is used in the same
way as 'die Zügel schießen' earlier. It implies that Christa T.
abandons her sceptical attitude towards the General, dis-
armed by his inspiriting predictions that she will one day
fulfil her potential. In other words, she is willing to suspend
her disbelief because there is an emotional reward for doing
so: the General's words bolster her fragile self-image. What is
surprising is that the previously sceptical narrator finds herself succumbing as well ('ich auch'). She evidently wants
Christa T. to have been comforted by the General because
she is acutely aware of her own failure to comfort her at the
time ('in diesen Wochen nur er'). Once again we see the
narrator's instinct to transform her friend's life for the better. This may explain why the narrator now stops interven-
ing in the narrative to point out what is going through the
mind of 'her General' and adopts instead the term 'unser
General': overcome by a feeling of solidarity with her friend,
she loses interest in undermining Christa's diary account.

Finally, however, the narrator returns to 'Christa's
General' who predicts that Christa will marry, have two
children, and live in a house outside the city. He continues:

In einer schönen, geraden Linie verläuft das Leben, hält Ihnen die
Möglichkeiten offen, Ihre reichen Charakteranlagen auszuschöpfen,
die seltene Mischung von romantisch-poetischer und pädagogisch-
praktischer Begabung . . .
  Nur zu, General, vergessen Sie nichts, uns dürstet nach der Aussch-
mückung! Werden wir ein Auto besitzen? Welche Marke? Oder ziehen wir
ein Himmelbett vor?
  Vielleicht hätte sie sich nicht anmerken lassen sollen, daß er sie schon
wieder verlor. Denn nun nimmt er zum letzten Mal die Hand. Übrigens
das Letzte noch, das Lebensende betreffend. (106)

Wolf's elliptical style makes this passage difficult to understand, but it seems to me that the brief paragraph beginning
'Nur zu' is another of the narrator's fictional additions
(rather than an extract from Christa T.'s diary), and that it
represents the narrator's idea of the reaction which a clairvoyant could normally expect from his clients. Thus, we can
only reconstruct the sense of the passage if we assume that
the narrator has the following imaginary scene in mind:

when the General begins (paragraph 1) to tell Christa T. exactly what she wants to hear (that her future life is full of possibilities and that she is richly endowed with gifts), her body language tells him that he is 'getting warmer'. However, he misinterprets this (paragraph 2) and assumes that like everyone else she wants to know all the details of her future prosperity and marital bliss. But, as we know, these are not Christa T.'s ideals, and this time her gestures (paragraph 3) make it clear that he is on the wrong track, and that he is losing her trust. Consequently, he makes one last attempt to engage her interest, and tells her that one of the partners in the marriage will die young, a prediction which Christa T. immediately assumes means that *she* will die young. In other words, the narrator wishes to ascribe purely human motives to what Christa T. saw as a supernatural power foretelling her early demise: in the narrator's view the General only tells Christa T. that the marriage will end with a premature death because his previous attempts to engage her belief in his powers have failed.[38]

The episode of the visit to the clairvoyant is well under way before the narrator interrupts to inform the reader that Christa T. had 'invented' the General, and that she proposes to do the same herself. This creates the impression that the narrator has realized something about this episode only during the process of writing. What exactly is this new insight? Probably the narrator has realized that Christa T., while she knew at some unconscious level of her great gifts and of her unfulfilled potential, lacked the confidence to acknowledge consciously her own worth. It therefore occurs to the narrator that, by ascribing supernatural powers to the general, Christa T. found a means of substantiating what she could not believe of her own accord (just as she had earlier

[38] Thomassen, not surprisingly, finds this scene confusing. She sees two insoluble contradictions: the first is the narrator's claim that *both* she and Christa T. have invented the General; and the second is the narrator's claim that Christa's visit to the clairvoyant was *both* a real event and invented. Having noted that the narrator ends her account of the visit by quoting the General's final words as they appear in Christa's diary, Thomassen comments: 'Offenbar findet [die Erzählerin] diesen Satz aus dem erklärtermaßen von ihr selbst erfundenen Gespräch paradoxerweise in dem Dokument Christa T.s und scheint sich nicht einmal hierüber zu wundern' (*Der lange Weg zu uns selbst*, 84). I hope my interpretation offers a way of making sense of this confusion.

required a third person to call her a 'Dichter' in a dream
(70)). The narrator's fictional additions to the story highlight Christa T.'s self-delusion (since they suggest that it was
easy to see through the General's charade). Yet at the same
time as wanting to hear about her potential, Christa T. evidently wanted to believe that she would die early, and this
apparently contradictory state of affairs suggests that Christa
T. needed a kind of 'escape clause' in her plans for her
future. For, in spite of the General's assurances, she must
have feared that her unfulfilled potential would never be
realized, and in that case death presented a way of both
escaping a hostile world and preserving her sense of her
own potential. Since, on my reading, the narrator's additions
to the story imply that Christa T. uses the General's words as
a smokescreen to hide from herself the fact that she *wants* to
die rather than let her gifts come to nothing, it would seem
that the narrator is coming round to the idea that Christa
T.'s death had less to do with illness than with a death-wish
(an idea which she at first resists because it forces her to
acknowledge her part in failing to rescue her friend from
despair). Moreover, in attempting to understand—through
fiction—the psychological mechanisms at work in Christa's
visit to the General, the narrator is atoning for her censorious attitude to the visit at the time (described on p. 97).

The next example of a fictional scene invented by the
narrator is an imaginary conversation between Christa T.
and the headmaster of the school where she teaches, about
the cynical lies told by her school class in their essays (129–
34). While the pupils pay lip service to Socialist ideals in
their essays, because they know it is expected of them, they
have no principles of their own. As with other invented
episodes, this conversation is preceded by some indication
of what the narrator thought 'damals'. Although Christa T.
had shown her the essays in question and invited her to
share her indignation at the schoolchildren's cynicism, the
narrator's only reaction had been: 'Was ist? [. . .] Warum
regst du dich auf?' (129). In the invented conversation
which follows, this unsympathetic response is exorcized by
being transferred to the headmaster, who likewise dismisses
Christa T.'s anger as a fuss over nothing. In contrast, the

narrator shows her sympathy for Christa T.'s anger, which she now sees as a positive aspect of her idealism, and the reader is left in no doubt that Christa T. is the moral victor in the dispute. For instance, the narrator makes the headmaster reproach Christa T. for wanting too many things at once, but it is clear from the thoughts then attributed to Christa T. that the narrator now sides with her friend: 'Ihr war nicht eingefallen, daß man das nicht alles sollte haben wollen. Plötzlich begreift sie: Das ist sein Fall. Er hat sich erzogen, nur so viel zu wollen, wie er erreichen kann [. . .]. Aber was man so leichtfertig hinsagt: Wie man denkt, soll man auch handeln, oder [. . .] die Wahrheit und nichts als die Wahrheit . . . Das alles lag hinter ihm' (132–3). The imagined conversation therefore functions as an attempt to compensate for the narrator's lack of understanding at the time of another crisis in Christa T.'s life. Her efforts to empathize with Christa T.'s feelings (to the extent of thinking her thoughts) are a way of 'doing penance' for her past behaviour; and as with the imagined interview with Gertrud Dölling, the narrator projects some of her own failings onto another person (the headmaster) in order to distance herself from them.[39]

Finally, the narrator invents a scene in which Christa T. arrives at a fancy-dress party without a costume, claiming to have come as Sophie la Roche (and later as la Roche's character, Fräulein von Sternheim) (148–52). The narrator invents this scene because she fears that she has not yet conveyed to the reader with sufficient clarity Christa's most important facet: 'Sie, Christa T., hat eine Vision von sich selbst gehabt' (148). The narrator claims to have known about this vision since the day as a child when she saw Christa T. roll up a newspaper and pretend to be blowing a trumpet, an early expression of Christa's creativity and capacity for self-expression which, as the reader already knows, made an indelible impression on the narrator. Christa T.'s choice of the role of a female writer must therefore be seen as an

---

[39] This scene differs from the interview with Gertrud, however, because the narrator (and behind her Wolf) is also using this opportunity to condemn an older generation, the original Socialists, for their inability to sustain their revolutionary idealism beyond the first phase of the establishment of the GDR.

attempt to demonstrate publicly to her peers, albeit by indirect means, her belief in her own creative potential. More
specifically, it is an attempt to communicate to her circle of
friends her perception of her relationship with Justus, who is
introduced to them at the party. For her friends (the narrator included) are surprised that Christa T., whom they
know as a nonconformist afraid of settling down, should
suddenly be willing to take on a conventional and provincial lifestyle: 'Ein bißchen wunderten wir uns ja auch. Eine
Tierarztfrau im Mecklenburgischen—das sollte es nun
also sein?' (148). Christa T. anticipates their misgivings and
responds to them through the figure of Sophie la Roche:
just as provincial life was unable to inhibit la Roche's creativity, inspiring her on the contrary to write her *Geschichte
des Fräuleins von Sternheim*, so Christa T. is determined not to
let provincial life inhibit her own creative impulses.

The narrator initially presents this fancy-dress party as a
real event, but subsequently admits that it is 'erfunden' (152).
Once again we might ask what the narrator hopes to achieve
by sending her dead friend to a party she never attended, and
once again the answer may lie in the narrator's desire to atone
for her neglect of Christa T. during her lifetime by changing
Christa's life for the better in her imagination. In this case, the
narrator's vision of Christa as Sophie la Roche is a clear case
of wishful thinking, for everything we have learnt of Christa
suggests that she lacked the confidence for such public self-
expression. The woman who cannot even admit to herself
that she wants to be a 'Dichter', requiring a third person to
reveal her vocation to her in a dream, is hardly likely to
announce her creative leanings so publicly. The narrator
seems to sense the implausibility of the scene when she
dismisses it as a fiction and undertakes an alternative and
more plausible version. In this alternative scene, Christa T. is
less self-assured and more eager for Justus's approval; and she
realizes that if, out of some misguided desire to remain
independent, she does not marry now, it may be too late. This
second scene does not, however, invalidate the first, whose
importance lies in allowing the narrator to explore an
alternative past in which Christa T. might have developed
more fully than in her real life.

Because the narrator's re-evaluation of her life is (as I mentioned earlier) an ongoing process which is still in progress as she writes, the fictions which she invents are not just a means of expressing already formulated insights about Christa T., but also a means of bringing tentative insights into clearer focus, in order to pin them down or make sure of them. Thus, although critics have sometimes argued that Wolf's intention in employing the kind of narrative techniques which I have examined in this chapter is to blur our picture of Christa T., in order to prevent us from taking away a 'graven image' of her, or in order to demonstrate the ultimate unknowability of the individual,[40] it seems to me that at the time of writing the narrator is working towards a definite 'image' of Christa T., and that she is trying to bring this image into focus (not to blur it) by inventing episodes in Christa's life.

In the course of Chapter 18, the narrator of *Christa T.* describes how she and her circle of friends reached an age at which they began to tell stories about their past:

Es war unvermeidlich, daß wir anfingen, uns Geschichten zu erzählen, Geschichten, wie sie in einem auftauchen, wenn die Wasser sich verlaufen. Dann ist man ein wenig erstaunt, daß diese Geschichten alles sein sollen, was übrigbleibt, und man sieht sich gezwungen, sie ein wenig auszuschmücken, eine hübsche kleine Moral in sie hineinzulegen und ihren Schluß vor allem, mag man davon halten, was man will, zu unseren Gunsten zu gestalten. [. . .] Wir arbeiteten an einer Vergangenheit, die man seinen Kindern erzählen kann. (211)

In this way the friends transform their pasts into anecdotes which bolster their preferred self-image. Frisch describes much the same process when he writes that 'jeder Mensch erfindet sich früher oder später eine Geschichte, die er für sein Leben hält. [. . .] Oder eine ganze Reihe von Geschichten.'[41] Both Frisch and Wolf see the desire to tell

---

[40] See for instance Thomassen: 'das Merkmal der "fiktiven Fiktion" hindert noch mehr als die schon vorher aufgezeigten Darstellungsmittel, Christa T. auf eine greifbare Identität festzulegen' (Thomassen, 85); Dennis Tate, who argues that Wolf is trying to 'confront the reader with the elusiveness of identity' (Dennis Tate, *The East German Novel. Identity, Community and Continuity* (Bath: Bath University Press, 1984), 143); and Birgitta Schuler: 'Durch die Dynamik des Wechselspiels von Authentizität und Erfindung wird dem Leser ein fertiges Bild der Christa T. vorenthalten' (Schuler, 95).   [41] Frisch, *Werke*, V. 49.

fictions about oneself as a fundamental human need. Wolf, however, contrives to set up a contrast between, on the one hand, this process of reducing the past to a series of anodyne stories which do not threaten one's self-image and, on the other, the narrator's less self-serving reflections, which, far from rendering the past innocuous and unthreatening, deliberately open up old wounds, undermining her self-image and bringing her face to face with her failings. The text suggests that even when she imagines herself having been more sympathetic to Christa T. than she actually ever was, she is not trying to rewrite the past in her *own* favour (the implication of 'zu unseren Gunsten' above), but in *Christa's* favour, showing a generosity of spirit which is held up for our admiration. Moreover, while it is true that the narrator's tendency to alter Christa's life retrospectively for the better is in some senses an impotent gesture (it cannot, of course, benefit Christa; and we may suppose that at best it serves as a therapeutic aid to lessen the narrator's grief) Wolf's intended message is anything but resigned: by using her narrator to argue the case for a re-evaluation of the GDR's values and to demonstrate the transformative power of a morally informed imagination, she hopes to enlist her contemporary reader in the creation of a more perfect society.

While this is undoubtedly the message which a contemporary readership was intended to draw from the text, more recent (post-*Wende*) interpretations of *Christa T.* have challenged this reading (and, at the same time, Wolf's reputation as a subversive writer). For while the narrator's celebration of her nonconformist friend was considered extremely radical in the context of GDR writing of the 1960s, what stands out from a post-communist perspective, it is argued, is the unnaturally intense effort which the narrator invests in trying to reappropriate her dead friend to the socialist cause. In other words, the narrator makes what appears now as a rather strained attempt to neutralize the potentially destabilizing effects of her friend's subversive behaviour by demonstrating that, for all her apparent nonconformism, Christa T. was a better Socialist than her contemporaries.[42]

---

[42] Two recent interpretations of *Christa T.* examine and enlarge on this new approach: Elizabeth Boa, 'Unnatural Causes: Modes of Death in Christa Wolf's

The reflective style of narration which Wolf perfected in *Christa T.*—and which is characterized by persistent self-questioning, associative (rather than linear) thought patterns, and fluid transitions between different time-levels and characters—has become the hallmark of her more mature works (most notably *Kein Ort. Nirgends, Kindheitsmuster, Störfall,* and *Was bleibt)*. We find it, too, in her latest novel, *Medea. Stimmen,* in which six voices take turns in telling the story of Medea's gradual marginalization and eventual expulsion from the corrupt city-state of Corinth. Though hardly a great technical innovation, these multiple perspectives are handled by Wolf with consummate skill. Not only does she make good use of the potential for inconsistency and contradiction inherent in a narrative told from different viewpoints; she also carefully dovetails the portions of narrative in such a way that each advances the plot, since each is narrated from a slightly later point in time. At the same time she cleverly conceals this contrivance behind a superficially disordered chronology which appears to be driven solely by the characters' jumbled chains of association.

Nachdenken über Christa T. and Ingeborg Bachmann's Malina', in Arthur Williams, Stuart Parkes, and Roland Smith (eds.), *German Literature at a Time of Change 1989–1990: German Unity and German Identity in Literary Perspective* (Berne: Peter Lang, 1991), 145–154; and Georgina Paul, 'The Return of the Political Unconscious: Rereading Christa Wolf's *Nachdenken über Christa T.*', paper delivered to the Conference of University Teachers of German, September 1996. Both women quite rightly distance themselves from the small band of critics which has attempted to discredit Wolf's work by accusing her of accommodation with a corrupt regime.

5

JUREK BECKER: *JAKOB DER LÜGNER*

> Ich wußte nichts von Moden und Trends und Theorien, die,
> was Schlüsse oder was Fabelführung angeht, aufgestellt
> waren, und ich war sehr verwundert, welche Zielströmungen
> ich alle berücksichtigt haben soll. Vielleicht habe ich es getan
> ohne es zu wissen, vielleicht hat mir der Zeitgeist die Feder
> geführt. (Becker on *Jakob der Lügner*)[1]

1. Introduction

Unlike Johnson, Frisch, and Wolf, who were already established writers by the 1960s, Jurek Becker, an East German
writer of Polish-Jewish origin, was still a novice at this time.
His literary début, the novel *Jakob der Lügner*,[2] was published
to great acclaim in 1969, at a time when the controversy over
Christa T. was still raging. Indeed, for the critic Volker Hage,
looking back after the *Wende*, these two novels together mark
a watershed in the development of GDR literature and can
be credited with having made West German critics take GDR
writing seriously. After 1969, Hage writes, a new attitude to
East German literature prevailed in the West: 'Die junge
Literatur, die in diesem Staat geschrieben wurde, war überhaupt noch zu entdecken—bis dahin hielt man bei uns alles,
was aus der DDR kam, für uninteressant.'[3] The fact that both
novels marked a decisive move away from the aims and
accepted forms of Socialist Realism and towards narrative
techniques already popular in the West no doubt played a
significant role in this sea change in critical thinking.

---

[1] Heinz Ludwig Arnold, 'Gespräch mit Jurek Becker', in Arnold (ed.), *Jurek Becker*, Text und Kritik, 116 (Munich: Edition Text und Kritik, 1992), 4–14 (7).

[2] Jurek Becker, *Jakob der Lügner*, Bibliothek Suhrkamp, 510 (Frankfurt/Main: Suhrkamp, 1976). All further references are included in the main text.

[3] Volker Hage, 'Die Wahrheit über Jakob Heym: Über Meinungen, Lügen und das schwierige Geschäft des Erzählens. Eine Lobrede auf den Schriftsteller Jurek Becker', *Die Zeit*, 15 March 1991, 73.

Despite tackling very different subjects, the two novels employ similar narrative techniques. In each case a first-person narrator tries to set down a record of the life of a third person (Christa T./Jakob), and in their reconstructions both narrators rely as much on the power of their imagination as on what they know (or can establish from available evidence), inventing situations which demonstrate how the central characters might have acted. Moreover, in both cases the subject of the biographical account is someone who also invents stories (Christa T. as a would-be writer, Jakob in his attempt to give hope to those around him), so that creativity and imagination are prominent themes for both authors.

According to Becker, his inspiration for the novel came initially from his father, as he explained to Heinz Ludwig Arnold in 1992:

Er [mein Vater] habe im Ghetto Lodz einen Mann gekannt, der ein großer Held gewesen sei, sagte er, und über diesen Helden sollte ich schreiben, ihm sozusagen ein Denkmal setzen. Ich fragte ihn, was war das für ein Mann, und er erzählte mir, es habe dort einen Mann gegeben, der hatte ein Radio versteckt, was bei Todesstrafe verboten war. Er hat mit diesem Gerät Radio Moskau, Radio London gehört und hat gute Nachrichten bei den anderen verbreitet, und somit quasi Hoffnung. Eines Tages ist das der Gestapo zu Ohren gekommen, wie nahezu alles Verbotene, durch Spitzel vielleicht, durch eine Unvorsichtigkeit, und dieser Mann ist verhaftet und erschossen worden; und mein Vater sagte, dieser Mann war ein Held, über ihn solltest du schreiben. Ich fand auch, daß dieser Mann ein Held war, aber ich hatte keine Lust, über ihn zu schreiben; denn fast immer, wenn ich über diese Zeit gelesen habe, war von diesem Mann die Rede, über solche Menschen und über solche bewundernswerten Helden. Es schien mir unergiebig, noch einmal darüber zu schreiben. Ich habe die Geschichte wieder vergessen, bis mir ein Einfall kam, den man vielleicht einen künstlerischen nennen könnte, der jedenfalls zu meinem ersten Buch geführt hat. Und mir fiel dieselbe Geschichte ein, mit dem Unterschied, daß die anderen nur denken, daß der Mann ein Radio hat, der hatte in Wirklichkeit aber keines.[4]

In adapting his father's story to his own purposes, by giving it a crucial twist (substituting an imaginary radio for the real one), Becker was clearly reacting not just against his father's personal view of what would make a worthwhile story, but

---

[4] Arnold, 'Gespräch mit Jurek Becker', 5.

against what he saw as a regrettable post-war vogue for resistance narratives. These were particularly fashionable in the GDR since they could be used to help legitimize the new East German state by suggesting that it grew naturally out of resistance (in particular socialist and communist resistance) to the Hitler regime.[5] Becker's novel therefore breaks away from established models of GDR fiction in both form and in content.

For all the innovations in its narrative technique (which will be explored later in this chapter), the novel has a fairly traditional plot. The eponymous protagonist, Jakob Heym, a modest, unheroic café owner, has been interned with hundreds of other people of Jewish descent in a ghetto in an unidentified Polish town. His trials begin when a Nazi sentry plays a trick on him, sending him to the much-feared ghetto police station (the 'Revier') to ask for a 'just punishment' for breaking the curfew (an offence he has not in fact committed). Against all expectations, Jakob escapes this ordeal unpunished, but while in the police station he hears a radio broadcast announcing that Russian troops have advanced to within 400 kilometres of the town. Although he delights in this news (for the Jews have been systematically starved of information from the outside world by the ghetto authorities) he hesitates to pass it on, fearing that his fellow Jews will suspect him of being an informer, as there is no other conceivable explanation for his safe return from the police station. However, when he sees his friend Mischa ready to risk his life to steal a few potatoes, Jakob uses news of the Russian advance to convince him of the folly of throwing

---

[5] I. A. and J. J. White refer to this East German tradition when they speculate that if Becker had taken his father's advice, 'so wäre daraus vermutlich ein Werk in der Tradition pathetisch-heroischen Widerstandes geworden wie etwa Bruno Apitz' *Nackt unter Wölfen*' (I. A. and J. J. White, 'Wahrheit und Lüge in Jurek Beckers Roman *Jakob der Lügner*', *ABNG* 7 (1978), 207–31 (208)). See also J. H. Reid, who writes that 'early presentations of the Third Reich [in post-war East German literature] tended to concentrate on the underground resistance movement, illegal printing presses producing antifascist leaflets, and the sabotaging of the war effort' (J. H. Reid, *Writing Without Taboos: The New East German Literature* (New York, Oxford, and Munich: Berg, 1990), 130). As I mentioned in Chapter 2, Johnson's *Karsch* also finds that East German publishers are eager for such resistance narratives (*Das dritte Buch über Achim*, 125–32).

away his life in pursuit of such petty rewards when liberation may be imminent. To make his story more convincing,
and to avoid awkward questions about his business in the
'Revier', Jakob claims to have a radio hidden in his house, in
defiance of the ghetto regulations. Since Mischa cannot keep
the good news to himself, it spreads through the ghetto, and
Jakob finds himself drawn into an increasingly elaborate web
of lies, obliged to supply the Jews every day with fresh 'news'
of the Russian advance. He must also satisfy the curiosity of
an orphaned girl, Lina, for whom he has taken responsibility,
and who will not rest until she has seen what a radio looks
like. Although Jakob's efforts earn him the status of a popular hero and he has the satisfaction of seeing the number of
suicides in the ghetto dwindle to zero, the tide begins to
turn against him when a Jew dies carrying the good news to
a truck-load of deportees which is passing through the camp.
When Jews in the ghetto are deported street by street Jakob
begins to despair of his role; but by unburdening himself to
his oldest friend, Kowalski, he only precipitates Kowalski's
suicide. Soon afterwards Jakob and the other inhabitants of
the ghetto are deported, presumably to an extermination
camp ('wir fahren, wohin wir fahren' is the narrator's understated comment (282)).

As it stands, this summary omits one essential element of
the narrative: the narrator. For Jakob Heym (who we assume has perished in the death camps) has passed on an
account of his experiences to a stranger, a fellow Jew whom
he chances to meet on the journey from the ghetto, and who
survives to tell the tale. This Jewish narrator, whose name we
never learn, is the main link with the other novels in this
study, as he freely and openly invents parts of his story. Early
in the novel he tells the reader plainly that his narrative combines his own imaginative vision with information
gleaned from witnesses:

Mein wichtigster Gewährsmann ist Jakob, das meiste von dem, was ich von
ihm gehört habe, findet sich hier irgendwo wieder, dafür kann ich mich
verbürgen. Aber ich sage das meiste, nicht alles, mit Bedacht sage ich das
meiste [. . .]. Immerhin erzähle ich die Geschichte, nicht er, Jakob ist
tot, und außerdem erzähle ich nicht seine Geschichte, sondern eine
Geschichte. [. . .] Einiges weiß ich noch von Mischa, aber dann gibt es

ein großes Loch, für das einfach keine Zeugen aufzutreiben sind. Ich sage mir, so und so muß es ungefähr gewesen sein, oder ich sage mir, es wäre am besten, wenn es so und so gewesen wäre, und dann erzähle ich und tue so, als ob es dazugehört. (43–4)

In his interview with Arnold, Becker echoed his narrator's words, saying of the novel: 'Hier erzählt ein Ich eine Geschichte, die es nur partiell kennt und deren Lücken es mit seiner Phantasie ausfüllt. Das geschieht das ganze Buch über.'[6] Both Becker and his narrator speak of filling in gaps ('Loch', 'Lücken'), but whereas a more conventional narrative employing limited perspectives might call attention to these gaps in order to emphasize the limits of our rational understanding, the narrator of this novel (like the narrators of *Das dritte Buch* and *Christa T.*) is able to fill in these gaps with the help of his imagination. He does so in two distinct ways. On some occasions he adopts the perspective of one of the characters in his story, in the manner of an omniscient narrator. Thus, for instance, he relays to the reader the thoughts of the 'Wachhabender' (18), Herschel Schtamm (86–7), Preuß and Meyer (196), Mischa (71), Kowalski (90), and Lina (141–9). He does this unobtrusively, without drawing attention to the artifice (which is presumably what he means by 'und dann erzähle ich und tue so, als ob es dazugehört'). On other occasions, however, he conjures up imaginary scenes and conversations and deliberately foregrounds their fictional status.

A typical example is the passage in which the narrator describes how Felix Frankfurter, father of Mischa's girlfriend Rosa, reacts to news that Jakob Heym has a radio which has broadcast news of a Russian advance (55–60). The narrator has heard part of the story from Mischa himself. But since Mischa leaves the house immediately after breaking the news, the narrator is deprived of an informant, and is obliged to *imagine* how the scene continues: 'Dann ist Frankfurter mit seiner Frau alleine, ohne Zeugen. Ich weiß bloß, wie es ausgegangen ist, ich kenne nur das Resultat, nichts dazwischen, aber ich kann es mir nur so oder ähnlich vorstellen' (55). The phrase 'so oder ähnlich' is reminiscent of

---

[6] Arnold, 'Gespräch mit Jurek Becker', 6.

phrases used by the narrators of *Das dritte Buch über Achim* ('Etwa so. So ungefähr') and *Nachdenken über Christa T.* ('So oder anders') and the imagined scene which follows (which I analyse more fully in Section 4 below) features many of the devices examined in earlier chapters of this study: the use of 'vielleicht' and the modal auxiliaries 'mögen' and 'können' to indicate possibility;[7] the presentation of choices with which the narrator is faced (and which are normally already made by the time the narrative is set down on paper), either in the form of undecided alternatives,[8] or a rejection of one or other alternative;[9] and the use of phrases equivalent to Frisch's 'Ich stelle mir vor' which indicate that the narrator is inventing what we read.[10] At the end of the scene, the events are cancelled out with one last modal auxiliary: '"Ich habe dir doch gesagt, daß ich nie gehört habe", könnte er ihr geantwortet haben' (60).

By far the most important invented passage is the alternative ending (258–72) in which Jakob is killed just hours before the Russians liberate the ghetto. Immediately after narrating Kowalski's suicide, the narrator reveals how, over the years, he has put together an alternative ending which he feels does justice to the story and its characters in a way that the real ending cannot. Because the narrator feels that Kowalski's suicide has no place in this alternative ending, he reels back the action to an earlier point and rewrites the

---

[7] '"Felix", könnte sie nach einer Weile leise gesagt haben' (56); 'Vielleicht sieht er aus wie ein Mann, der einen wichtigen Entschluß gefaßt hat' (56); 'Vielleicht sagt er ihr jetzt schon, was er vorhat' (56); 'vielleicht betrachtet er für einen Moment das gerahmte Bild mit allen Angehörigen des Theaters' (58); 'Sie mag nicken, verwundert über seinen Zorn' (58); 'Sie schreit vielleicht leise auf, sie ist vielleicht entsetzt, bestimmt erschrocken' (59).

[8] 'Sie wischt sich die Tränen weg [. . .] oder sie wischt sie nicht weg' (55); 'könnte sie nach einer Weile leise gesagt haben [. . .]. Oder sie könnte gesagt haben: [. . .]' (56); 'Frankfurter [. . .] nimmt eine Tasse oder ein Kästchen heraus und findet darin den Schlüssel' (56); 'er sucht sich ein Stück Sacktuch oder einen Sack mit Löchern, den er zerreißt, oder, wenn kein Sack da ist, er zieht die Jacke aus und hängt sie vor die Tür' (57).

[9] 'Vielleicht sagt er ihr jetzt schon, was er vorhat [. . .] aber das ist unwahrscheinlich, er hat sie nie groß um ihre Meinung gebeten [. . .] Nehmen wir also an, er schließt wortlos den Schrank, geht zur Tür, dreht sich dort zu ihr um und sagt nur: "Komm"'(56).

[10] 'Ich denke mir, daß er für einen Augenblick den Finger auf den Mund legt' (57).

scene: 'Kowalski darf Auferstehung feiern, Fensterkreuz und Schnur werden von ihm keines Blickes gewürdigt, denn Jakob verzichtet auf das Geständnis. Sie unterhalten sich an dem bewußten Abend über belangloses Zeug, obwohl Jakob der Sinn nach anderem steht, aber Kowalski braucht davon nichts zu merken' (258). In this respect, the narrator is reminiscent of the *Buch-Ich* in *Gantenbein* who reels back the action in a similar way, cancelling out parts of the narrative which do not suit his purposes (and who also twice cancels out a 'Geständnis' in which one character confesses to having deceived another character, though the deception is of a different nature).[11]

As with the scene in the Frankfurters' house, the narrator deliberately draws attention to the fictional status of his alternative ending. Once again, foregrounding devices include the use of *Konjunktiv II* and the modals;[12] equivalents of Frisch's 'ich stelle mir vor';[13] undecided alternatives;[14] the act of selecting one of a series of possible alternatives[15] (or, indeed, a refusal to select one: 'ich kann mir kein Herz fassen und Jakob auf einen von ihnen festlegen. Also biete ich sie zur Auswahl an', (269)); and implicit references to

---

[11] Frisch, *Werke*, V. 184, 199.

[12] 'Zum Beispiel könnte er befürchten, daß [. . .]' (259); 'in der Ferne könnte er meinetwegen seinen Scheinwerfer erkennen' (268); 'lieber Gott, wäre das eine Nacht gewesen' (270).

[13] 'Ich stelle mir einen Moment lang vor, Jakob wäre auf die simple Idee gekommen zu behaupten, das Radio sei ihm gestohlen worden. [. . .] Ich stelle mir vor, ein ganzes Ghetto sucht den gewissenlosen Dieb [. . .] Ich stelle mir weiter vor, die Suche nach dem Dieb nimmt beängstigende Formen an' (259); 'ich denke mir, daß Kowalski und Mischa ihm bleiben' (261); 'Mischa verspricht es, bestimmt in der Hoffnung auf weitere gelegentliche Neuigkeiten, wie ich mir seine Taktik erkläre' (266); 'Nach ungefähr zwei Stunden, denke ich, ist Jakob entschlossen' (267); 'ich stelle mir weiter vor, daß das Ghetto längst noch nicht zur Ruhe kommt. Ich male mir die Rache für Jakob aus' (270).

[14] 'Er wird im Zorn erschlagen [. . .] oder er wird nicht erschlagen, das tut nichts zur Sache' (260); '"Es gibt nichts Neues", sagt er dann [. . .]. Oder noch wirksamer, er sagt [. . .]' (261); 'Ich habe mir keine Gedanken darüber gemacht, wie ich selbst mich in dieser Angelegenheit verhalte, auf welcher Seite ich stehe, ob ich Jakobs Freund bin oder Feind' (262); 'am besten wohl Kowalski, aber auch ein Nachbar oder ich oder sonst einer vom Bahnhof könnte es sein' (271).

[15] 'Nehmen wir an, ich plädiere entschieden, sich durch das Gerede nicht verwirren zu lassen' (262); 'Weil meiner Willkür keine Grenzen gesetzt sind, lasse ich es eine kühle und sternenklare Nacht sein' (268); 'Dann die Grenze, ich habe für Jakob den denkbar günstigsten Ort ausgewählt' (268).

the 'real' ending.[16] Moreover, every mention of the resurrected Kowalski is a reminder of the 'real' story, in which we have already read of his death, and therefore calls attention to the artificiality of this alternative scenario.[17]

The alternative ending is cancelled out when the narrator reluctantly returns to the 'real' story:

> Aber nach dem erfundenen endlich das blaßwangige und verdrießliche, das wirkliche und einfallslose Ende [. . .].
>
> Kowalski ist unwiderruflich tot, und Jakob lebt vorerst weiter, verschwendet keinen Gedanken daran, Lina fremden Leuten aufzuhalsen, entblößt seine Jacke nicht von vorgeschriebenen Sternen, läßt die Zange in der Schublade, falls er überhaupt eine besitzt, verleitet also auch keinen Posten auf dem alten Gemüsemarkt in kühler und sternenklarer Nacht zu Schüssen, die ein so gewaltiges Echo auszulösen imstande sind. (272)

Once again, the narrator reels back the story, and the deliberate enumeration of the scenes which he had previously conjured up and which he now makes disappear draws attention to the contrivance.[18]

What I have said of the other novels discussed in this study—that the reader cannot be kept permanently aware of the fictional status of a scene (and does not necessarily want to be)—holds true for the scenes described above. Whenever the conjectural frame recedes into the background, the reader becomes immersed in the scene and experiences it as real.[19] In fact, in *Jakob der Lügner* our reading experience is

---

[16] 'Weder im wirklichen Ende [. . .], noch in meinem' (260), 'bei mir' (260); 'jedenfalls findet der Einbruch nicht statt, nicht in meinem Ende' (263); 'an einem wichtigen Abend in meinem Ende' (264); 'das kommt auch meinem Ende zustatten, man wird sehen' (268); 'legen wir in diesem hochdramatischen Augenblick meines Endes eine kurze Pause ein' (268); 'das alles und mehr ist mir nicht wichtig genug, um dafür Platz in meinem Ende zur Verfügung zu stellen' (271).

[17] 'Die folgenden Nächte, die ja nun durch das Wegfallen aller Selbstvorwürfe wegen Kowalskis Tod frei werden' (259); 'Ganz von Wohlgesonnenen ist er aber nicht verlassen, ich denke mir, daß Kowalski und Mischa ihm bleiben' (261); 'irgendeiner steht in der Nähe, der Jakob kennt. Am besten wohl Kowalski' (271).

[18] Again, the *Buch-Ich* in *Gantenbein* uses a similar device. See my analysis on p. 72 above.

[19] I would therefore question Heinz Wetzel's suggestion that we experience a *constant* alienation from the story: 'wobei die Fiktionalität der Geschichte, die Gründe für das Erzählen und die Art des Erzählen *ständig* reflektiert werden: Daß und wie weit es sich um Fiktion handelt, bleibt *nie* zweifelhaft' (Heinz Wetzel, '"Unvergleichlich gelungener"—aber "einfach zu schön"? Zur ethischen und ästhetischen Motivation des Erzählens in Jurek Beckers Roman *Jakob der Lügner*', in

encoded in the text itself, in the behaviour of the orphan girl Lina, a figure reminiscent of the naïve narratees employed by both Frisch (Knobel in *Stiller*, Camilla in *Gantenbein*) and Grass (Bruno in *Die Blechtrommel*). With the natural credulity of a child, Lina is at first taken in when Jakob imitates a radio broadcast for her, failing to notice the obvious absurdity of an English presenter and an English politician (Sir Winston Churchill) conversing in German. Yet although we are able to view Lina's behaviour from an ironic distance, we may have more in common with her than we think. Far from feeling disappointed when she discovers Jakob's pretence (after peeping behind the screen that separates them), she continues to delight in his mimicry ('das Vergnügen am Zuhören ist nicht kleiner geworden' (170)). Moreover, the broadcast does not seem to become any less real for her once she knows that it is false: for when Mischa's fiancée Rosa accuses Jakob of lying, Lina protests indignantly that she has heard his radio with her own ears. By implication, then, a story does not become less real to the naïve reader for being exposed as a fiction. And though we may like to flatter ourselves that we are infinitely more sophisticated than a child such as Lina, it seems to me that we experience a similar effect when we read episodes whose fictional status is deliberately foregrounded.

As with all the novels examined in the present study, it makes little sense to explore this particular aspect of *Jakob der Lügner* in isolation: it has to be considered in the broader context of the novel's narrative technique. Critics are agreed that the question of story-telling and its motivation is one of the central thematic concerns of the novel.[20] In what follows

Albrecht Schöne (ed.), *Kontroversen, alte und neue. Akten des VII. Internationalen Germanisten-Kongresses, Göttingen, 1985*, 11 vols. (Tübingen: Niemeyer, 1986), VII. 107–14 (109); my italics.

[20] See, for instance, Heinz Wetzel, 'Fiktive und authentische Nachrichten in Jurek Beckers Romanen *Jakob der Lügner* und *Aller Welt Freund*', in Roland Jost and Hansgeorg Schmidt-Bergmann (eds.), *Im Dialog mit der Moderne. Zur deutschsprachigen Literatur von der Gründerzeit bis zur Gegenwart* (Frankfurt/Main: Athenäum, 1986), 439–51: 'Jurek Becker [. . .] macht die Diskrepanz zwischen Wahrheit und Fiktion, wie auch die Motivation zum Lügen zu einem Hauptthema seiner Romane, am deutlichsten in *Jakob der Lügner*, wo die moralischen Implikationen der Mimesis das zentrale Problem bilden' (440).

I argue that the overt invention of scenes and conversations is just one of a series of narrative strategies in *Jakob der Lügner* which reflect the narrator's obsessive desire to tell a good story. In order to argue this, it is necessary to define precisely what the narrator understands by a 'good story' (and this is one of the tasks of Section 2 below). I also propose two new approaches to the interpretation of the double ending, seeing it firstly as symptomatic of the narrator's attitude to storytelling; and suggesting secondly that a hidden motive may underlie his preoccupation with inventing 'ein ordentliches Ende', namely, a need to find strategies for coping with the emotional trauma of the Holocaust.

2. The Story-Teller and his Stories

The narrator of *Jakob der Lügner* has a distinctive personality, his most salient characteristic being the evident satisfaction he derives from telling a story well. Sometimes the pleasure comes from interrupting the main action to 'chat' to the reader about himself: 'Wir wollen ein bißchen schwätzen, wie es sich für eine ordentliche Geschichte gehört, laßt mir die kleine Freude' (24). At other times, he takes obvious pleasure in narrating the individual episodes which make up the main story. When he tells us 'Mischa kommt mit Rosa in sein Zimmer, und das ist eine ganze Geschichte für sich' (60), we sense that he relishes the prospect of relating this anecdote. Towards the end of the novel the narrator recalls meeting a former Nazi officer who told him the story of the suicide of a Jewish doctor, prompting the narrator to comment: 'Er hatte gut erzählt, lückenlos und plastisch' (212). From this and other comments it is clear that the narrator considers story-telling to be a craft, and aims to excel at it. In this connection, Wolfgang Joho speaks quite rightly of the narrator's 'Freude am Fabulieren und an beiläufig mitlaufenden kleinen Geschichten und Anekdoten'.[21]

This attitude to story-telling extends moreover to the characters of *Jakob der Lügner*, for although the eponymous liar,

---

[21] Wolfgang Joho, 'Lüge aus Barmherzigkeit', *NDL* 17/12 (December 1969), 151–3 (153).

Jakob Heym, is by no means a natural *raconteur*, he too experiences briefly the thrill of telling a story well, walking to work 'gehobenen Herzens' after inventing his first story of any substance (about the imaginary 'Schlacht an der Rudna'). Shortly afterwards, when to satisfy Lina's curiosity he imitates a radio broadcast (producing something which is part performance and part narrative), he gradually loses his inhibitions and is overcome, as Heinz Wetzel puts it, by 'Freude am Hervorbringen des schönen Scheins um seiner selbst willen'.[22] Another character, Felix Frankfurter, is a celebrated and enthusiastic *raconteur*, who is particularly fond of stories constructed in such a way that everything leads up to a final flourish, or *Pointe*: 'Frankfurter hat nichts lieber als eine Geschichte mit einer Pointe am Ende. [. . .] Gleich wird Frankfurter eine Anekdote erzählen, eine seiner Geschichten, an deren Ende er immer so vergnügt tut, daß er sich auf die Schenkel schlägt' (48).

The enthusiasm for story-telling exhibited by all three men—the narrator, Jakob, and Frankfurter—can be traced back to their creator, Becker, who had a particular liking for anecdotal stories rounded off by a final twist or *Pointe*. In an interview with Marianna Birnbaum in 1988, Becker admitted that his novels were full of 'short stories', and commented: 'Mir hat einmal jemand vorgeworfen, ich hätte ein aphoristisches Verhältnis zur Wirklichkeit. Ich liebe Pointen sehr, und ich weiß, daß ich da auch in Gefahr bin: daß ich manchmal, wie es heißt, für eine Pointe meine Großmutter verrate.'[23] Indeed, the anecdotal stories of which Becker speaks here were not confined to his prose works. In the interview with Birnbaum, for instance, he told an anecdote with a characteristic sting in its tail to illustrate the human weakness which leads people in even the closest of relationships to keep secrets from one another:

Ich will Ihnen dazu eine kleine Geschichte erzählen. Ich kenne jeman-den, der kam eines Tages nach Hause, und seine Frau hatte sich das Leben genommen, nach zwanzigjähriger Ehe. Sie lag auf der Erde, sie

---

[22] Wetzel, '"Unvergleichlich gelungener"—aber "einfach zu schön"?', 111.
[23] Jurek Becker, '"Das Vorstellbare gefällt mir immer besser als das Bekannte": Gespräch mit Marianna Birnbaum (1988)', in Irene Heidelberger-Leonard (ed.), *Jurek Becker* (Frankfurt/Main: Suhrkamp, 1992), 89–107 (105).

war 50 Jahre alt, und ihr war das Gebiß aus dem Mund gefallen. Mein Bekannter erzählt: 'Das Erschütterndste für mich war, daß ich nicht wußte, daß sie ein Gebiß hatte.'[24]

Similarly, when answering questions at a Canadian symposium on *Jakob der Lügner*,[25] Becker offered to explain why the research he did on life in the ghetto never actually found its way into his novel, saying: 'I can tell a little story which explains this problem very well.'[26] Indeed, 'Ich will Ihnen dazu eine kleine Geschichte erzählen' was evidently something of a catchphrase of Becker's.[27] Moreover, in his interview with Arnold, Becker made it clear that, however much critics may have wished to ascribe more profound or more intellectual motivations to him, the desire to tell a good story was always the primary motivation when he embarked on a new writing project. He rejected both the notion that his novels were written to express political views and the idea that his writing acted as a kind of emotional release:

Eine Geschichte verträgt nur insoweit meine Überzeugung, wie es fürs Geschichtenerzählen notwendig ist, und das ist ein sehr geringes Maß. Ich schreibe ja nicht eine Geschichte, um mir Ansichten aufzuladen und diese Ansichten ein Stück weiter zum Leser zu transportieren. Darunter

---

[24] Jurek Becker, 'Gespräch mit Marianna Birnbaum', 95.

[25] Jurek Becker, 'Answering Questions about *Jakob der Lügner*', *Seminar*, 19 (1983), 288–92.

[26] 'Answering Questions about *Jakob der Lügner*', 290. The story itself is another neat, rounded anecdote with a punchline: 'I have a friend, he is an actor. And when Bertolt Brecht lived in his last years, this actor was eighteen years old. He had to play a very minor role in a play by Erwin Strittmatter, the East German author. The play is called *Katzgraben*, and it was directed by Brecht. And there was a little scene: My friend had to play a song on the guitar, that was all he had to do. He played a young farmer. And Brecht came to the rehearsal, and during the scene he stopped and said, listen, you play terribly, what's wrong with you? And my friend said, I am not playing a guitarist, I am playing a farmer. Mr. Eisler wrote a very complicated song with eight different harmonies. I'm just able to play five of them, but is that so important? And Brecht was impressed, and he said to him, you know, you're right. Please learn the other three harmonies and then leave them out' (290).

[27] The phrase was chosen as the title of an interview in which Becker had used it: Jurek Becker, 'Ich will Ihnen dazu eine kleine Geschichte erzählen', in Wolfgang Geisler and Peter E. Kalb (eds.), *Einmischung: Schriftsteller über Schule, Gesellschaft, Literatur* (Weinheim/Basel: Beltz, 1983), 56–66. The 'little stories' which he told the interviewer were intended to demonstrate: 'daß zum Geschichtenerzählen nicht unbedingt die Beherrschung einer Sprache gehört. Es ist eher eine bestimmte Haltung, auch eine bestimmte Lust' (59–60).

würde mir fast jede Geschichte zusammenbrechen. [. . .] Eigentlich schreibe ich nicht, um mich zu befreien, also wie man eine Notdurft verrichtet, oder um mir das Herz zu erleichtern. Das Motiv für Bücher ist das Finden einer Geschichte, die ich für erzählenswert halte.[28]

Here, Becker makes explicit that 'die Geschichte' and 'das Geschichtenerzählen' take precedence over other considerations. Critics have tried repeatedly to establish links between the 'Freude am Fabulieren' which characterizes Becker's narrative style in *Jakob der Lügner* and Jewish literary tradition. Early reviewers such as Joho who believed they saw in *Jakob der Lügner* the influence of the Yiddish writer Sholom Aleichem (1859–1916)[29] were contradicted by Becker, who played down the importance of his Jewish background for his writing and claimed not to have read any of Aleichem's works until *after* he had written *Jakob*.[30] This has not prevented critics from continuing to cite Aleichem as an influence on Becker.[31] Indeed, even those critics who accept Becker's claim not to have read any Yiddish literature before writing *Jakob der Lügner* persist in seeing a Jewish influence on his narrative style. Manfred Karnick, for instance, maintains that a story-telling culture prevails in the ghetto of *Jakob der Lügner* which was typical of the Jewish 'Schtetl'.[32] Susan

---

[28] Arnold, 'Gespräch mit Jurek Becker', 9–10.

[29] 'Nicht von ungefähr wird zweimal in dem Buch Scholem Alechem beschworen: Beckers Buch ist diesem großen Erzähler in seinen besten Partien verpflichtet und nicht unebenbürtig' (Joho, 'Lüge aus Barmherzigkeit', 153).

[30] 'Tatsache ist, daß ich zum erstenmal Scholem Alejchem las, nachdem ich das Musical *Der Fiedler auf dem Dach* gesehen hatte, eine Weile nach dem Buch' (Jurek Becker, 'Wäre ich hinterher klüger? Mein Judentum', *FAZ*, 13 May 1978, supplement: *Bilder und Zeiten*, 4).

[31] Most recently Russell Brown: 'Becker chose to write a comic novel of Jewish *shtetl* life in the Sholem Aleichem tradition' (Russell E. Brown, 'Radios and Trees. A Note to Jurek Becker's Ghetto Fiction', *Germanic Notes*, 19 (1988), 22–4 (23)).

[32] Manfred Karnick, 'Die Geschichte von Jakob und Jakobs Geschichten', in Irene Heidelberger-Leonard (ed.), *Jurek Becker* (Frankfurt/Main: Suhrkamp, 1992), 207–21. Karnick bases this view on the work of two American sociologists, Zbrowski and Herzog. Interestingly, their work suggests that the dual ending of the novel and the narrator's foregrounding of alternatives may also reflect the idiosyncratic logic of East-European Jews, of whom they write: "'Jeder Stock hat doch zwei Enden". [. . .] Fragt man einen Juden nach dem Weg [. . .], so muß man sich eine [. . .] Rede anhören über all die Wege, die man nicht gehen sollte. [. . .] Zahllose Anekdoten, erzählt von oder über osteuropäische Juden, beruhen auf der tief verwurzelten Überzeugung, "daß es in jeder Situation immer zwei

Johnson offers evidence that Becker came into contact with
this aspect of Jewish culture in post-war Berlin, where his
father met regularly with Jewish neighbours to exchange
stories. In an unpublished interview of 1984 Becker claimed
that by joining in these sessions he learnt the tricks of his
trade: 'With each gathering Becker learned more both by
telling stories and by listening, and preparing stories during
the interim period became a favorite preoccupation. Just
telling a story was not enough. Becker wanted to tell a
good story, and as his skills improved, he laid the foundation
for a writing career.'[33] Johnson's account is corroborated by
Becker's interview with Arnold, in which he claimed to have
learnt from his father 'gewisse Techniken des Geschichtenerzählens, die fand ich toll'.[34]

If, then, there was a specifically Jewish influence on Becker
it was probably due to the natural impact of his environment,
rather than to Becker's conscious emulation of any literary
model. However, in their attempts to place Becker in
a Jewish tradition, critics have tended to neglect the role
played by another, non-Jewish influence: Max Frisch. Becker
publicly acknowledged his indebtedness to Frisch, first in his
1978 article 'Wäre ich hinterher klüger',[35] and then in
his 1988 interview with Birnbaum,[36] and Frisch's influence
seems to me to be especially evident in Becker's narrative
technique, both authors favouring short, self-contained, and
carefully structured stories and anecdotes.[37] This brings me

Möglichkeiten" gibt. Sollte das Schlimmste kommen, so gibt es immer noch zwei
Möglichkeiten; und sollte das Schlimmere dann eintreten, so liegen darin auch
noch zwei Möglichkeiten—und so weiter' (quoted by Karnick, 214).

[33] Susan M. Johnson, *The Works of Jurek Becker: A Thematic Analysis* (New York:
Peter Lang, 1988), 2–3.

[34] Arnold, 'Gespräch mit Jurek Becker', 6.

[35] 'Ich empfinde keinen Stolz darüber, daß Kafka Jude war, obgleich ich ver-
mute, daß seine Literatur für mich von bestimmender Bedeutung gewesen ist. Ich
ärgere mich nicht darüber, daß Max Frisch kein Jude ist, obgleich seine Bedeutung
für mich eine ähnliche ist' (Becker, 'Wäre ich hinterher klüger', 4).

[36] 'Als ich Student war und noch Bücher lesen konnte wie ein normaler Mensch,
hat mir Max Frisch viel bedeutet' (Birnbaum, 106).

[37] Typical 'kleine Geschichten' in Frisch's works include: 'Die kleine Geschichte
von Isidor', the story of Stiller/White's elopement with the mulatto-girl Florence,
the fairy-tale 'Rip van Winkle', and the cave story (all from *Stiller*); the stories of
Otto the milkman, the Pechvogel, the Bäckermeister in O., the Ambassador, Ali
and Alil, Philemon und Baucis, the man who went to his own funeral, and the story

to my last point here, that while critics have been quick to draw attention to the pleasure which the narrator takes in 'Fabulieren', and quick to attribute his inventiveness to Becker's Jewish origins, they have been conspicuously slow to identify the specific characteristics of his particular brand of story-telling, despite the fact that this is what makes the narrative tone of *Jakob der Lügner* so distinctive.[38] In other words, when they speak of the narrator's (or Becker's) desire to tell a 'good story', they take it for granted that we all know what is meant by this term, whereas, in fact, it means very little until we define it.

My own analysis of the narrative will show that it is made up of anecdotal episodes of a very traditional kind: each is structured in order to create maximum suspense and excitement; each is complete in itself (neither fragmented nor open-ended); and most lead up to some kind of *Pointe*, often a strange twist of fate or reversal of expectations. Although the stories are designed to invite emotional involvement they are far from sentimental since the narrator has a keen eye for the quirks and frailties of human nature, which he gently satirizes.[39] Thus, the delight which the narrator takes in

of the floating corpse (all from *Gantenbein*); the stories of Marion the puppeteer and 'Der andorranische Jude' (both from *Tagebuch 1946–1949*).

[38] While Martin Kane's analysis of the narrator's comic technique (in particular of his use of farce) is very persuasive, Kane chooses not to analyse any of the narrator's other story-telling techniques, despite praising Becker's 'endless inventiveness, a talent for spinning an interesting yarn which make him one of the best story tellers to emerge from the GDR' (Martin Kane, 'Tales and the Telling: The Novels of Jurek Becker', in Kane (ed.), *Socialism and the Literary Imagination: Essays on East German Writers* (New York and Oxford: Berg, 1991), 163–78 (166)).

[39] Two representative examples of such frailty will illustrate the technique. In the first instance, the narrator imagines that when Jakob's predictions of an imminent liberation do not come true, his admirers will turn against him, and, in order to justify this about-face to themselves, will delude themselves that they always knew he was a bad lot: 'das Eis, das er verkauft hat, wird allmählich schon immer das schlechteste in der ganzen Stadt gewesen sein, sogar sein berühmtes Himbeereis, und seine Kartoffelpuffer noch nie ganz koscher' (27). In another instance, we learn that while Jakob's friend Kowalski likes to think that he is no less brave than Jakob ('Wer hätte an deiner Stelle anders gehandelt', he tells Jakob in an interior monologue (90)), he is horrified by the suggestion that he should hide Jakob's radio in his own house while Jakob's street is subject to a power cut. But since cowardice is not part of Kowalski's self-image, he hides his fear from his friends (and from himself) by pretending that he would be perfectly happy to hide the radio if only the idea were not foolish and imprudent and likely to endanger

story-telling is not limited to the pleasure of perfecting the story's 'mechanics': he takes just as much pride in demonstrating his powers of human observation and his empathetic understanding of human frailty. Finally, the narrator is set apart from the other narrators who feature in this study by his unintellectual outlook on life (his studies in human nature, for instance, though they sometimes illustrate the complex relationship between the conscious and unconscious mind, show no formal knowledge of the theories or terminology of psychoanalysis). Thus, one might describe his stories as 'naïve'.[40] In fact, he is very like the story-teller as defined by Walter Benjamin: a craftsman and dispenser of wisdom, who invents compact stories unencumbered by psychological analysis.[41]

These naïve story-telling techniques can be illustrated with reference to a typical 'kleine Geschichte' from *Jakob der Lügner*. As I mentioned above, the narrator promises us that the episode in which Mischa persuades Rosa to sleep with him will be 'eine ganze Geschichte für sich' (60). The story is in fact told in two instalments, but each part is complete in itself, leading to a *Pointe*, though the second *Pointe*, as befits the story's finale, is more poignant and forceful than the first. The narrator begins the first instalment by anticipating its highlights:

Mischa kommt mit Rosa in sein Zimmer, und das ist eine ganze Geschichte für sich. Wenn es eine Geschichte ist, wie jemand belogen werden muß, damit er ein bißchen glücklich sein kann, nichts anderes geschieht mit Rosa, wenn es eine Geschichte ist, wie verwegene Listen angewendet werden müssen, und Angst vor Endeckung ist im Spiel, und kein Fehler darf um Himmels willen unterlaufen, und das Gesicht muß immer ernst und harmlos dabei bleiben, wenn alles das eine brauchbare Geschichte

the lives of others (91–4). Both examples highlight the human capacity for self-delusion.

[40] Erdmann Waniek speaks of the narrator's '"naiver" Erzählstil' and of 'das naive Erzählen', without defining either term (Erdmann Waniek, '"Aber warum verbieten sie uns die Bäume?" Frage und Antwort in Jurek Beckers *Jakob der Lügner*', *Seminar*, 29 (1993), 279–93 (285, 291)).

[41] Walter Benjamin, 'Der Erzähler. Betrachtungen zum Werk Nikolai Lesskows', in Benjamin, *Gesammelte Schriften*, ed. Rolf Tiedemann and Hermann Schweppenhäuser, 7 vols. (Frankfurt/Main: Suhrkamp, 1974–89), II. 2 (1977), 438–65.

hergibt, dann ist es auch eine Geschichte, wie Rosa und Mischa in sein Zimmer kommt. (60)

At first sight the narrator may appear unsure of the merits of his story, but this is merely a ruse: in reality he knows perfectly well that his anecdote contains all the ingredients of a good story, and he is simply whetting our appetite by promising us both a paradoxical situation (in which deception, contrary to expectations, is used to make others happy)[42] and suspense (aroused by the threat of discovery). The story which follows fulfils both these promises: in order to persuade Rosa to sleep with him in his room despite the presence of his room-mate, Fajngold, Mischa tells Rosa that Fajngold is deaf and dumb, and will therefore be oblivious to their love-making. But no sooner has this lie begun to pay dividends, than Mischa's difficulties begin. First, Fajngold lets on that he has heard some of the lovers' private conversations, and, as a result, Mischa feels constrained to ensure that Fajngold is asleep before he turns his attention to Rosa, even though this strategy risks forfeiting her affection (and therefore undoing his whole scheme), since she feels 'Enttäuschung, warum er sie so lange warten läßt' (64). Secondly, Fajngold talks in his sleep one night ('ungeachtet der Tatsache, daß Taubstumme auch im Schlaf taubstumm zu sein haben' (64)), thus threatening to expose the deception.

The narrator recognizes in this situation some classic elements of comedy, calling it 'das winzige Lustspiel' (64). For the *Pointe* he homes in on a particular night, on which Rosa insists on fantasizing about the future, to the annoyance of her weary fiancé. After Rosa has painted a lovingly detailed picture of their future home, right down to the spices on the kitchen shelf, the *Pointe* adds a subtle twist: 'Weiter weiß ich nicht, in dieser Gegend ist mein Gewährsmann Mischa end-

---

[42] Clearly this aspect of the anecdote mirrors what happens in Jakob's story, since he too deceives others in order to make them happy. A further variation on this situation is found in the fairy-tale which Jakob tells to Lina, in which a princess's happiness depends on her being deceived by a young gardener at her father's palace (171–4). Lina, in turn, is being deceived by Jakob who is attempting to entertain her by pretending to be a 'Märchenonkel' telling stories on the radio. These clever Chinese-box effects seem to be attributable to Becker rather than to the narrator.

gültig eingeschlafen, mitten unter den Gewürzen. Vielleicht hätte mir Fajngold mehr erzählen können über diese eine Nacht, vielleicht hat er wach gelegen vom Keller bis zum Dachboden, aber ich habe ihn nicht gefragt' (67). This ending leaves us with an awareness of human imperfection (for Mischa, instead of sharing in his fiancée's hopes and dreams, gives in to the less noble but very human desire for sleep), and provides the added amusement of a comic injustice: we are asked to imagine that while her future husband slips into a welcome sleep (and thus becomes 'taubstumm'), the unfortunate 'Taubstummer' Fajngold is forced to listen to Rosa's domestic fantasies (which are a matter of total indifference to him), unable to protest without exposing his friend's deception.

In the second instalment of this story (174–81) the narrator describes Mischa and Rosa lying in bed together and then cleverly creates suspense by imputing curiosity to the reader:

Man wird zu Recht fragen, warum flüstert er nicht? Und man wird fragen, warum der Schrank nicht mehr in der Zimmermitte steht, sondern ganz normal an der Wand, und warum der Vorhang wieder das Fenster verdeckt, anstatt den Raum in zwei Hälften zu teilen? Wo die spanische Wand geblieben ist, wird man sich wundern, und vor allem, warum Rosa auf einmal nackt liegt, obgleich das Licht noch brennt, wieso geniert sie sich nicht mehr? Dann wird man gütigst einen Blick auf das zweite Bett werfen, wird es leer finden und alle Fragen gehen auf in einer: Wo ist der taubstumme Isaak Fajngold mit den scharfen Ohren? (174)

The narrator resolves this suspense fairly quickly with the revelation that Fajngold has disappeared without trace and that his friends fear the worst (arrest or execution by the Nazis), but there is a further moment of suspense when Mischa appears to betray the truth about Fajngold, suggesting to Rosa that the supposed 'Taubstummer' might have forgotten about the curfew while 'chatting the evening away' ('sich verplauschen' (174)). Here too, the tension is quickly dissipated, as Mischa thinks of an ingenious, if implausible, explanation for his words (that deaf mutes can communicate just like everybody else: using sign-language).

Next, the narrator employs one of his favourite storytelling devices: a reversal of expectations. The reader naturally assumes that Fajngold's disappearance will have a liberating effect on the lovers, freeing them to conduct their relationship without fear or shame. Instead, Rosa feels inhibited in the new situation. The narrator's commentary suggests three reasons for her unexpected reaction: first, a strong unconscious association has been forged in Rosa's mind between Fajngold's silent presence on the other side of the room and her sexual desire, so that in his absence her desire evaporates;[43] secondly, Rosa cannot look at Fajngold's empty bed without thinking of his probable fate at the hands of the Nazis, and these morbid thoughts also take away her sexual appetite; and thirdly, Rosa has caught herself rejoicing at Fajngold's disappearance, and this selfishness makes her feel guilty. I am not persuaded by Erdmann Waniek's interpretation of this scene, namely that Rosa's refusal to profit by Fajngold's absence is a sign of her compassion: 'der Preis für die Veränderung zum "Normalen" hin, Fajngold das Opfer, ist zu hoch.'[44] For what this passage exemplifies is not the narrator's admiration for human altruism, but, on the contrary, his fascination with human frailty. Thus, Rosa's experience teaches us some important lessons about human nature, none of them particularly flattering: first, our motives are often less pure than they may appear to others (Mischa—like Waniek—thinks Rosa's 'compassion' for Fajngold is a credit to her);[45] secondly, while selfishness is instinctive to us, we are prevented from enjoying our selfish desires by the moral codes which have been instilled in us; and thirdly, we are at the mercy of uncontrollable Pavlovian responses (for Rosa's sexual arousal has become dependent on Fajngold's presence in the same way that salivation became dependent on ringing bells for the dogs in Pavlov's most famous experiment). Rosa's unconscious response is all the more striking because both the narrator and Mischa had previously insisted on her strict principles of decency

[43] 'In diesem Zimmer hat Rosa zu lieben angefangen, in Fajngolds Gegenwart, er war von der ersten Sekunde an dabei, die Heimlichkeit vor ihm war fester Bestandteil aller Zärtlichkeiten' (176).

[44] Waniek, 286.

[45] Wetzel sees Jakob's motives as similarly impure, a complex mixture of altruism and egoism (Wetzel, '"Unvergleichlich gelungener"—aber "einfach zu schön"?', 106).

and decorum. She would not contemplate making love to Mischa in the presence of another man, we were told, because 'sie ist nicht so ein Mädchen' (61). Yet now she cannot contemplate making love to him *without* another man in the room. In this way, her subliminal desires undermine her self-image of modesty and respectability.

The narrator uses the story's *Pointe* to heighten our sense of the paradoxes inherent in human behaviour and to round off his story in a satisfying way. At their first assignation after Fajngold's disappearance Rosa initially refuses Mischa's sexual advances, only to wake him in the middle of the night to ask him to move the furniture back to where it was when Fajngold lived there. Mischa, who has heard that women are subject to strange whims and fancies which must at all costs be nipped in the bud, refuses to comply unless she can give him a sensible reason, which she cannot. This leads to a lovers' quarrel; but the tension appears to be resolved when they apologize to one another the next day and seal their reconciliation by making love, albeit rather unsuccessfully. The narrator, who adopts the narrative pose of 'taking leave' of the pair, then delivers his *Pointe*:

Hören wir noch, wie Mischa auf der Woge des Vertragens lächelnd fragt, was er lieber nicht gefragt hätte: 'Möchtest du immer noch, daß ich das Zimmer wieder mit Schrank und Vorhang teile?'.

Das sagt er, und vor allem lächelnd, weil für ihn kein Zweifel ist, daß Rosa nun die Dinge anders sieht, daß sie von dummen Launen antworten wird, sie wüßte selbst nicht, was in sie gefahren wäre gestern, und daß der leidige Zwischenfall sich bestens zum Vergessen eignet. Und vernehmen wir noch, wie Rosa sagt: 'Ja bitte'. (181)

This pay-off involves another reversal of expectations: Mischa thinks that reason has triumphed over female caprice, but his desire to hear Rosa actually admit that she has capitulated backfires on him, and instead he finds himself forced to indulge her whim, a satisfying punishment for his desire to see her humbled. Not only does the ending reinforce our sense of Rosa's frailty (her wish—despite her public image of respectability—to pretend that there is a second man in the room while she makes love), there is also a neat sense of circularity, since Rosa's happiness now depends on her deceiving herself, a situation which recalls the narrator's opening remarks: 'Wenn es eine Geschichte ist, wie jemand belogen werden muß, damit er ein bißchen glücklich sein kann' (60).

An analysis of any episode in the novel would reveal the use of similar narrative strategies to those described above. The sections which follow demonstrate that whenever the narrator allows himself the freedom to invent, or to see into the minds of other characters, he does so in order to achieve effects similar to those just described.

3. 'Gönnen wir uns eine freiere Sicht': Playing with Perspectives

I have already mentioned the narrator's tendency to grant the reader access to the thoughts of various characters in the manner of an omniscient narrator, thereby breaching the normal 'rules' of perspective, according to which a first-person narrator cannot see into the minds of others. Although the narrator does not draw attention to this particular contrivance, it is not difficult to identify those points in the narrative at which the narrator plays with perspectives in this way, and two examples are analysed below. But first I want to consider the narrator's motives for this inconsistent use of perspective.

A clue to his motives can be found in the scene in which Elisa Kirschbaum is arrested at her home in the ghetto. The arrival of a car in the ghetto sends Jews in the street running for cover to the nearest doorway, from which they watch what happens with great curiosity. Initially, we observe events through the eyes of Rosa (whose report of what she sees reaches the narrator via Mischa). Rosa's is a classic limited perspective inasmuch as she views the scene through a key-hole. But when the narrator finds this point of view too restrictive, he abandons it: 'Gönnen wir uns eine freiere Sicht, begeben wir uns auf die Straße' (243). Thus, the narrator adopts a standpoint which suits him better, but from which neither he nor any of his 'witnesses' can have actually seen the event (since we are told specifically that the street had emptied of Jews who were too afraid to come face to face with a member of the SS). The narrator's insistence on a 'freiere Sicht' suggests that he resents the restrictions imposed on him by what he has seen himself or learnt from others because he is reluctant, as an accomplished story-teller, to let the laws of logic and truthfulness cramp his style. In this particular case, the switch in perspective seems to be motivated by a desire to encourage the reader's emotional involvement in Elisa Kirschbaum's fate;[46] but 'Gönnen wir uns eine freiere Sicht' could also stand as a comment on the narrator's attitude to his narrative in general, for he allows himself the freedom of an omniscient perspective wherever it serves the needs of his story. Two further examples will illustrate this point.

The first scene takes place in the ghetto police station, where Jakob has been sent by a malicious sentry to beg for 'just punishment' for breaking the eight-o'clock curfew. Once inside the police station the petrified Jakob is directed to a particular office where he finds the duty officer (the 'Wachhabender') asleep and discovers from the clock that it is in fact only half past seven, so that he has not broken the curfew at all. After some hesitation, he attempts to wake the officer by knocking loudly at the door. The narrator continues:

Jakob klopft noch einmal, kann man denn so fest schlafen, er klopft stark, der Wachhabende sitzt, bevor er richtig aufgewacht ist, reibt sich die Augen und fragt: 'Wie spät ist es denn?'.

[46] By this point the narrator has built up a certain amount of suspense, for the Nazi soldiers have entered the house in which Jakob lives, and the reader, along with the Jews huddled behind the door of the house opposite, fears that Jakob is to be arrested. However, this expectation is frustrated when a woman is brought out of the house. The watching Jews do not know who she is (she is referred to as 'eine Frau'), but the 'freiere Sicht' afforded by the street allows the narrator to break the suspense at this strategic point and to reveal that the woman is Elisa Kirschbaum. We know already that Elisa's brother, a doctor, has poisoned himself rather than treat the ghetto Commandant, and we suspect therefore that she is now to be punished for his defiance. Moreover, Elisa has earned our respect by standing up to two Nazi officers in an earlier episode (196–203). Thus, it is only by revealing the identity of the woman brought out of the house that the narrator can elicit our sympathy for Elisa, a sympathy which is heightened when the Nazi soldiers play a trick on her, moving their van just as she is about to step up into it, so that she falls to the ground. In fact there is a deliberate contrast between our sympathy for her, and the indifference of the many witnesses who are simply passing by on their way home from work, and for whom this kind of injustice is an everyday occurrence.

'Es ist einige Minuten nach halb acht', sagt Jakob.

Der Wachhabende ist fertig mit dem Augenreiben, sieht jetzt Jakob, reibt sich noch einmal die Augen, weiß nicht, ob er böse sein soll oder lachen, das hat es überhaupt noch nicht gegeben, das glaubt einem ja kein Mensch. (18)

Initially the reader is, as it were, standing in Jakob's shoes: the question 'kann man denn so fest schlafen' only makes sense if it issues from Jakob's consciousness, for it is he (and not the narrator) who is disconcerted when his knock fails to produce the expected effect. Moreover, the particle 'denn' indicates—as German particles often do—that this is a piece of interior monologue rather than a part of the narrator's (more literary) discourse (see Chapter 1, note 8). Thus far, then, we assume that the narrator is merely relaying Jakob's version of these events to the reader (though the interior monologue skilfully reduces our sense of the narrator's role as mediator). However, when the duty officer wakes up, the narrator switches to his point of view: the words 'sieht jetzt Jakob' relocate the narrative standpoint in the duty officer's consciousness, and the words 'das hat es überhaupt noch nicht gegeben, das glaubt einem ja kein Mensch' clearly belong to the duty officer's thoughts. Again, the use of a particle ('ja') indicates that this is a piece of interior monologue rather than a narratorial statement. Of course, the narrator cannot really know what the officer was thinking, but that is immaterial; what matters is that he uses the switch in perspective to heighten our sense of the danger which threatens Jakob and thereby to increase our suspense to a considerable degree. The officer's utter disbelief is evident from his actions (he rubs his eyes once to wake himself and again because he thinks he may still be dreaming), and might therefore have been reported to the narrator by Jakob; but it is reinforced by the improvised interior monologue, which suggests that such a violation of the prevailing racial pecking-order (a Jew entering the office of a sleeping German officer unannounced and daring to wake him) is completely unheard of ('das hat es überhaupt noch nicht gegeben, das glaubt einem ja kein Mensch'). This, in turn, suggests that any punishment which is meted out by the officer will be accordingly severe, and our fear for

Jakob's life increases. Moreover, by assuming an omniscient perspective, the narrator is able to tell us that the officer is uncertain what he should do, so taken aback is he by this unprecedented situation: 'weiß nicht, ob er böse sein soll oder lachen'. This uncertainty is passed on to the reader, who must wait to discover whether Jakob is punished or not. Had the narrator not used his imagination freely to supply the thoughts of the duty officer, the scene would be much less compelling.

The second example is taken from a scene in which Jakob risks his life while stealing some scraps of newspaper from a Nazi latrine. By this point in the story, Jakob is running out of 'news' stories which might plausibly be broadcast on his imaginary radio. When he sees a soldier leave behind a newspaper in the latrine, he recognizes an opportunity to procure some genuine news and lets himself into the wooden hut, which is out of bounds to Jews. A farcical, though potentially fatal scenario ensues: after secreting several pages of the newspaper under his shirt, Jakob peeps out through the heart-shaped opening in the door (a ridiculously homely detail in the inhospitable world of the ghetto) and sees a Nazi soldier approaching. The narrator creates suspense about the outcome of this situation in two complementary ways. On the one hand he gives the reader a sense of the urgency of the situation (something must happen soon because the soldier is in a hurry to relieve himself: 'Seine Finger hantieren schon am Koppelschloß, in Gedanken sitzt er bereits und fühlt sich wohler', and because he has only a short distance to walk: 'er hat noch acht ganze Schritte [. . .] er hat noch fünf Schritte' (105)). On the other hand the narrator deliberately draws the scene out, an effect achieved by forcing us to follow Jakob's painfully slow deliberations. Three possible plans for escape are rejected in turn (locking the door, breaking down the back wall, squeezing through a small hole), and Jakob appears to have run out of time. At this climactic moment, however, the narrator abandons Jakob's perspective and switches to the soldier's point of view:

Der Soldat öffnet die Tür, die sich nicht sträubt, zu seinem Verdruß sieht er eine aufgeschlagene Doppelseite Zeitung vor sich, in Maßen zitternd, was aber in solch peinlichem Moment nicht weiter auffällt.

'Oh, Verzeihung!', sagt er und macht die Tür schnell zu. (105)

Having shared Jakob's thoughts and vision all the way through the scene, we are suddenly deprived of them, and stand where the soldier stands instead. This may not be entirely faithful to Jakob's account of the episode, as it was passed on to the narrator (for Jakob cannot have seen himself from the outside), but it is much more exciting. How much duller it would be if the narrator continued the scene in the same vein—following Jakob's train of thought—and told us that Jakob had the inspired idea of hiding behind the ill-fated newspaper. We would then know, even before the door opened, that he was safe from the soldier. By denying us that knowledge he leaves us in great suspense: either Jakob has not thought of a plan, in which case he will certainly be executed, or he has thought of a plan and will get away with it. In this second example, then, the breach of the 'rules' of perspective is less flagrant than in the 'Revier' scene—the narrator does not add any obviously *invented* details to Jakob's account. But by momentarily adopting the soldier's visual perspective the narrator again demonstrates his rejection of a more logical single perspective in the interests of a good story.

4. The Role of Invention in the Text

An analysis of those passages in which the narrator deliberately draws attention to the process of fictionalization shows that they are part of the same narrative strategy: their invention is motivated by the desire to tell 'eine ordentliche Geschichte'.

On pp. 259–60, for instance, the narrator invents a variation on Jakob's story, in order to explore an intriguing possibility: what would have happened had Jakob told his 'listeners' that his radio had been stolen? In this imaginary scene Jakob's claim brings out the worst in human nature: neighbours become suspicious of one another, and find a welcome justification for previously unfounded dislikes ('hat er [der Nachbar] nicht schon immer so etwas Eigenartiges im Blick gehabt, wovor einen die innere Stimme gewarnt hat?' (259)). A group of vigilantes conducts a house-to-house search, discovers a radio, and even—depending on which version we choose—lynches the supposed culprit.[47] The narrator is conscious that his story is flawed, for if the man had listened to his radio, he would know that Jakob had been lying, and it is highly improbable that he would have kept silent for so long. Nevertheless, he asks us to bear with him: 'denn jener Mann ist gewissermaßen nur ein Hirngespinst, eine flüchtige Spielerei' (260). Like other episodes in the novel, this story leads up to a punchline, in this case a visual punchline: 'Das Radio bringt man zu Jakob, dem rechtmäßigen Besitzer, die Vorstellung seines Gesichts ist den ganzen Einfall wert' (260). The pay-off, then, is the look on Jakob's face when the Jews return 'his' radio to him. Although the narrator does not explain why this sight makes the whole anecdote worth while, we can guess, for we are by now familiar with the narrator's fondness for stories involving a reversal of expectations. In this case, Jakob's expression of horror is the exact opposite of the joyful expression which the Jews had expected to light up his face when they returned his cherished radio. At the same time, Jakob's visible dismay underlines a cruel twist of fate: his ploy to rid himself of his onerous duties has backfired, leaving him considerably worse off than he was before (since he now risks being found in possession of a radio, a capital offence under ghetto regulations). The ending thus possesses a satisfying kind of symmetry since the expectations of both sides —Jakob and his fellow Jews—are reversed. Although the narrator subsequently cancels out this episode ('Aber genug damit, Jakob kommt nicht auf die Idee mit dem Diebstahl' (260)), the invented scene illustrates perfectly the fact that nothing fires the narrator's imagination so much as the possibility of a good *Pointe*.

The desire to tell a good story also motivates the im-

---

[47] A typical open alternative of the kind we have seen already in *Das dritte Buch*, *Gantenbein*, and *Christa T.*: 'er wird im Zorn erschlagen, [. . .] oder er wird nicht erschlagen, das tut nichts zur Sache' (260).

provisation of the scene in Frankfurter's cellar (55–60), without which another anecdote would lack the suspense which builds up to its crowning moment. Having briefly apprised us of the details of Mischa's courtship of Rosa, the narrator homes in on a particular evening, the evening on which Mischa brings the good news from Jakob's radio to Rosa and her family (46). But before Mischa is allowed to pass on the good news, our expectation is carefully built up. Having already experienced the joyful reactions of Mischa and Kowalski to the news of the Russian advance, we naturally anticipate that Felix Frankfurter will react in the same way. Moreover, certain details deliberately encourage this expectation. First, Frankfurter says in conversation that he regards the birth of a baby in the neighbourhood as a misfortune (because a child born in the ghetto is likely to have a short life) and, hearing that the parents have resolved to have the child's name registered officially 'wenn alles vorbei ist', he mocks their plans for the future: 'Wenn alles vorbei ist, lebt das Kind nicht mehr, und die Eltern leben nicht mehr. Wir alle werden nicht mehr leben, dann ist alles vorbei' (50). Thus, the reader (already in possession of the 'good news') anticipates that news of the Russian advance will make Frankfurter see the baby's birth in a more positive light and dispel his gloom about the future. A few minutes later, when Mischa unexpectedly asks Frankfurter for his daughter's hand in marriage, Frankfurter objects on the grounds that a ghetto is no place to hold a wedding, and that their first priority should be survival. But the reader feels sure — as Mischa does — that Frankfurter's objections to the marriage of Mischa and Rosa will evaporate once he hears the news from Jakob's radio. This careful preparation is clearly intended to mislead the reader into expecting a positive reaction from Frankfurter, in order to increase our surprise when this expectation is reversed.

At the same time as he builds up these expectations, the narrator draws the scene out, increasing the tension by obliging us to wait for Mischa's revelation and its effect on the family. First, Mischa racks his brains for a clever or entertaining way to pass on the good news, for he knows that Frankfurter likes to listen to stories which have a *Pointe*. But before he has thought of a suitable anecdote, Mischa mis-construes Rosa's question 'Hast du überhaupt schon das Neueste gehört?' (49) and assumes the news has reached them already, only to find that they are talking about something entirely different. Even once this misunderstanding has been cleared up, Mischa remains tongue-tied, fearing that the Frankfurters will now be suspicious because he did not tell them the news as soon as he arrived. Eventually he calculates that by asking Frankfurter's permission to marry Rosa he can create a suitable opportunity to announce Jakob's news, and a suitable excuse for his hesitation (a fine example of Becker's unsentimental character portrayal, since Mischa's motives for proposing are thus far from romantic). Finally, then, after this series of skilfully motivated retarding devices, the narrator allows Mischa to deliver the news; Frankfurter sinks into his chair, covering his face with his hands (apparently in a gesture of relief); and Rosa and Mischa leave him to take in the implications of the news.

At this point, the reader might think the story is ended, but not so, for the narrator has kept something up his sleeve: he has since learnt that Felix Frankfurter had a radio hidden in his cellar. Of course, if he wanted to, the narrator could impart this information in a single sentence, but that would certainly be an anticlimax after such a careful build-up. As an expert story-teller he naturally wants to make the most of this revelation because it adds an interesting twist to the whole episode. So, in order to maximize the effect of his *Pointe*, the narrator uses his imagination to conjure up the scene which passed between Frankfurter and his wife once Rosa and Mischa had left the house (55).

The first function of this imagined scene is to upset the reader's expectations. As we have seen, the reader has been deliberately misled into thinking that Frankfurter would be overjoyed at the news from Jakob's radio. Moreover, Frankfurter's immediate reaction to the news (collapsing in his chair and covering his face with his hands) is portrayed in a deliberately ambiguous way which allows the reader to believe that he has been overcome with relief or inexpressible joy. Suddenly, however, we discover that far from being elated, Frankfurter is anxious and preoccupied (55–

6). While the reader searches for a reason to explain this unexpected behaviour, the narrator manipulates our curiosity, deliberately denying us access to Frankfurter's thoughts and using a whole series of retarding devices to delay the answer (these include: variant possibilities; an unnecessarily detailed description of Frankfurter's cellar, to which he and his wife now descend; a flashback to the day on which the Frankfurters had to move their belongings to the ghetto; and Frau Frankfurter's speculations as to what her husband is looking for). The reader's confusion is further heightened when Frankfurter declares: 'Dieser Jakob Heym ist ein Trottel' (58) and we share Frau Frankfurter's puzzlement as to why the bringer of good news should be so maligned, before finally we are enlightened as Frankfurter uncovers and then destroys his radio.

The narrator is not, however, solely interested in the effect of surprise. The closing paragraphs of the scene also draw attention to the doubly paradoxical outcome of the situation: first, Mischa, who had hoped to bring joy to Frankfurter, has instead brought terror, for if the Gestapo hears of the existence of a radio in the ghetto and conducts a house-to-house search, Frankfurter will almost certainly be executed; and second, Jakob's fraudulent claim to possess a radio has caused what is perhaps the only real radio in the ghetto to be destroyed. As Fritz Raddatz writes, 'die gelogenen Nachrichten haben die Chance auf echte verdrängt.'[48] Moreover, like other episodes in the novel, this one is used to illustrate human weaknesses. We learn that, having taken the apparently courageous step of bringing his radio to the ghetto in defiance of the regulations, Frankfurter has been unable to reap the rewards of his daring, being too scared to listen to it and constantly troubled by fears of discovery. And therein lies another irony: while the man who has no radio pretends to listen to one, the man who does have a radio avoids listening to it at all costs. The episode ends with one further illustration of human frailty,

---

[48] Fritz Raddatz, 'Eine neue sozialistische Literatur entsteht. Jurek Becker, Brigitte Reimann, Christa Wolf, Manfred Bieler, Fritz Rudolf Fries', in Raddatz, *Traditionen und Tendenzen. Materialien zur Literatur der DDR* (Frankfurt/Main, 1972), 372–400 (373).

as Frau Frankfurter forgets her righteous indignation (that her husband has risked the lives of his family by concealing a radio, without even having the decency to tell her) and gives in to a venial desire to hear her hopes about the Russian advance confirmed, regardless of the risk that might have been run to get the information: 'Hast du auch gehört, daß die Russen fast in Bezanika sind?' (60). Becker suggests that our moral principles give way easily to human impulses such as curiosity and the need for reassurance.

As we have seen, the narrator's fictional reconstruction of the scene in Frankfurter's cellar prevents his carefully constructed story from fizzling out. Like Mischa, he feels a duty to his listeners (or, rather, his readers) to tell his story properly. The desire to shape each episode of the novel into a neatly rounded anecdote is not, however, the only impulse which drives the narrator to invent, as two examples will show. The first example is the culmination of the opening episode in which Jakob visits the ghetto police station. As he makes his apparently miraculous escape, Jakob hears the sentry responsible for his ordeal speaking on the telephone, apparently to a superior officer, as his only words are 'Jawohl', repeated several times. The narrator has no way of knowing the details of this conversation, but *imagines* that the sentry is receiving a reprimand for the trick he has played on Jakob:

Vielleicht hat ihn ein anderer Posten angerufen, der sich auch langweilt. Aber zu dem sagt er nicht andauernd 'jawohl', das ist ausgeschlossen. Also der Anführer der Postensteher, der irgendwelche Anweisungen gibt? Eigentlich ganz unwichtig, aber nehmen wir den günstigsten Fall, der Wachhabende ist an der Leitung. Was fällt Ihnen ein, sind Sie verrückt geworden, armen unschuldigen Juden einen solchen Schreck einzujagen! ('Jawohl') Haben Sie denn nicht gesehen, daß der Mann ganz verstört war, seine Beine haben vor Angst gezittert! Daß mir das nicht noch mal passiert, verstanden? ('Jawohl'). Beim vierten Jawohl ist die Ecke da, soll er weiterreden, bis er schwarz wird, dann ist Jakob, keine zehn Minuten, zu Hause. (22)

This short passage constitutes another piece of undisguised invention. At one level it serves the story-teller's aims, allowing him to round off an episode which would otherwise peter out with Jakob's return home. Not only does the con-

versation create a satisfying sense of circularity (because we
return once more to the deception which set the action in
motion): the ending also gives the reader the *moral* satisfaction of seeing justice done. The transgression which
triggered the initial crisis (the sentry's malicious trick) is
punished by the 'Wachhabender'. The good man is
rewarded, the wicked man chastised, and a kind of harmony
is restored: a traditional device familiar from the German
novella.

However, this passage does more than just put the finish-
ing touches to the opening episode. What is striking—and
what sets it apart from the examples which I have looked at
so far—is that it is a clear case of wishful thinking. For in
the light of what the reader knows of the duty officer it is
extremely improbable that he should reprimand the sentry
at all, let alone so harshly. Although Jakob calls the duty
officer a 'freundlicher Mensch' (18), his perspective is seriously distorted by his desire to survive, and Becker does not
intend that the reader should share it. In other words, Jakob
regards the duty officer as 'friendly' because he is not the
monster that fear and prejudice have led him to expect,
whereas from the reader's more objective viewpoint the duty
officer is sarcastic and condescending, and it is clear that if
he does not exactly relish his position of power, he does at
least take it for granted. For instance, he addresses Jakob
with the ironic remark: 'Was verschafft mir die Ehre?' (18).
Although Jakob is relieved at the officer's relatively light-
hearted tone, to the reader the remark betrays contempt for
the Jews, implying as it does that it is *not* an honour for a
German soldier to be visited by a Jew, and that the German
is necessarily superior. For the officer, it is also a way of
asserting his authority, since Jakob cannot reply in kind (i.e.
ironically) without fear of severe punishment. Moreover,
even though he is younger than Jakob ('ein recht junger
Mann, höchstens dreißig' (16)), the officer treats the Jew in
a familiar manner, addressing him as 'du' and with phrases
one might use to a child ('Nur keine falsche Scham [. . .]
Immer raus mit der Sprache' (18)). Jakob of course, has to
speak deferentially, and use 'Sie'. Finally, the officer makes
no excuse for keeping Jakob waiting (and in suspense) while

he writes something down on a piece of paper and coolly smokes a cigarette, before finally letting him go. There is no sign that the duty officer is reluctantly following orders or in any way uncomfortable in his role. It is therefore highly improbable that he should use the words 'arme unschuldige Juden', as he does in the imagined telephone conversation, or that he should enter so readily into Jakob's sufferings and fears. The invented conversation therefore has a utopian dimension: it encourages the hope that human values can prosper even at a time when cruelty and dehumanization have been legitimized by the ruling powers. It is a refusal to let brutality have the last word, and also, perhaps, part of the narrator's strategy for coping with his feelings of frustration and helplessness by exercising his power as narrator and taking his revenge, in his imagination, on the sentry.

A similar motivation may be discerned behind the narration of the story of Herschel Schtamm. Schtamm, a deeply religious orthodox Jew, is one of the many inhabitants of the ghetto who oppose Jakob's news broadcasts because they fear that discovery by the Nazi authorities will lead to reprisals. From the beginning, Schtamm is painted as a weak, unheroic man. Although he deliberately keeps himself aloof from his workmates whenever they discuss Jakob's news, and indeed directs disapproving glances at them, the narrator suspects that he is careful to keep within earshot of their discussions (84–5). Thus, while Schtamm might like to think of himself as a man of integrity, who is not prepared to put the lives of innocent people at risk, he is as susceptible to curiosity as everybody else, and his aloofness may have as much to do with cowardice as with principle. He is also naïve in his religious beliefs, believing that God orchestrates a power cut in the ghetto in direct response to his prayer for the destruction of the radio. This portrait of Schtamm will later prove to be a deliberate ploy designed to build up false expectations which are then overturned.

A little later in the novel, Schtamm takes centre stage in a scene at the railway station where he, Jakob, and the narrator are working (126–41). Having been severely reprimanded for trying to open the door to a railway wagon which the Jews have been forbidden to touch, Schtamm crosses the

railway yard to tell Jakob that he has heard voices coming
from the wagons, and the two men acknowledge tacitly the
horrific truth that the wagons are full of Jewish deportees
on their way to the death camps. While Schtamm's first
encounter with the railway wagon seems to have been a
genuine, if rather dangerous, mistake, Schtamm's workmates watch in horror as he deliberately approaches the
wagon a second time (despite having been warned that the
next person to go near it will be shot) and talks to the people
inside. At this point the narrator is once more forced to
resort to his imagination:

Ich kann nicht hören, was Herschel redet und was die drin ihm sagen,
dafür ist die Entfernung viel zu groß, aber denken kann ich es mir, und
das hat nichts mit vagen Vermutungen zu tun. Je länger ich überlege, um
so klarer weiß ich seine Worte, auch wenn er sie mir nie bestätigt hat.

'Hallo! Hört ihr mich?' sagt Herschel als erstes.

'Wir hören dich', muß eine Stimme aus dem Wageninneren antworten.
'Wer bist du?'

'Ich bin aus dem Ghetto', sagt Herschel dann. 'Ihr müßt aushalten, nur
noch kurze Zeit müßt ihr aushalten. Die Russen sind schon bei Bezanika
vorbei!'

'Woher weißt du das?' fragen sie von drinnen, alles ganz logisch und
zwangsläufig.

'Ihr könnt mir glauben. Wir halten ein Radio versteckt. Ich muß wieder
zurück'.

Die Eingeschlossenen bedanken sich fassunglos, ein weißes Täubchen
hat sich zu ihnen in die Finsternis verirrt, ihre Worte sind unerheblich,
sie wünschen ihm vielleicht Glück und Reichtum und hundertzwanzig
Jahre Leben, bevor sie hören, wie seine Schritte sich entfernen. (137–8)

Once more, this piece of undisguised invention could be
interpreted as a skilful manœuvre on the part of the story-
teller-narrator, for having carefully primed the reader to see
Schtamm as a weak and cowardly man, he now engineers a
reversal of expectations, showing Schtamm performing an
act of astounding bravery in order to alleviate the suffering
of the deportees. The story is given a further twist because
Schtamm's principled opposition to Jakob's news broadcasts
is now overturned as he himself takes on Jakob's role. It
might appear, therefore, that the narrator is simply using
Schtamm as an instrument, that he is more interested in the

story-value of this scene than in Schtamm's death. But it seems to me that on the contrary, he is using the mechanics of his story to point up the bravery of Schtamm (which is all the more striking because we have been led to expect something different). And here, too, there may be an element of wishful thinking. We sense that the narrator needs to believe that in a place where suffering had become commonplace men were still capable of being so touched by the anguish of others that they were prepared to forget their principles and risk their lives to bring relief to the sufferers. The fact that the narrator wants to convince himself of this is suggested by his uncharacteristic insistence on the facts of this case. Gone are the tentative modal auxiliaries and variants which normally accompany such imagined scenes (although they return briefly in the last sentence, once Schtamm's bravery has been established); instead we are given statements of fact ('sagt Herschel', 'fragen sie von drinnen'), and the narrator insists that these are certainties, not 'vage Vermutungen'. As with the imaginary telephone conversation between the sentry and the 'Wachhabender', the narrator is motivated not just by a desire to tell his story to maximum effect, but also by the need to sustain his personal belief in the individual's potential for humanity.

5. 'Ein Ende, bei dem man blaß werden könnte vor Neid': The Double Ending

The double ending is a rather more complicated case than any of the scenes analysed so far, and we can begin by considering the established interpretations. According to the most commonly held view, Becker supplies an alternative, optimistic ending in order to inspire hope and to counteract the negative, unproductive reactions of despair and resignation;[49] or (put slightly differently) in order to preserve the reader from a feeling of powerlessness in the face of historical events (a reaction which would lead to

---

[49] Arthur M. Lesley, 'Jacob as Liar in Jurek Becker's *Jakob der Lügner*', *Seminar*, 19 (1983), 273–9: 'This defamiliarization of the inevitable and well-known ending through suggestion of an alternative prevents our resignation to it' (279).

political apathy), by investing his narrator with the power to change events, if only in his imagination.[50] Wetzel sums up these views when he writes:

> Es ging ihm [Jurek Becker] darum, dem Fatalismus zu wehren, indem er durch das Gestalten einer glaubhaften Alternative zur historischen Wirklichkeit deren Determiniertheit leugnete und mit der Freiheit der Entscheidung auch die Möglichkeit des sinnvollen Handelns postulierte. [. . .] Der Analogieschluß ist erlaubt, daß sich Jurek Becker durch die Figur seines Erzählers der Möglichkeiten eines Erzählens versichern wollte, das der Mutlosigkeit und Verzweiflung wehren könnte. So wären die mehrfach ineinander geschachtelten schönen Geschichten—diejenigen Jakobs von der baldigen Befreiung, diejenige des Erzählers von Jakob, dem mutigen Verkünder der Hoffnung, und diejenige Jurek Beckers von dem sorgfältigen und engagierten Chronisten und Erfinder von Jakobs Geschichte—aus dem Bedürfnis nach Hoffnung entstanden und, da Hoffnung von ihrer Verbreitung lebt, zugleich aus dem Bedürfnis, Hoffnung zu verbreiten.[51]

As a general statement of Jurek Becker's aims and achievement in *Jakob der Lügner*, this is certainly convincing: the humanity of all three story-tellers (Jakob, the narrator, Jurek Becker) does indeed offer hope in the face of the inhumanity of the Holocaust; and we have already seen how the narrator's wishful thinking (in the imaginary telephone conversation between the sentry and the duty officer, and in the story of Herschel Schtamm's bravery) brings alive the possibility that humanity can thrive even in times of tyranny. I am less convinced that this statement can be applied to the alternative ending, that is, that the alternative ending is likewise intended to inspire hope; for, as I will show, the imagined ending is hardly optimistic.

In his interview with Arnold, Becker implied that the narrator's motives for inventing a second ending were, in the first place, aesthetic. This can be inferred from the

---

[50] Werner Zimmermann writes that the double ending: '[dient] der erzählerischen Grundintention, gegen die "Absurdität der historischen Abläufe" das Prinzip Hoffnung zu setzen' (Werner Zimmermann, 'Jurek Becker: *Jakob der Lügner*', in Zimmermann, *Deutsche Prosadichtungen des 20. Jahrhunderts: Interpretationen* (Düsseldorf: Schwann, 1988), III. 10–39 (16)). Similarly, Karnick suggests: 'Gerade gegenüber der brutalen Übermacht des Tatsächlichen wird ein Raum der eigenen Entscheidung und Abstandnahme aufgemacht' (Karnick, 215).

[51] Wetzel, '"Unvergleichlich gelungener"—aber "einfach zu schön"?', 112–13.

following passage (in which Becker makes no distinction between the narrator's motivation and his own):

Was das Ende angeht, so steht es im Grund als einziges in der ganzen Geschichte fest, denn man weiß, was das Schicksal von Juden im Krieg gewesen ist. Aber zu der schönen Geschichte, die [der Erzähler] sich da zum Teil ausgedacht hat, will es ihm nicht gefallen. Also führt er vor, was für ein Ende er gewählt hätte, wenn er es zu entscheiden gehabt hätte. Ich gebe ja nicht das Bild der Historie, wie sie gewesen ist, sondern ich erzähle eine Story und benutze die Geschichte des Weltkriegs auf eine Weise, wie ich sie für die Geschichte brauche.[52]

In fact, Becker is here echoing the words of his narrator, who, when introducing the fictitious ending, tells us plainly that he is interested in 'eine schöne Geschichte':

Bei aller Bescheidenheit, ich weiß ein Ende, bei dem man blaß werden könnte vor Neid, nicht eben glücklich, ein wenig auf Kosten Jakobs, dennoch unvergleichlich gelungener als das wirkliche Ende, ich habe es mir in Jahren zusammengezimmert. Ich habe mir gesagt, eigentlich jammerschade um eine so schöne Geschichte, daß sie so armselig im Sande verläuft, erfinde ihr ein Ende, mit dem man halbwegs zufrieden sein kann, eins mit Hand und Fuß, ein ordentliches Ende läßt manche Schwäche vergessen. (258)

Our interpretation of both these passages depends very much on how we understand 'eine schöne Geschichte'. Even though the narrator confesses that his ending is 'nicht eben glücklich', many critics seem to suppose that 'eine schöne Geschichte' is a story which ends happily, or at least one in which poetic justice is done.[53] However, certain phrases used by the narrator in the second passage ('gelungen', 'eine schöne Geschichte, [die] so armselig im Sande verläuft', 'ein Ende [. . .] mit Hand und Fuß') clearly imply that for the narrator, 'eine schöne Geschichte' is not a story with a *happy*

---

[52] Arnold, 'Gespräch mit Jurek Becker', 6.

[53] Wetzel, for instance, calls this alternative ending 'ein versöhnliches Ende' and speaks of 'die fiktionale Alternative mit ihrer kolportagehaften Handlung und dem happy ending' ('"Unvergleichlich gelungener"—aber "einfach zu schön"?', 113). Nancy Lukens argues that the Russian liberation 'zeigt, wie sehr der Erzähler—wie die Juden im Ghetto, und seine Leser wohl auch—an der Vorstellung einer poetischen Gerechtigkeit hängt, die ein "Happy-End" garantiert' (Nancy Lukens, 'Schelm im Ghetto: Jurek Beckers Roman *Jakob der Lügner*', *ABNG* 20 (1985–6), 199–218 (216)). Joho calls the alternative ending 'eine Art Happy-End' ('Lüge aus Barmherzigkeit', 153).

ending, but a story with a *good* ending, an aesthetically pleasing ending, such as should crown a well-told tale. After all, only a well-crafted ending is capable of arousing pride in the story-teller (implied in the phrase 'bei aller Bescheidenheit') and a corresponding envy (in rival story-tellers); envy of a happy ending would make no sense. Similarly, the narrator judges the 'real', historical ending in aesthetic terms, introducing it with the words: 'Aber nach dem erfundenen endlich das blaßwangige und verdrießliche, das wirkliche und einfallslose Ende' (272). Not only does the historical ending peter out as no good story should ('daß sie so armselig im Sande verläuft'), it also lacks excitement ('blaßwangig') and is unimaginative ('einfallslos').

Seen from this viewpoint, the double ending appears to be another manifestation of the principle which guides the narrator throughout, namely that the aesthetics of his story take priority over facts; and an analysis of the alternative ending will bear this out. Like other episodes already examined in this chapter, it is contrived in such a way as to provide a crowning *Pointe* which the deportation of the Jews from the ghetto fails to offer.

The alternative ending begins auspiciously, with the 'resurrection' of Jakob's friend Kowalski (258). The narrator then imagines Jakob searching for ways to free himself from the ever more demanding task of keeping alive the hopes of his fellow Jews. As a first measure, Jakob refuses to answer any more questions about the state of the hostilities, explaining to persistent questioners that he is not prepared to risk being found out and executed when the ghetto may be liberated any day. Tension mounts as some of the Jews accuse him of cowardice, and Mischa hears rumours that a group of men is planning to take the radio by force from Jakob, so that someone more courageous can operate it. Forced to take evasive action, Jakob attempts to escape from the ghetto but is shot dead by a sentry as he cuts the barbed wire of the boundary fence. This is what the narrator means when he concedes that the alternative ending is 'ein wenig auf Kosten Jakobs'. It seems that if Becker would sell his granny for a *Pointe*, as he put it,[54] his narrator will happily sacrifice his

---

[54] Becker, '"Das Vorstellbare gefällt mir immer besser als das Bekannte"', 105.

hero for one. This attitude also explains why the narrator offers no definite motivation for Jakob's flight ('Bei mir will er eben fliehen und basta' (269)): the *reason* for the flight is much less important than the *fact* of it, which is essential if the punchline is to work.

But Jakob's death is not itself the *Pointe*. Indeed, any readers foolish enough to think that the death of the hero is a suitable event with which to end a narrative are quickly put in their place by the more expert story-teller-narrator: 'Jakob ist tot und am Ende sämtlicher Mühe. Doch damit nicht genug, was wäre das auch für ein Ende' (270). He goes on to tell us that this is the night on which the Russians liberate the ghetto from the Nazis;[55] but he does not dwell on the details of the liberation because his narrative has a clear goal and can brook no digressions:

> Wie Mischa denkt, daß es Jakob nun bestimmt besser gehen wird, wie er Lina zu ihm bringen will und ihn nicht antrifft, wie das Brot schmeckt, das uns reichlich gegeben wird, was mit den armen Deutschen geschieht, die uns in die Hände fallen, das alles und mehr ist mir nicht wichtig genug, um dafür Platz in meinem Ende zur Verfügung zu stellen. Wichtig ist mir nur eins. (271)

This is another example of the projection and cancellation of narrative possibilities (a device common to all the novels examined in this study), but the narrator's words also call into question the view that the alternative ending is 'ein versöhnliches Ende'.[56] Not only is there nothing positive about Jakob's death (it is neither heroic nor glamorous, and achieves nothing), but the narrator is not even interested in the positive consequences of liberation, which, as he says here, do not merit space in his ending. If his aim were to offer an optimistic alternative to the harsh reality of deportation and extermination, we would surely expect him to make the liberation and its effect on the Jews the main

---

[55] Kane argues that Becker uses the narrator's rather clichéd description of the Russian liberation to ironize 'a whole tradition of literature in which the Soviet army is presented as the glorious liberators' (Kane, 'Tales and the Telling', 166). This tallies with my comments on Becker's rejection of the hackneyed resistance narrative (see Section 1 above). It seems unlikely, however, that the more naïve narrator—who shows no knowledge of contemporary literature—is aware of this irony.

[56] Wetzel, '"Unvergleichlich gelungener"—aber "einfach zu schön"?', 113.

focus of the dénouement. Instead, he chooses a different focus: 'Wichtig ist mir nur eins'.

This unspecified 'one important thing', is, it seems to me, the *Pointe*, and, accordingly, a character is chosen to deliver it ('am besten wohl Kowalski, aber auch ein Nachbar oder ich oder sonst einer vom Bahnhof könnte es sein, jedenfalls irgendeiner, der ihn kennt, Lina ausgenommen' (271)). The narrator then contrives that this man should join a group of Jews gathered around the dead man. Jakob's acquaintance recognizes him and expresses his astonishment, but the other bystanders see nothing remarkable in the death, assuming that the dead man tried to flee because he did not realize how close the Russians were. Their ignorance creates a convenient information-gap which allows Jakob's acquaintance to point out their mistake:

Und der eine, dem sich die Kehle zuschnürt, unternimmt den hoffnungslosen Versuch zu erklären, was ihm auf ewig unerklärlich bleiben wird.

'Das ist doch Jakob Heym', sagt er. 'Versteht ihr? Jakob Heym ist das. Warum wollte er fliehen? Er muß verrückt geworden sein. Er wußte doch genau, daß sie kommen. Er hatte doch ein Radio . . . '

Das ungefähr sagt er und geht kopfschüttelnd mit den anderen hinaus in die Freiheit, und das ungefähr wäre mein Ende. (272)

The devices which the narrator uses in this ending are by now familiar to us. He unifies or rounds off his story, in this case with one last reminder of the lie which set the whole plot in motion ('Er hatte doch ein Radio . . . '); and he engineers a reversal of expectations: the acquaintance expects Jakob to be the first to rejoice at the liberation which he himself has foretold, but instead he appears to have thrown away his life. Moreover, Jakob dies only hours before the arrival of the liberators renders the need to escape redundant, and in doing so destroys the myth of his privileged access to information at the very moment when his predictions are about to 'come true'. The reader derives pleasure both from the neatly paradoxical nature of this situation and from the satisfying feeling, akin to dramatic irony, that we possess the key to the puzzle which the acquaintance will never be able to solve.

This analysis suggests that the narrator imagines an alternative to the deportation of the Jews, not from any noble motives (such as a desire to fight against resignation and apathy), but because he cannot abide a story which lacks a proper ending. This explanation may seem unappealing, even perplexing—which might explain why critics have ignored it—but the evidence for it is certainly there in the text. It is noticeable that the few critics who address this aspect of the novel directly appear to feel uncomfortable with the narrator's attitude. Their comments are interesting because they raise general questions about Holocaust literature. Martin Krumbholz asks whether silence, or at least a fragmented story, would not be a more appropriate reaction to the horrific reality of the Holocaust than the narrator's obsession with a good story:

> Der kritische Leser mag sich allerdings fragen, ob das Interesse an der Geschichte im Sinne einer kompakten Erzähleinheit angesichts des grauenhaften Inhalts nicht von vornherein unangemessen erscheint; ob es nicht gerade die Leerstellen, die Brüche und Risse im Erzählten, kurz; die *Verweigerung einer Geschichte* wären, die einer solchen kruden Realität am ehesten gerecht würden.[57]

Joho expresses similar misgivings, objecting specifically to the use of the words 'blaßwangig' and 'verdrießlich' to describe the Holocaust. It would have been better, he writes:

> hätte Jurek Becker auf die Varianten verzichtet und es bei dem wirklichen Ende belassen, von dem wir alle ohnehin wissen, und das—alle makabre Ironie in Ehren—nicht 'blaßwangig' genannt und, auch wenn man noch so untertreibt und aus guten Gründen falsches Pathos vermeiden wollte, nicht nur als 'verdrießlich' bezeichnet werden sollte.[58]

Given that one of these two passages is taken from a review written in the year of the novel's publication, and the other from a recent article on Becker's novels, it is fair to say that this uneasiness is a persistent feature of the novel's *Rezeptionsgeschichte*.

Krumbholz's comments imply that only a fractured or fragmented form can adequately express the experience of the Holocaust. I am sceptical of this prescriptive attitude.

---

[57] Martin Krumbholz, 'Standorte, Standpunkte: Erzählerpositionen in den Romanen Jurek Beckers', in Heinz Ludwig Arnold (ed.), *Jurek Becker*, Text und Kritik, 116 (Munich: Edition Text + Kritik, 1992), 44–50 (45).

[58] Joho, 'Lüge aus Barmherzigkeit', 153.

Thomas Keneally's *Schindler's Ark*, for instance, uses traditional story-telling techniques similar to those used in *Jakob der Lügner*, presenting the reader with a series of neatly rounded episodes, full of drama and suspense, featuring characters with whom we are asked to identify emotionally. The purpose of this technique is not to commercialize or sentimentalize the Holocaust, but to make it accessible to those who have no direct experience of it, for Keneally believes that story-telling is a more effective means of passing on wisdom and experience than documentary literature.[59] In *Die Blechtrommel*, too, the narrator Oskar Matzerath is very conscious of his role as a story-teller or spinner of yarns, and offers us many skilfully constructed anecdotes, yet this in no way diminishes the novel's power to evoke the experiences of the Nazi years. Traditional story-telling is, in my view, by no means incompatible with a provocative account of the horrors of the German past. Becker, too, was aware that he was writing chiefly for those who did not live through the Holocaust,[60] and his concern to tell 'a decent story'[61] must in part have been influenced by the need to make the Holocaust accessible to this audience. It should also be remembered that Becker was following the example of his father and his father's friends, who apparently dealt with their own experience of the Holocaust in precisely this way, using the traditional story-telling techniques employed by Becker in his novel (since he claimed to have learnt the tricks of his trade from them).[62] In other words, he has captured for us in the novel one way in which Jewish survivors coped with their

---

[59] Keneally expressed these views in an interview with the *Independent* in 1994: 'When he researched the story in the early Eighties, Keneally decided to write it as a novel rather than a biography because he wanted to reach the widest readership for polemical reasons. "I was aware that to some the Holocaust is unutterable but I also felt that Europe had not accepted responsibility for its anti-Semitism. The Holocaust is a Gentile problem, not a Jewish one"' ('The Long Ambiguous Journey into the Ark: Peter Guttridge Talks to Thomas Keneally', *Independent*, 19 February 1994, 29).

[60] Becker told his father, who was angry that the novel did not reflect his own experience of the ghetto: 'books about such things are not written for the witnesses, why should I tell them stories. Books are written precisely for the others' (Jurek Becker, 'Answering Questions about *Jakob der Lügner*', 288).

[61] Jurek Becker, 'Resistance in *Jakob der Lügner*', *Seminar*, 19 (1983), 269–73 (272).

[62] Johnson, 2–3.

experiences after the War (whether or not he has accurately captured the experience of ghetto life itself).[63] Finally, Krumbholz ignores the fact that the end of the novel *is* fragmented, that for all the narrator's attempts to tell a story 'im Sinne einer kompakten Erzähleinheit', there remains an obvious gap between his version and what really happened. As Wetzel puts it: 'Es bleibt schließlich dabei, daß die Schlüsse auseinanderklaffen.'[64] Thus, Becker does not let the 'schöne Geschichte' have the last word. John Fowles, who published his double-ended novel *The French Lieutenant's Woman* in the same year as *Jakob der Lügner*, writes that the second of two endings—in Becker's case the deportation of the Jews from the ghetto—will always seem more real, 'so strong is the tyranny of the final chapter'.[65]

To return to Joho's comments: he implies that the aesthetic term 'blaßwangig' has the effect of denying the moral and emotional dimension of the Holocaust—for all humane and civilized people its most important dimension—and that the use of an understatement like 'verdrießlich' trivializes the Nazi crime of genocide. While I agree with Joho that Becker is trying to avoid 'falsches Pathos' in the novel, I am inclined to account for the narrator's evident irritation with the Holocaust's lack of story-value differently. For it goes without saying that the narrator's treatment of his subject-matter is inappropriate. When the narrator says 'eigentlich jammerschade um eine so schöne Geschichte, daß sie so armselig im Sande verläuft' (258), there is a clear disparity between the feeling he expresses (mild regret that the deportation and extermination of the Jews spoils a good story) and the feeling we expect him to express (intense horror at the fate of the Jews). However, the disparity is so glaring that it provokes the reader. It alienates the Holocaust by presenting it as a story with a third-rate ending. But this technique arguably tests our reactions much better than the kind of resistance literature which Becker rejects and which,

---

[63] Two critics have drawn on historical evidence to show that Becker's picture of conditions in the ghetto is very far from the historical truth: see Brown, 22–3, and Johnson, 21–7.

[64] Wetzel, '"Unvergleichlich gelungener"—aber "einfach zu schön"?', 114.

[65] John Fowles, *The French Lieutenant's Woman* (London: Pan, 1992), 349.

by arousing well-rehearsed emotions, may eventually make us insensitive to the crimes of the Nazis, training us to produce the right emotions in an entirely mechanical way, or, as Becker put it, at the press of a button.[66] Instead, Becker goads us into a more conscious reaction to the fate of the Jews, one which, because it does not rely on our sharing the emotions of the narrator, is not vicarious, but forces us to feel emotion for ourselves.

I have suggested one way in which Becker might be defended against the charge that a concern with story-telling is inappropriate to Holocaust writing. But a more realist reading of the text also suggests a possible psychological motivation for the narrator's obsession with story-telling— particularly as manifested in the alternative ending—namely that it is part of his strategy for coping with the emotional pain of his past.

We know that the narrator is still traumatized by his experiences during the Nazi era. He speaks of 'mein ganzer privater Kram mit den Bäumen [. . .] und meine schlimme Rührseligkeit und die Freigebigkeit meiner Tränensäcke' (99). Indeed, he cannot think about trees without crying (44). The nature of this trauma is complex. On the one hand he is troubled by intense feelings of guilt that so few Jews in the ghetto were brave enough to offer resistance to the Nazis (99); on the other hand he feels anger and bitterness at the inhumane ghetto regulation which prohibited trees:[67]

Hardtloff hat sich das ausgedacht, warum weiß der Teufel, vielleicht wegen der Vögel. Dabei sind tausend andere Sachen auch verboten, Ringe und sonstige Wertgegenstände, Tiere zu halten, nach acht auf der Straße sein, es hätte keinen Sinn, alles aufzählen zu wollen. [. . .] Für

[66] Arnold, 'Gespräch mit Jurek Becker', 6.

[67] Waniek sees this regulation as symptomatic of the Nazis' desire to dehumanize and then exterminate the Jews: 'Das einfache Verbot der Bäume ist das Konzentrat der lebensabwürgenden Einschränkung auf eine [. . .] Insel des Unrechts. [. . .] Es ist die hybride und erschreckend erfolgreiche Anmaßung, selektiv das Leben zu verbieten' ('"Aber warum verbieten sie uns die Bäume?"', 289). Other critics who analyse the symbolic status of trees in the novel are: John P. Wieczorek, 'Irreführung durch Erzählperspektive?: The East German Novels of Jurek Becker', *MLR* 85 (1990), 640–52 (642); and Wetzel, 'Fiktive und authentische Nachrichten', 443–4.

alles habe ich Verständnis, ich meine, theoretisch kann ich es begreifen,
ihr seid Juden, ihr seid weniger als ein Dreck, was braucht ihr Ringe, und
wozu müßt ihr euch nach acht auf der Straße rumtreiben? Wir haben das
und das mit euch vor und wollen es so und so machen. Dafür habe ich
Verständnis. Ich weine darüber, ich würde sie alle umbringen, wenn ich es
könnte, ich würde Hardtloff den Hals umdrehen mit meiner linken Hand
[. . .] doch es geht in meinen Kopf. Aber warum verbieten sie uns die
Bäume? (9)

Given that even the more comprehensible of the ghetto
regulations inspire murderous thoughts in the narrator it is
not surprising that the emotions aroused in him by the
pointless prohibition of trees are so strong as to defy direct
description, so that he must resort to a comparison to evoke
them. Similar emotions are aroused in him by the reactions
of post-war Germans to the Holocaust. Whenever a German
acquaintance tries to prove that he was not a Nazi, the
narrator is overcome by a fury which is all the more striking
for being out of character: '"Leck mich am Arsch", sage ich,
stehe auf und gehe. Nach fünf Schritten werde ich wütend
über mich selber, weil ich so grob geworden bin, so unnötig
ausfallend, und er hat sich nichts dabei gedacht. Aber ich
drehe mich nicht um und gehe weiter' (25). Similarly, the
narrator is infuriated when his girlfriend Elvira pities him
because he has spent time in a concentration camp: 'Ich
höre das Mitleid in ihrer Stimme und werde verrückt. Ich
gehe ins Bad, setze mich in die Wanne und fange an zu
singen, damit ich nicht etwas tue, wovon ich genau weiß, daß
es mir nach fünf Schritten leid tut' (25).

Clearly, then, we are in no sense dealing with a dispas-
sionate or unemotional narrator. But the narrator's method
of dealing with his pain seems to be a somewhat unhealthy
combination of repression and introversion on the one hand
('mein [. . .] privater Kram', 'das ist einzig und allein meine
Sache' (44)), and violent outbursts (weeping, verbal abuse)
on the other. Thus, when the narrator comes to describing
the most emotionally charged events of the novel (the deportation of the ghetto Jews to a camp where most of them
will meet their death), we might expect another violent
outburst. Instead, he retreats behind the detached role of
the professional story-teller, maintaining that he judges the

deportation primarily in terms of its aesthetic defects. It seems possible, then, that the narrator directs his energies into story-telling at this juncture in order not to have to confront directly the final horror of the concentration camps. Just as singing to himself in the bath is the only way he can stop himself venting his anger on his girlfriend Elvira, so he has to concentrate on telling a good story in order not to be overcome by his 'schlimme Rührseligkeit'—that is, in order to be able to tell the story at all.

We cannot assume, however, that Becker's motives for telling the story were identical to those of his narrator, namely that he was struggling to contain his own emotion. Unlike the much older narrator, Becker had no memories of the ghetto[68] and confessed that he disliked the way in which Holocaust survivors and chroniclers tried to elicit from others an emotional response to the fate of the Jews under the Nazi regime. When Arnold asked him in 1992 whether the relationships between fathers and sons in his work reflected his own relationship with his father, Becker replied:

Was Sie aus den Büchern oder Geschichten, die mit ihm zu tun haben, ersehen können, ist vielleicht eine Art zu revoltieren gegen seine Art, Geschichten zu erzählen, mit der ich nicht so einverstanden war. Er hatte gewisse Techniken des Geschichtenerzählens, die fand ich toll, aber Geschichten hatten für seine Begriffe ein Quantum an Rührung zu enthalten, das mir nicht gefiel. Das hat sicher mit unserem unterschied-lichen Alter und auch mit unseren unterschiedlichen Biographien zu tun. Wissen Sie, mein Vater hatte eine Art Knopf auf der Brust, und wenn man da draufdrückte, kam, beim Erwähnen bestimmter Themen, die Rührung. Ich habe diesen Knopf nicht, und nicht nur das; wenn jemand diese Rührung zu produzieren versucht, werde ich mürrisch und unge-duldig und fühle mich eigentlich unangenehm berührt.[69]

Nevertheless, the text of *Jakob der Lügner* suggests that Becker did not favour an entirely unemotional response to the Holocaust. In fact, what we find in the novel is a kind of compromise: the narrator has the same 'Knopf auf der Brust' as Becker's father, but he does not attempt, at least not blatantly, to find the same spot in the reader. He controls

---

[68] Becker, 'Wäre ich hinterher klüger', 4.
[69] Arnold, 'Gespräch mit Jurek Becker', 6.

his emotions without actually denying them, so that his anger and sadness remain in the background without losing any of their power to move. As Marcel Reich-Ranicki put it: 'Beckers Gelassenheit hat nichts mit lauwarmer Versöhnlichkeit zu tun. Hinter seiner Heiterkeit verbirgt sich nichts anderes als Schmerz und Schwermut.'[70]

I have shown that for the narrator of *Jakob der Lügner* telling fictions is both a skill which he delights in demonstrating and a means of coping with painful experiences from the past. But the narrator's story-telling also has a moral quality. His depiction of human folly and frailty, which is gently satirical without ever being censorious or judgemental, promotes tolerance. Without abandoning a moral code (for the Nazi atrocities are quite clearly condemned), the narrator encourages us to be lenient and magnanimous in the face of minor human imperfections—petty selfishness, cowardice, self-delusion. This spirit of tolerance seems to be a deliberate counter-force to the hatred spread by Nazi propaganda, based as it was on ideals of racial and physical perfection.

Becker returned to the theme of the Holocaust and its legacy in later novels (*Der Boxer* and *Bronsteins Kinder*). In Gregor Bienek, hero of *Irreführung der Behörden*, he also created another gifted and passionate story-teller, albeit one facing rather different problems (attempting to reconcile his wayward imagination with the demands of the GDR's cultural authorities). While the works which followed *Jakob der Lügner* are relatively conventional in their narrative technique (with the possible exception of *Der Boxer*, in which the dialogue between an interviewer and his interviewee provides for a certain amount of tension), Becker's final novel, *Amanda herzlos* (1992), is something of a technical *tour de force*. Not only does it offer three contrasting male perspectives on the central figure, written in a variety of styles (monologue, dialogue, narrative, and diary), and each in its own way flawed (Becker gives his misogynists just enough rope to hang themselves with); Becker contrives to complicate the individual perspectives even further. In the second narrative,

---

[70] Marcel Reich-Ranicki, 'Roman vom Getto: Jurek Becker, *Jakob der Lügner*', in Reich-Ranicki, *Zur Literatur der DDR* (Munich: Piper, 1974), 145–8 (148).

for instance, the writer Fritz Hetmann, furious that a *Novelle* based on his (now defunct) relationship with Amanda has been erased from his computer, attempts to recall the plot from memory, interweaving it with the story of their real relationship. Becker plays on the way in which these two strands converge and diverge, making excellent use of the comic potential inherent in the consequent narrative entanglements[71] and ironizing Fritz's attempts to rewrite his life.

[71] For instance, where the two narratives converge, Fritz writes about himself, Amanda, and their fictional counterparts as if all four were present simultaneously, which conjures up some amusing pictures: 'als wir im Bett lagen (wir vier)'. Similarly, his feelings of humiliation are heightened by the absurd thought that Amanda and her fictional double Louise are ganging up on him and his *alter ego* Rudolf: 'Wir saßen zerknirscht im Bett, Rudolf wie ich, wir ließen alle Züchtigungen über uns ergehen und warteten darauf, daß das Unwetter sich verzog. [...] In meiner Vorstellung berieten sich die Frauen, bevor sie das Verfahren fortsetzten, sie suchten nach einer letzten Demütigung für uns' (Jurek Becker, *Amanda herzlos* (Frankfurt/Main: Suhkamp, 1992), 163, 165).

6

GÜNTER GRASS: *ÖRTLICH BETÄUBT*

1. Introduction

While on the campaign trail for the SPD in 1965, Günter Grass told an audience: 'Es liegen "Demokratische Geschichten" in der Luft',[1] signalling his intention, in his next literary work, to abandon the era of National Socialism, which had provided such fertile material for his first three prose works, *Die Blechtrommel, Katz und Maus,* and *Hundejahre,* and to turn his attention instead to contemporary West Germany. Having conceived the subject-matter for his new work, Grass gave it two distinct forms, one dramatic (the play *Davor*)[2] and one narrative (the novel *örtlich betäubt*).[3] Both works tell the story of a Berlin schoolteacher, Eberhard Starusch, who, while undergoing a course of orthodontic treatment to correct a congenitally misaligned bottom jaw, attempts to dissuade his pupil Philipp Scherbaum from setting fire to his pet dog in front of a café on Berlin's Kurfürstendamm, in protest at the use of napalm in Vietnam. While Starusch is determined, as a liberal and an educator, to thwart his pupil's plan, his resolve is weakened both by his infatuation with the boy (of which more will be said later in this chapter) and by his pride in his own youthful anarchist activity (as Störtebeker, the leader of the *Stäuber* gang who played a prominent role in *Die Blechtrommel*). Nevertheless, in both

---

[1] Günter Grass, 'Es steht zur Wahl', in Grass, *Werkausgabe in zehn Bänden,* ed. Volker Neuhaus (Darmstadt and Neuwied: Luchterhand, 1987), IX. 76–87 (87). All works by Grass are referred to in this edition, hereafter abbreviated to *Werkausgabe.*

[2] *Werkausgabe,* VIII. 479–555.

[3] Günter Grass, *Werkausgabe,* IV. 6–264. All further references to the novel are included in the text. Although some critics 'correct' the spelling of the title to *Örtlich betäubt,* I have followed the orthography used by the publishers and by Günter Grass in a letter to me: both use a lower-case letter for 'örtlich'. Grass describes his experiment with parallel texts in an interview with Henning Rischbieter: 'Die Krise des Berufes, der sich Theaterkritik nennt', *Werkausgabe,* X. 63–73 (72).

works Scherbaum is eventually persuaded, with the help of Starusch's dentist, to abandon his violent protest in favour of more peaceful, democratic engagement (as a campaigning editor of his school magazine).

While in *Davor* this storyline is given a relatively straightforward dialectical structure (a series of debates between the five characters), *örtlich betäubt* is an altogether more complex undertaking, not least because Grass has access to the mind of his narrator, whose fantasies he paints for us in vivid detail. In the novel, then, the dog-burning dilemma is just one strand of a much more involved plot. For most of Books I and III, which record two separate stages in his dental treatment, Starusch sits immobilized in the dentist's chair facing a television screen (aimed at distracting nervous patients) onto which he projects a combination of memories and imaginings. Even when freed from the dentist's chair, however (notably in Book II, when he returns to his school), Starusch continues to invent scenes and conversations.

Much of the material for these imaginings and projections is provided by Starusch's relationships with women: with his present partner, Irmgard Seifert, with his pupil Vero Lewand (Scherbaum's girlfriend), and, most importantly, with Sieglinde (or Linde) Krings, daughter of the former Nazi Field Marshal Ferdinand Krings. According to Starusch's stories, he and Linde were engaged in the 1950s (at a time when he was working as an engineer in her father's cement works), until her affair with the electrician Heinz Schlottau brought the engagement to an end. Linde and Schlottau's alliance is more than merely sexual: they also join forces against Linde's father, who indulges his fantasy that he is capable of winning all the battles which other Nazi generals lost by constructing a huge sandbox full of toy soldiers in which to rehearse military manœuvres. Having defeated her father in these wargames, Linde breaks off her engagement with Starusch, who returns again and again in his mind to the scene of their parting: the Rhine Promenade at Andernach (a motif reminiscent of the scene in the deserted apartment in *Mein Name sei Gantenbein*).

Besides this relatively coherent and linear story, the novel contains a host of fragmentary imagined scenes, many of which are a confusing blend of Starusch's projected fantasies, pictures broadcast on the television, and the magazine stories he reads in the dentist's waiting-room. While many of these scenes appear unconnected, they include a recognizable series of fictional fantasies in which Starusch, in various guises, murders his fiancée.

No doubt a real experience of a broken relationship lies behind Starusch's ramblings about Linde and her counterparts (we suspect, for instance, that there really was a parting on the Rhine Promenade). However, the exact details cannot be established, because Grass is less interested in the fiancée than in Starusch's sexual and emotional inadequacies. What distinguishes *örtlich betäubt* from its stablemate, *Davor*, is therefore more than just the addition of a sub-plot (the story of Linde and Krings): the novel form, with its first-person narrator, allows Grass considerably more scope for psychological study. Through Starusch's fantasies he is able to explore the emotional effects on Starusch of the professional dilemma posed by the dog-burning plan and to situate this dilemma within a wider crisis of confidence in the life of the middle-aged schoolteacher. Some of the most persuasive studies of the novel are those which examine the relationship between Starusch's fantasies and his neuroses.[4] My own analysis (in Sections 3 and 4 below) offers new insights into the mechanics of this relationship. However, Grass is not an author whose main interest lies in the study of human psychology for its own sake: all his works testify to an overwhelming concern with history and with the interaction of the individual with social and historical processes. Accordingly, Section 5 below shows that Grass's exploration of Starusch's fictions is closely related to his concern with Germany's Nazi past, with the 1960s protest movement, and with modern mass popular culture.

---

[4] These include two articles by Gertrud Bauer Pickar: 'Spielfreiheit und Selbstbefangenheit: Das Porträt eines Versagers. Zu Günter Grass' *örtlich betäubt*', in Manfred Durzak (ed.), *Zu Günter Grass* (Stuttgart: Klett, 1985), 96–114, and 'Starusch im Felde mit den Frauen. Zum Frauenbild in Grass' *örtlich betäubt*', *CG* 22 (1989), 260–82. See also John Reddick, 'Action and Impotence: Günter Grass's *örtlich betäubt*', *MLR* 67 (1972), 563–78; and Ann L. Mason, *The Skeptical Muse: A Study of Günter Grass' Conception of the Artist* (Berne: Herbert Lang, 1974), 86–128.

2. Starusch's 'krause Fiktionen'

Many of the devices by which Grass foregrounds the fictional status of Starusch's fantasies are by now familiar to us. In his murder fantasies, for instance, Starusch (like the *Buch-Ich* of *Gantenbein*) often switches between 'ich' and 'er', a device which indicates his desire to identify with the invented persona of the murderer.[5] The version in which a taxi-driver kills his fiancée is typical: 'Da ist er und will Punkte mit einem Armeerevolver setzen [. . .]. Mit der guten alten Sechsschüssigen, die ich als Taxifahrer, nachdem es in Hamburg zum dritten Mord an einem Taxifahrer innerhalb eines Monats gekommen war, ziemlich teuer erstanden hatte, [. . .] verließ ich kurz nach siebzehn Uhr unser Schlafzimmer im Schlafanzug' (73).[6] In the final murder story, this process is reversed: Starusch begins by calling the murderer 'ich', later switching to 'er' (259–63). Since these fictional variations on the murder of Starusch's fiancée cannot all simultaneously be true, they also cancel one another out. Each is 'erased' when the next murder fantasy is narrated.

On occasions, Starusch draws attention to the fact that he is playing with variants ('Ob sich diese Szene, ohne Fahrrad, Landschaft und Auto, in den Grauen Park verlegen ließe?' (49)) and to the fact that the details of his stories are not fixed, but can be changed at will ('Krings kommt mit Koffer —vielleicht schiebt er doch das Rad' (49)). Elsewhere he draws attention to discarded possibilities: as director of an imaginary film about Krings's homecoming, he first describes and then erases a particular scene ('aber das muß man nicht zeigen' (44)) and declares that a series of

---

[5] Starusch claims to have read the initial 'Verlobtenmörder' story (52–5) in the newspaper *Welt am Sonntag* (*WamS*). However, the fact that he ascribes many of his own characteristics and circumstances to the murderer (his future father-in-law, his job as an engineer, his visits to the Rhine Promenade at Andernach, his knowledge of Seneca, and even his toothache), suggests that Starusch has invented this character (no doubt inspired by a story in *WamS*). See my comments below about Starusch's tendency to project his own image onto his characters and his tendency to borrow from popular forms in his fictions.

[6] Cf. the version in which a photographer is responsible for the death of his fiancée, Arantil: 'er wartete, bis sie sich zu Nacht gekleidet hatte und endlich [. . .] eingeschlafen war. Jetzt erst verließ ich mein Versteck' (61).

conversations between Schlottau and his companions 'sind Verschnitt' (44). In the metaphor of the film, they will end up on the cutting-room floor. There is even one example in which an imagined scene is prefaced by 'Man stelle sich vor' (195), echoing Frisch's 'Ich stelle mir vor', and two further episodes are related in *Konjunktiv II* (139 and 147–8), which, as I have shown in previous chapters, is used to indicate possibility and supposition.

Other foregrounding devices are unique to Grass's novel. The dentist, for instance, plays a role in exposing Starusch's imaginings as fictitious. Not only does he reprove Starusch for telling 'die beliebigsten Fiktionen' (107) and 'krause Fiktionen' (234), he also does a little detective work and discovers that there is no such man as Ferdinand Krings, that Starusch was never a qualified engineer, and that while he did once take a summer job in a cement works he was never engaged to the boss's daughter. These revelations cancel out retrospectively Starusch's stories about Linde and her father.

Starusch's imaginings are not confined to individual scenes and anecdotes, however: the protracted conversation with the dentist is itself an invention, for while the dentist is working on his teeth, Starusch's jaw is locked open, rendering him 'tonlos' (8). Given this enforced silence, his lively conversations with the dentist must be interpreted as an inner monologue (or rather dialogue).[7] The reader receives repeated reminders of the fictional status of this dialogue. For instance, Starusch speaks of inviting the doctor into his head, where they can hold a conversation: 'während ich, nein, wir beide in meinem Köpfchen, das gerne Besuch hat: "Was meinen Sie, Dokter, [. . .]?"' (18).[8] The following passage describes how the dentist's assistant prepares Starusch for treatment: 'Da waren sie wieder, die Mohrrübenfinger. Hängten den Speichelabsauger ein, drückten die Zunge ins Hinterstübchen. (Zubeißen wollen. Tätig werden. Oder bei Seneca Muße suchen: "Was meinen Sie,

---

[7] Grass has made clear that this was his intention: '[Starusch] erfindet einen inneren Dialog zwischen Zahnarzt und Patient' (Rischbieter, 'Die Krise des Berufes, der sich Theaterkritik nennt', 72).

[8] The temporal clause introduced by *während* is grammatically incomplete: Starusch does not supply a verb.

Dokter, ob nicht gewisse geschichtliche Entscheidungen vom Zahnschmerz beeinflußt gewesen sein mögen")' (77). Given that Starusch has an instrument for removing saliva in his mouth and is deprived of the proper use of his tongue, his words to the dentist are clearly imagined.[9] No doubt there is a real dentist in the background ('real', that is, within the world of the text), for somebody is certainly there, fixing Starusch's teeth, but the dentist we hear in the text debating, discoursing, advising, and reproving is, I would argue, Starusch's invention.[10]

So far I have listed some of the more overt textual indicators which draw the reader's attention to Starusch's tendency to fantasize. Even without them, however, Starusch's inventions would be fairly transparent, since he tends to project his own idiosyncrasies, anxieties, and aspirations onto the characters and situations which he invents. His complaint that he cannot outsmart the dentist in an argument about revolution because 'der Zahnarzt ist ähnlich belesen' (101) underlines the fact that he has given his imaginary dentist a classical, humanist education which is a mirror-image of his own. Not only can the dentist trace the history of dentistry back to Hippocrates and Pliny; he is also an authority on Seneca, Nietzsche, Hegel, and 'Marxengels' (as Grass collectively dubs the authors of the *Communist Manifesto*).[11] Starusch also ascribes to the dentist his own fondness for impromptu lectures ('mein Zwang, Stegreifvorträge halten zu müssen' (65–6)). Thus, when Starusch regales his dentist with detailed descriptions of the geology of the Voreifel region or of the processes involved in cement

---

[9] See also pp. 104, 242.

[10] Analysing the text becomes a laborious task, however, if one is obliged to explain at every mention of the dentist that Starusch is putting words into his mouth or controlling his actions. In what follows I occasionally write about the dentist as though he were a 'real person': I ask the reader to take it as read that Starusch, as puppeteer, is pulling the strings.

[11] In objecting to the frequency with which the dentist quotes Seneca, Manfred Durzak makes the mistake of treating the character as an autonomous individual: 'Der Zahnarzt ist pragmatischer Intellektueller—seine Bildung signalisieren seine übermäßigen Seneca-Zitate vielleicht allzu augenfällig' (Manfred Durzak, 'Abschied von der Kleinbürgerwelt. Der neue Roman von Günter Grass', *Basis*, 1 (1970), 224–37 (230)). I identified a similar problem for critics of *Mein Name sei Gantenbein* (see above, p. 52 n. 14).

manufacture, the dentist reciprocates with lectures on tartar or the nervous system of teeth. Nor is the dentist the only fictional character to whom Starusch lends his own intellectual profile: Krings knows his Seneca (22 and 254), as does the *Verlobten-Mörder* (55); the bogus lifeguard reads Nietzsche and the *Communist Manifesto* (260); and Linde is an expert on military history (82, 105–6, 110–14).

Later in this chapter I will argue that Starusch is an avid, though closet, consumer of popular culture and that, despite (or perhaps because of) his unwillingness to admit to popular tastes in public, his fascination with popular forms finds expression in his private fantasies. Consequently, whenever elements of popular culture find their way into Starusch's stories we can be fairly sure that we are dealing with a fabrication. This is very obviously true of the quiz-show scene (in which Vero, Scherbaum, and Krings pit their wits in a television quiz on military history, hosted by Krings's daughter Linde), and of the tale of Krings's military confrontation with his daughter in the sandbox (which contains such spy-thriller staples as double agents, Mata-Hari-style seductions, the dissemination of false information to confuse the enemy, and the photographing of secret documents). Other instances are more subtle. In Book I Starusch relates a story from his student days, when he took a job distributing ration coupons in a tenement in Aachen (87–90). The job turns into a sexual apprenticeship, as he is seduced by (and later learns to sell his sexual services to) a whole series of willing women. While the episode contains some intensely realistic details (such as the smell of Brussels sprouts and the sight of a sickly budgerigar), which suggest that it has a basis in memory, various clues point to the fact that the sexual adventures it describes are an invention. The narrator switches between 'ich' and 'er', a device which Starusch uses on other occasions, as I demonstrated above, to define his relationship to an invented persona. Moreover, as Gertrud Bauer Pickar has pointed out, the story's fairy-tale beginning ('Es war einmal ein Student' (88)) hints that it is an idealized account, while the fact that Starusch suffers from anxieties about his sexual potency may lead us to suspect that this is a compensatory fantasy.[12] What Pickar over-looks in an otherwise excellent analysis is the fact that the story also borrows clichés from third-rate erotic fiction—the sexually naïve young man who is initiated into the adult sexual world by an older woman, the bored and over-sexed housewives who lure passing young males into their homes —which give a strong indication that Starusch has invented this account of his sexual exploits.

3. The Power of Fiction (I): Fantasy as Compensation

One way in which Starusch uses his fantasies is to express urges which he feels obliged to repress in his professional life. When the dentist suspects him of harbouring violent thoughts, Starusch protests: 'Als Studienrat für Deutsch und also Geschichte sind mir Gewaltaktionen verhaßt, zutiefst verhaßt' (32). Starusch's role as an educator, and more specifically the humanist tradition to which, as a teacher of literature, he is an heir (and which, it is implied, informs his interpretation of history) force him to take a principled stand against violence. Yet, as the dentist points out, Starusch's fantasies are full of violent scenes. Not only do the various fiancée-figures meet violent deaths, Starusch also dreams of political revolution, bulldozing Western consumer society with the aid of an imaginary bulldozer (100–2) in order to create a *tabula rasa* from which to reconstruct a better world. Starusch knows, however, that these revolutionary urges will never be translated into reality, describing himself as 'der an sich liberale und nur uneigentlich radikale Studienrat' (102). Similarly, although Starusch is an implacable opponent of Kurt Georg Kiesinger, whose chancellorship he considers to be compromised by his Nazi past, his fantasies reveal a fascination with the figure of the incorrigible Nazi general Ferdinand Krings. The dentist observes drily that Starusch speaks of Krings 'mit nur mühsam ironisierter Begeisterung' (66) and Linde also accuses him of admiring her father (68). While it is true that Starusch

---

[12] Pickar, 'Starusch im Felde mit den Frauen', 272, and 'Spielfreiheit und Selbstbefangenheit', 110.

sympathizes with Krings for personal rather than political reasons (Krings is attempting to turn past defeats into victories, something Starusch would also like to achieve), his secret flirtation with the figure of an unregenerate ex-Nazi nevertheless undermines his public political stance. In this way, Starusch's fantasies reveal one of his defining characteristics: his tendency to think one thing and do another. A single sentence of the narrative (which occurs at a moment when he is debating whether to push his fiancée from the roof of a high building) epitomizes Starusch's inability to reconcile intentions with actions: 'Aber ich dachte nur und tat nichts' (238).

The most significant way in which Starusch uses his fantasies is to correct or compensate for what he perceives as personal failings. Paradoxically (and this is, of course, Grass's intention), these compensatory fantasies merely serve to draw attention to the inadequacies which Starusch hopes to efface. For instance, Starusch's interior monologue reveals that he has doubts about his teaching abilities and professional credibility (he is haunted by Scherbaum's question: 'Warum unterrichten Sie eigentlich?' (50) and by his fiancée's taunt: 'Und sowas darf unterrichten!' (102)). Yet Starusch's fear of professional failure is evoked most forcefully by means of its antithesis: his fantasies of professional *success*. In Book I, for instance, Starusch invents for himself a past in which he was a highly successful industrial engineer, whose meteoric rise in the cement industry (described on pp. 27–8) was due in large part to his single-handed development of a method of recycling cement dust, a process which simultaneously rationalized cement production and assuaged local concerns about the environmental impact of dust emissions (21–2).[13] Indeed, Starusch the industrial engineer is *so* successful that he can affect modesty about his achievements: '*Ich gebe zu, daß* mein Vortrag Krings *bewogen haben mag*, der Installierung elektrischer Ofenentstauber zuzustimmen' (23; my italics). The phrasing of this statement implies a certain reluctance—real or feigned—to take credit for the rationalization of the Krings cement factory;

---

[13] Cf. Reddick, 'Action and Impotence', 566–7.

yet this modesty fantasy is an obvious compensation, for the real Starusch is so bereft of talent and dynamism that modesty is not an option open to him: he feels the need to boast about the slightest evidence of his 'abilities' (his skill at putting together school timetables (91) or his spontaneity in slapping his partner Irmgard across the face (198)).

Even in his criminal fantasies, Starusch is a *successful* criminal. Had the 'Verlobtenmörder' not given himself up voluntarily, the police, we are told, would never have caught him, such was his mastery of disguise (52). He is also an accomplished housebreaker, carrying out his burglaries 'ohne besonderes Werkzeug, dennoch perfekt' (52) and he combines this criminal expertise with a specialist knowledge of both Seneca and cement manufacture (53).

Another of Starusch's perceived failings is his inability to finish academic projects. On top of his writing desk—to which he returns periodically between visits to the dentist and days at school—sit pieces of work which he has begun but not finished. We are told, for instance, of 'einige Bände *An*gelesenes' (31) and 'meine *begonnene* Denkschrift zur Schülermitverantwortung' (31; my italics). In fact, even when he is considering whether or not to read a book, Starusch evidently cannot envisage reading it from cover to cover, but only starting it: 'Bücher aufschlagen, *an*lesen?', he suggests to himself (172; my italics again). He also alludes repeatedly to a partly written study of the Nazi General Schörner (the prototype of the imaginary Krings). The first, unspecific, allusion to this manuscript, 'die ärgerlich dünne Mappe' (31), takes the form of a self-reproach, suggesting Starusch's irritation with his slow progress on the work. There is some indication that his personal problems are to blame for disturbing his concentration: 'Zu Hause lag unverrückt das Angefangene. Ich öffnete die Mappe, überflog das Kapitel "Schörner auf der Eismeerstraße", strich einige Adjektive, schloß die Mappe und entwarf dann ein Gutachten, das der Verteidiger des angeklagten Schülers Philipp Scherbaum anfordern mochte, wenn es soweit war' (191).[14] As his erasure of a few adjectives suggests, however, it is not

---

[14] See also pp. 168, 177, 187, 221, 225.

just Scherbaum's plan which interferes with the work, but a tendency to rework constantly and pointlessly what he has already written, as confirmed by the following description of his method of working: 'Einen breiten Rand lassen für Zusätze, die später gestrichen werden' (186). Not surprisingly, at the end of his dental treatment, the Schörner manuscript is still 'das Angefangene' (263). Moreover, a comment on p. 230: 'Das Angefangene bewegen oder meine Forster-Studien wieder aufnehmen', indicates that the work on Schörner is not the only project which Starusch has started but not finished.

Although these references to Starusch's slow progress on his writing projects appear at relatively frequent intervals, they occur at some of the novel's least memorable moments and might go unnoticed were it not that the fictions he invents (in which he compensates for this shortcoming by imagining his various personae successfully completing pieces of written work) betray a deep-seated insecurity about his intellectual staying-power. For instance, when his toothache finally forces him to turn himself in, the 'Verlobtenmörder' is able to hand over 'ein in zwölf Jahren gewachsenes Manuskript von beträchtlichem Umfang: *Der frühe Seneca als Erzieher des späteren Kaisers Nero*' (55). Similarly, in his fictitious account of his past life as an engineer, Starusch claims to have written a study concerning 'Erfahrungen mit Tiefbohr- und Traßzementen beim U-Boot-Bunkerbau in Brest' (27). Finally, Starusch fantasizes about completing a dissertation for his engineering degree, describing his briefcase as 'geschwollen von meiner für gut befundenen Examensarbeit über die Entstaubung von Zementwerken' (90). The exaggerated size of the fictitious works ('von beträchtlichem Umfang', 'geschwollen') is clear evidence of an attempt to compensate for the modest dimensions of Starusch's half-finished Schörner manuscript ('die ärgerlich dünne Mappe'). The phallic associations of the phrases 'von beträchtlichem Umfang' and 'geschwollen' may only become apparent when they are taken out of context, but might nevertheless suggest an unconscious association in Starusch's mind between intellectual and sexual prowess.

Another of Starusch's insecurities is his fear of not finding sympathetic listeners. While he has a captive audience in Class 12a (and readily seizes the opportunity to expound his latest concerns to them),[15] a captive audience is not necessarily an appreciative one and Starusch suspects that some of the pupils are secretly mocking him, or at least that Scherbaum, whose opinion matters most to him, thinks he is a crank or a bore: 'Diese Angst, nicht ernst genommen zu werden, ist Beisitzer [. . .] meiner Unterrichtsstunden: Das Lächeln einiger Schüler—oder wenn Scherbaum, als sei er um mich besorgt, den Kopf schräg hält—läßt mich stocken, abschweifen' (23). In an attempt to escape his fears, Starusch fantasizes about eager and interested listeners. These include the audience at a cement manufacturers' conference (27), a group of visitors whom he shows around the cement factory (114), and his fiancée's father: 'Krings, der sich meinen Vortrag über die Entwicklung der deutschen Traßzemente während des letzten Krieges mit Interesse angehört hatte' (66). Moreover, when he imagines a world governed by a dentist and a schoolteacher, it is a world in which 'der eine hört auf den anderen, der andere auf den einen' (196).

Since the compensatory fantasies which I want to discuss next shed light on the relationship between Starusch and Scherbaum, it is necessary at this point to acknowledge unequivocally (as no critic seems yet to have done) Starusch's infatuation with his pupil.[16] Starusch betrays an obsessive interest in Scherbaum, whom he addresses repeatedly in his interior monologue.[17] He cannot think of his school class

---

[15] For instance, his interest in pollution: 'Später habe ich meine 12a mit den Problemen der zunehmenden Luftverschmutzung bekanntgemacht' (22); in Second World War bunkers: 'Das müßte meine 12a interessieren' (66); and in the military campaigns of the Second World War: 'Doch wer interessiert sich heute noch für Demjansk? Etwa meine 12a?' (72).

[16] Of the few critics who even mention the infatuation, Neuhaus makes the understated comment: 'auch Starusch empfindet mehr für Scherbaum, als er selbst zugeben will' (Volker Neuhaus, *Günter Grass* (Stuttgart: Metzler, 1979), 109), while Reddick states that Starusch has a 'dubious love' for Scherbaum which is '"Ersatzliebe", an exiguous substitute for a genuine involvement between two people that are mature and equal' (Reddick, 'Action and Impotence', 569).

[17] This habit of addressing Scherbaum in his mind, as if his whole interior monologue were for his pupil's benefit, suggests that Starusch dreams of Scherbaum being a companion with whom he can share his thoughts: e.g. 'Schauen Sie,

without thinking immediately of Scherbaum;[18] and he craves
his pupil's admiration as much as he fears his disapproval.[19]
Moreover, there are hints of homoerotic attraction in
Starusch's (albeit ironic) use of terms of affection for Scherbaum ('mein Philipp' (e.g. 112, 186), '[mein] Scherbäumchen' (e.g. 171, 187)); in his references to Scherbaum's
dimples (157, 171); and in his fantasy of a fight with Scherbaum (197). Indeed, on one occasion, when he hopes to use
an anti-Vietnam demonstration as a pretext for spending
time with the boy, Starusch sounds like a rather timid young
man asking a girl for a date, hiding his vulnerability behind
a mask of indifference to Scherbaum's response: 'Wir könn-
ten gemeinsam hingehen. Ich hatte ohnehin vor . . . ' (217).
Although Starusch at one point comes close to admitting the
strength of his feelings for Scherbaum, he still hides behind
a light-hearted, ironic tone:

Ist etwa mein Verhältnis zu Scherbaum vergleichbar dem Verhältnis eines
Hundeliebhabers zu seinem Hündchen?—Ich besitze ein Scherbaum-
Foto. Aus einer Klassenaufnahme ließ ich ihn und seine Lachgrübchen
vergrößern. In einen Wechselrahmen, der seit Jahren leersteht, schiebe

Scherbaum, auch das will beschrieben werden' (19); 'So, Scherbaum, sah mein
Reichsjugendführer aus' (72); 'Sehen Sie, Scherbaum, in Ihrem Alter ahnt man
noch nicht, welches Gewicht Zahnersatz in der wägenden Hand eines vierzig-
jährigen Studienrates haben kann' (79).

[18] Starusch's mental habit of singling out Scherbaum from the rest of Class 12a is
an important—but as yet unrecognized—stylistic device: 'Später habe ich meine
12a mit den Problemen der zunehmenden Luftverschmutzung bekanntgemacht.
Sogar Scherbaum war beeindruckt' (22); 'Das Lächeln einiger Schüler—oder
wenn Scherbaum, als sei er um mich besorgt, den Kopf schräg hält—läßt mich
stocken, abschweifen, und oft genug muß mich einer der Schüler, muß
mich Scherbaum mit einem lässigen "Wir waren bei Stresemann stehengeblieben"
zurückrufen' (23); 'Gedankensprünge zurück in die Zahnarztpraxis und von dort
in meine 12a, denn kürzlich noch sprachen wir über den Archetyp des Heim-
kehrers: "Meine Generation wurde von Borcherts Beckmann geprägt. Wie
stehen Sie zu Beckmann, Scherbaum?"' (47); 'Das müßte meine 12a interessieren.
"Glauben Sie mir, Scherbaum [. . .]"'(66); '"Was meinen Sie, wäre das nicht ein
Aufsatzthema [for class 12a]?" Mein Schüler Scherbaum möge sich vorstellen
[. . .]' (91); and 'Meine Schüler lächeln, sobald ich die Lehrbücher in Zweifel
ziehe: "Da ist aber kein Sinn, sondern nur organisiertes Chaos".—Warum lächeln
Sie, Scherbaum?' (128).

[19] He imagines Scherbaum reproving him for his self-absorption, for instance:
'Sie mit Ihren Zahnschmerzen. Und was ist im Mekong-Delta los?' (15); and worries about Scherbaum's perception of him: 'Gewiß hielt mich Scherbaum für einen
weltfremden Spinner' (21).

ich manchmal, wie etwas Verbotenes, das postkartengroße Porträt: mein Scherbäumchen, wie es den Kopf schräg hält . . . Und sagte nicht Irmgard Seifert: 'Ihr Verhältnis zu Scherbaum ist mir nicht distanziert genug. Sie können den Jungen nicht an der Leine führen . . .'. (171)

Despite the ironic tone, the fetishistic veneration of Scherbaum's photograph suggests a deep-rooted and obsessive attachment. It is not surprising, then, that Starusch feels pangs of jealousy as Scherbaum comes under the influence of his dentist (186 and 194–5).

To ignore the intensity of Starusch's fixation on Scherbaum is to miss out on the humour which derives from Starusch's doomed attempts to impress the boy. But more importantly, an understanding of Starusch's secret attachment is a prerequisite to understanding some of his fantasies. For while we gather from their conversations that Scherbaum is sceptical of Starusch's political beliefs and teaching methods,[20] we gauge how deeply Starusch is wounded by this rejection only because he fantasizes about Scherbaum's *admiration* for him. During the imaginary quiz show in which Scherbaum and Vero compete against Field Marshal Krings, Starusch has Scherbaum attribute his passion for History to Starusch's inspirational teaching (111). That this is a case of wish-fulfilment is made clear when Starusch draws attention to the disparity between the fictional quiz, where Philipp shows a keen interest in the subject, and the real schoolroom, where he does not: 'Ich gebe zu, daß mich jede richtige Antwort meines Philipp stolz machte. (Warum hier aufgeschlossen und beim Unterricht abweisend: "Was gehen uns Ihre Clausewitz Ludendorff Schörner an?")' (112). The answer to Starusch's parenthetical question is obvious: Scherbaum is uncharacteristically communicative at the quiz

---

[20] For example: 'Verstehe nicht, warum Sie Lehrer geworden sind, wo Sie doch bei der Entstaubung viel mehr hätten leisten können' (22); 'Meine Schüler lächeln, sobald ich die Lehrbücher in Zweifel ziehe: "Da ist aber kein Sinn, sondern nur organisiertes Chaos.—Warum lächeln Sie, Scherbaum?" "Weil Sie trotzdem unterrichten und [. . .] trotzdem einen Sinn in der Geschichte suchen"' (128). Scherbaum also mocks Starusch for suggesting that he channel his creative energies into protest songs because these will have a more lasting effect than the ephemeral dog-burning, commenting scornfully to Vero: 'Old Hardy glaubt an Unsterblichkeit. Haste gehört: Ich soll für die Ewigkeit schreiben' (166).

show because Starusch is indulging in a gratifying, but fanciful, daydream.

Not only do Starusch's fantasies compensate for his real life by offsetting what he feels to be his failings; as John Reddick has pointed out, they also allow him to take revenge, to redress perceived injustices which continue to rankle with him.[21] In particular, they allow him to punish his ex-fiancée for ending their relationship by sending her to her death in a variety of gruesome scenarios: she is strangled by a bicycle chain (52); pushed to her death from the walls of Perugia (60); killed when her photographer-fiancé takes a snapshot of her as she sleeps (61–2); shot by her taxi-driver fiancé (73–6); buried under a pile of wet cement (239); and finally drowned in a swimming pool with the aid of a wave-machine (259–63). Moreover, the portrayal of Linde as a heartless, scheming woman who uses sex as a weapon and employs brutal methods to destroy her father's cherished illusions is in itself a form of revenge, a way of punishing the woman who once spurned him by depicting her as a monster.[22]

One episode in the novel, the story of the painter Anton Möller (256–8), has been interpreted by critics as a statement about the role of the artist and the necessity of artistic compromise[23]—a reading which is invited by Starusch's own interpretation of the story. However, Starusch is not presented primarily as an artist-figure, so that his pronouncements on art are rather out of character.[24] I prefer to see the Maler Möller anecdote in the context of Starusch's revenge fantasies. The story, the last of the tales which Starusch tells

[21] Reddick, 'Action and Impotence', 567.

[22] See the dentist's comments on p. 235: '[Ihre Verlobte], die Sie sich als Monstrum neu erschaffen wollen'.

[23] e.g. Durzak, 237; Neuhaus, 117; James C. Bruce, 'The Motif of Failure and the Act of Narrating in Günter Grass's örtlich betäubt', MFS 17 (1971), 45–60 (54–5); Mason, 91; and Renate Gerstenberg, Zur Erzähltechnik von Günter Grass (Heidelberg: Winter, 1980), 87–119 (96).

[24] Although Mason chooses Starusch as a character with whom to contrast earlier Grass artist-figures in her study The Skeptical Muse, even she must admit that: 'in being a schoolteacher, Starusch is only marginally an artist, a representative of the imagination' (Mason, 124) and that he is at best 'an intellectual with an artistic mentality' (86). She therefore considers the comparison which Starusch sets up between himself and Anton Möller to be rather contrived (91).

to his dentist, concerns a Danzig painter who, while engaged to the daughter of Danzig's Bürgermeister, is commissioned to paint a mural of the Last Judgement for the City Council.[25] Möller's use of a young girl of low status and ill repute to model for the naked figure of Sin sends his fiancée into a jealous rage. The city fathers give him an ultimatum: obliterate the face of the rafter's daughter or relinquish his fee and his claims to his fiancée's hand in marriage. Möller's answer is to paint his fiancée's face over that of the rafter's daughter, thus publicly associating his fiancée with nakedness and sin. Pressed to withdraw this second outrage, Möller covers his fiancée's face with a glass bell, behind which she remains visible, though distorted, and paints the City Council and Mayor in a boat, floating downstream on their way to Hell. This anecdote is told in answer to the dentist's question as to whether Starusch has at last 'buried' his fiancée. 'Es ist mir gelungen', says Starusch, 'wie seinerzeit der Maler Anton Möller' (255). The answer to the dentist's question, is thus a resounding 'No': Starusch cannot resist one further chance to take revenge on his ex-fiancée, albeit vicariously, by recounting the story of Möller's vicious revenge on *his* fiancée.[26]

4. The Power of Fiction (II): The Fantasies Bite Back

While Starusch apparently has the power to confer on himself in his fantasies all the qualities he most misses in himself, or to confer on others the qualities he would most like to

[25] The original of Möller's 'Last Judgement' (painted 1602–3) hung in the Artushof in Danzig until the Second World War, when it was lost. Grass's anecdote is based on well-known apocryphal stories about the mural, but he supplies one or two fictional details, including the engagement between Möller and the Mayor's daughter (which is clearly intended to echo Starusch's situation). Art historians interpret the glass bell covering the face of the most prominent female figure as a globe, which serves to identify her as 'die Weltlust' (Walter Gyssling, *Anton Möller und seine Schule. Ein Beitrag zur Geschichte der niederländischen Renaissancemalerei* (Strasbourg: Heitz, 1917), 108).

[26] The epithet 'ziegenhaft', used on a number of occasions of Sieglinde Krings (16, 25, 35, 62, 105) and subsequently of Möller's fiancée (257), invites us to equate the two women. In this way, Starusch further disparages his ex-fiancée, associating her implicitly with the peevishness of the Mayor's daughter and—through Möller's painting—with Sin.

see in them, this power is not absolute, for he is not entirely in control of his imagination. Consequently, like other
narrator-figures analysed in this study, he becomes a kind of
sorcerer's apprentice in his own narrative. Having set his
fantasies in motion, he is obliged to stand by and watch
them bring to life the very fears and anxieties from which
they are meant to help him escape. In this way, a double
process is at work in the novel, whereby aspects of Starusch's
personality are repressed and then resurface, so that gratifying fantasies are first projected and then undermined.[27] As
Pickar points out, the freedom apparently offered by Starusch's fantasies is limited since he remains trapped within
himself: 'Statt der erwünschten Befreiung bieten ihm seine
Phantasien nur Bestätigung für sein Selbstbildnis. So bleibt
er in dem Netz seines eigenen Phantasierens verfangen.'[28]

Earlier I explained that Starusch compensates for his fear
of being a bore by inventing sympathetic listeners. We may
suspect that by projecting onto the dentist his own tendency
to give lectures on obscure topics, Starusch intends to supply
himself with the perfect listening partner (in much the same
way that Nathanael, hero of E.T.A. Hoffmann's *Der Sand-
mann*, creates in Olimpia a narcissistic projection of himself
who reflects exactly his own interests). Instead, Starusch
brings into sharper focus the difficulty of finding an audience for the hoard of curious and little-known facts which he
has stocked up in his mind: for since the dentist shares his
intellectual approach to life, he naturally also shares with
him this same insecurity. His patients are evidently quick to
tire of his scientific and philosophical ramblings, since he
observes to Starusch: 'Sie gehören zu den wenigen Patienten, die sich für die Ursachen und den Weg der Schmerzen
mit Ausdauer interessieren' (65); and his lectures on dental
decay at the *Volkshochschule* are, on his own admission, 'leider
nur mäßig besucht' (67). Moreover, the dentist is really no

[27] In fact the process is not necessarily sequential: Starusch may *simultaneously*
project a favourable image of himself and undermine that image. Indeed, Reddick
suggests that Starusch's 'driving sense of failure' becomes obvious *before* he projects
his fantasies of success (Reddick, 566). The notion of a sequence (repression
followed by the return of the repressed) is simply a metaphor which I find helpful
in attempting to make concrete a complex and abstract narrative process.
[28] Pickar, 'Spielfreiheit und Selbstbefangenheit', 113.

more interested in Starusch's lectures than Starusch is in his, so that they often talk past one another, as in the following exchange (Starusch speaks first):

'Der Bims gehört geologisch zu den Laacher Trachyttuffen . . .'
Er sagte: 'Das gründliche Nachpolieren verbürgt, daß das Schmelzober-
häutchen geschlossen wird . . .'
Ich erzählte vom mittleren Alluvium, von weißen Trachyttuffen und
der zwischengelagerten Britzbänke; er wies noch einmal auf meine freilie-
genden Zahnhälse hin und sagte: 'So. Erlöst, mein Lieber. Nun wollen wir
mal den Spiegel . . .' [. . .] Ich sprach dagegen an: 'Schon unter einem
Meter Humus liegt der Bims . . .'—aber mein Zahnarzt blieb bei der
Sache: 'Zwar ergibt unser Status, daß die zu überbrückenden Zähne
positiv sind, doch muß ich sagen: Sie haben eine echte, und echt heißt
angeborene Progenie, auf deutsch: einen Vorbiß.' (29)[29]

Although the two men exist in a kind of mutual depend-
ence (each allows the other to expound his favourite topic),
neither wants to listen to the other. 'Nicht wahr, Dokter, Sie
interessieren sich doch für Bims', says Starusch at one point,
to which the dentist replies: 'Wie Sie sich für den Karies-
zuwachs im Pflichtschulalter interessieren' (33), in other
words, not a great deal. The two men have entered into a
kind of pact like the characters in Sartre's *Huis clos*: Starusch
can only expect interest from the dentist if he shows interest
in return, but in both cases this interest is feigned. In the
latter part of the novel Starusch begins to acknowledge the
hollowness of this contract, first when he admits that he is
bored by the dentist's repetitive stories ('Schon befürch-
tete ich, seine Charité-Anekdoten—vier Mann gegen einen
Patienten—hören zu müssen' (185)) and secondly when he
speaks of the dentist 'paying him back' during a telephone
conversation in which Starusch gives a long account of a
teachers' conference which he is attending:

Als ich mit meinem Lagebericht am Ende war, begann mein Zahnarzt mir
heimzuzahlen: Er gab mir genauen Bericht vom Kieferorthopädischen
Kongreß in St. Moritz, indem er Zitate aus dem Eröffnungsvortrag über
Mißbildungen im Kieferbereich mit Landschaftsschilderungen und detail-
lierten Angaben über Wanderwege durch Lärchenwälder und über
Alpenwiesen mischte [. . .].

---

[29] See also pp. 13 and 122.

Mit einem Wort: wir blieben uns am Telefon nichts schuldig; durch eine Leitung sprachen wir aneinander vorbei. (195)[30]

Having created the dentist in his own image, Starusch inevitably finds himself looking into a mirror at his own shortcomings.[31] In his review of the novel, Marcel Reich-Ranicki takes exception to the many lectures on arcane subjects given by Starusch and his dentist, writing that the characters are 'meist von einer fixen Idee befallen, was für den Leser noch kein Unglück wäre, wenn sie sich nicht immer wieder darüber verbreiten müßten'.[32] Similarly, D.J. Enright argues that 'there is a distinct discrepancy between the space this information occupies in the novel and its significant contribution to the novel'.[33] Yet the technical lectures *are* central to the exploration of Starusch's psychology and if the reader finds them dull (rather than amusing), then Grass has failed to communicate their importance to Starusch's predicament.

Another example of the psychological double-bind in which Starusch is caught involves his insecurity about his sexual potency. The self-flattering virility fantasy about his seduction of Aachen housewives (87–90) is not sufficient to suppress this insecurity, which resurfaces in his invention of a rampantly virile sexual rival, Schlottau. On first meeting Linde, Schlottau confidently advertises his virility to her by telling her a smutty joke about a farmer who takes his cow to the bull (45); later, only minutes after having sex with her, he is ready to start again: 'Ich glaub, ich kann wieder' (81).

---

[30] Even outside the dentist's surgery, Starusch is haunted by the dentist's urge to silence him: 'Auch hinterm Schreibtisch und umgeben von privatem Kleinkram—Fetische, die mich schützen sollten—klatschte er mir, sobald ich "Linde" sagte, mehrere Löffel rosa Modellgips ins Maul' (86).

[31] Another of Starusch's inventions, Linde, also proves to be an unwilling listener. On the way to Normandy to visit wartime bunkers, Starusch gives a running commentary on the architecture of the region: 'Linde winkt ab. Sie kennt meinen Zwang, Stegreifvorträge halten zu müssen: "Hör endlich auf mit dieser elenden Kunsterziehung!"' (65–6).

[32] Marcel Reich-Ranicki, 'Eine Müdeheldensoße', in *Günter Grass. Aufsätze* (Zürich: Ammann, 1992), 91–101 (95).

[33] Dennis J. Enright, 'Always New Pains: Günter Grass's *Local Anaesthetic*', in Enright, *Man is an Onion: Reviews and Essays* (London: Chatto & Windus, 1972), 96–102 (97).

During this encounter, Linde remains detached, fixing her gaze on the factory chimneys in the distance: 'Sie guckt ihm über die Schulter und sieht die beiden Kamine der Krings-Werke und deren Zementstaubauswurf. Fertig. Er ist fertig!' (80). These gigantic phallic symbols (complete with ejaculations—'Auswurf') also reflect Starusch's awe at Schlottau's prodigious sexual powers.[34] Moreover, when he imagines a freezer-full of characters from his past, Starusch pictures 'Schlottau, die Hand am Geschlecht' (100), a clear signal that he equates Schlottau with sexual potency. And finally, in a paranoid fantasy in which Starusch imagines that Schlottau and Linde have disguised themselves as the dentist and his assistant, Schlottau openly demonstrates his sexuality despite the inappropriate setting of the surgery: 'Geile Vertraulichkeiten. Jetzt hat er sie ins Gesäß gekniffen' (116). Starusch's fantasies rebound on him here because these exaggerated images of sexual potency confront him with his own sexual inadequacy: the more he exaggerates his rival's sexual powers, the more unfavourably his own inferior powers compare.[35]

During the description of his fantasy career as an engineer, Starusch is keen to depict himself as socially adept: he chats amiably to Sieglinde Krings and her formidable Aunt Mathilde, observes the correct etiquette by dancing 'mehrmals aber nicht zu oft' with Linde at the cement manufacturers' ball, and shows restraint by offering her 'ein einziges Küßchen' when they part (28). This gratifying self-image is undermined even as Starusch projects it. The following sentence describes (in the third person) the way in which Starusch (here called by his American nickname Hardy) charms the cement heiress Sieglinde Krings: 'Hardy versteht es, nicht nur von Fliehkraftentstaubern, sondern auch von der Schönheit romanischer Basaltarchitektur zwischen Mayen und Andernach zu plaudern' (28). The

---

[34] It may be more than just coincidence, therefore, that Schlottau's name (which Starusch has invented) contains the word 'Schlot', denoting a very tall chimney (usually a factory chimney). Cf. the similarly phallic name which the jealous *Buch-Ich* of *Gantenbein* invents for his rival ('Einhorn').

[35] Bruce interprets the figure of Schlottau differently, arguing that Starusch uses the figure to *excuse* his own inadequacy (for what man, Bruce implies, could possibly succeed against such a sexual giant?) (Bruce, 59).

verb, 'versteht es', has positive connotations, suggesting that Starusch has a special expertise, in this case a social expertise, namely the ability to talk equally entertainingly (as implied by the verb 'plaudern') on a number of disparate subjects. However, there is a discrepancy between the impression which Starusch wants to convey, and the impression formed by the reader, which is that he is hopelessly inadequate in his attempts to relate to women. For not only are his chosen topics of conversation unlikely to charm a young woman; they also involve abstruse detail of the kind hardly compatible with social chit-chat.

The fantasy of his correct and restrained behaviour at the outset of his relationship with Linde is further undermined by an episode from Book II. Having succumbed once to his pupil Vero Lewand's sexual advances, Starusch tries to imagine himself facing up to a renewed seduction attempt with the fortitude which he has promised Scherbaum that he will exercise in future ('Ich bleibe eisern', 220). However, even in his imagination he cannot make the situation turn out as he would wish: as he practises what he would say to Vero, should she arrive on his doorstep, he struggles to disguise his sexual desire, which surfaces after only a couple of innocuous sentences: 'Wollen Sie nicht ablegen, Vero?— Wie schön, daß Sie da sind und meine Einsamkeit aufbrechen.—Ich muß Ihnen gestehen, daß ich, so groß mein Verlangen sein mag, weiterhin gewillt bin, Ihrer verwirrenden Unmittelbarkeit zu widerstehen, wenngleich ich nicht abgeneigt wäre, aber das kann soll darf wohl nicht sein' (221). Although Starusch admits his weakness for Vero in the concessive clause 'so groß mein Verlangen sein mag', the main thrust of the sentence, up to the words 'zu widerstehen', is nevertheless that he intends to resist her advances. However, this message is completely undermined by the addition of a second, stylistically superfluous, concessive clause—'wenngleich ich nicht abgeneigt wäre'—which suggests that he is not at all as convinced of the merits of restraint as he would like to appear. Similarly, although the second main clause—'aber das kann soll darf wohl nicht sein'—is an attempt to reassert the necessity of restraint, it indicates instead the confusion that Starusch feels in fighting against his evidently strong desire. 'Kann soll darf' suggests that he is searching for compelling reasons why he should not sleep with her, and 'wohl' confirms that he is not particularly convinced of these reasons himself. Subsequently, he is able to recover his equilibrium sufficiently to hold a conversation with Vero, but his mind turns inevitably to sexual subjects (Georg Forster's adulterous wife; Linde's affair with Schlottau). One final, desperate attempt to talk about neutral, technical matters (the electrics in Krings's sandbox) is to no avail and Starusch gives in. His last question appears to be an enquiry about contraception: 'Aber das sollte unter uns bleiben, Vero. Hörst du? Und muß ich wirklich nicht vorsichtig sein?' (221). Thus, even in his imagination— for this scenario is only a mental practice for a possible approach by Vero—Starusch has no control over his sexual desires.

Even Starusch's relationship with Scherbaum cannot be falsified for long. Despite Scherbaum's outstanding performance in the fantasy quiz show, which is depicted as a triumph for Starusch's inspirational history teaching, it is Scherbaum who, in another imagined scene, delivers the most stinging rebuke to Starusch. At one point in Book II, while Starusch is struggling both with Scherbaum's stubborn determination to burn his dog and with his own mixed feelings towards the plan, he prepares yet another admonitory speech to Scherbaum and rehearses it, as is his wont, in front of his shaving mirror (172). The tone of the speech is resigned, for his own experience, he says, has shown that rebellion as a teenager leads only to passivity and conservatism in later life. However, Starusch seems to have no great confidence in his own arguments and the speech ends tentatively, with the rhetorical question: 'Warum sage ich nicht: laß ihn brennen?!' In Starusch's mind, Scherbaum answers this question as follows:

Weil Sie eifersüchtig sind und selber möchten, aber nicht können. Weil mit Ihnen nichts mehr los ist. Weil Ihnen die Angst fehlt. Weil es gleichgültig ist, ob Sie es machen oder nicht. Weil Sie fertig sind. Weil Sie schon alles hinter sich haben. Weil Sie sich Ihre Zähne für später reparieren lassen. Weil Sie immer Abstand gewinnen wollen. Weil Sie sich die Folgen ausdenken, bevor Sie handeln, damit die Folgen Ihren Berechnungen entsprechen. Weil Sie sich nicht mögen. Weil Sie vernünftig sind, dabei sind Sie dumm. (173)

Since there is no reason to believe that Scherbaum has such a low opinion of his teacher (even if he occasionally shows an astute understanding of his weaknesses)[36] and since Scherbaum, for all his political passion, has been painted as a polite young man incapable of such invective, this passage must be interpreted as an expression of Starusch's self-loathing rather than as a realistic estimation of Scherbaum's likely response to such a question. In this way, Starusch's fantasies of Scherbaum's admiration for him are undermined by his (equally irrational) delusions of Scherbaum's contempt for him.

Starusch often portrays himself in his fantasies as a dynamic force, both in the world of work and in his role as the 'Verlobtenmörder'. Yet this fantasy, too, eventually turns against him. In one of his final imaginings, Starusch takes on the mantle of political activist and carries out Scherbaum's plan to burn his dog on the Ku-damm (247–9). This ought to be a moment of triumph for Starusch who, towards the end of Book II, finally comes out openly in favour of Scherbaum's plan, claiming that he would have done the same at Scherbaum's age; but his own imagined protest deteriorates into a comic interlude in which he loses all dignity. At first everything goes to plan: the dog, which has been doped with valium, remains docile while Starusch douses it with petrol. However, in the process of setting it alight, Starusch burns the palm of his hand and is reduced to blowing on it furiously but ineffectually in an attempt to dull the pain. Then, as the dog goes up in flames, Starusch is set upon by irate bystanders and beaten up, losing his spectacles in the process. After standing his ground for a few minutes, he abandons all pretence at heroism and tries to make a run for it, but is tackled and brought to the ground. He hopes to be rescued by the police, and indeed he is, but not before they have joined in the attack. Fear then gives way to embar-

---

[36] Scherbaum understands, for instance, that Starusch has difficulty translating his intentions into actions, and is therefore untroubled by his threat to report him to the police: 'Das halten Sie gar nicht durch, den Weg zum Revier und so . . . ' (145).

rassment and in a final *Pointe*, when Starusch gives his profession as 'schoolteacher', one of the policemen knocks his spectacles from his face (presumably because he considers him a disgrace to his calling). The spectacles, which had miraculously survived the tussle on the Ku-damm, are broken by the fall. In this fantasy, then, the energetic and successful man of the earlier fantasies is reduced to a clownish bungler.

One final example encapsulates the double process by means of which Starusch both controls and is controlled by his fantasies. In the course of the novel, Starusch gradually loses his hold over the figure of the dentist, whose behaviour he finds increasingly exasperating. Not only is Starusch bored by the dentist's stories and jealous of his influence over Scherbaum; the dentist also has an irritating habit of playing the psychiatrist, deconstructing Starusch's personality and exposing his inadequacies. When the dentist advises Starusch that his present sexual impotence is a direct result of his earlier defeat at the hands of his sexual rival, Schlottau (242), Starusch decides that the dentist has gone too far and launches a counter-attack, 'exposing' (that is, imagining) the dentist's guilty secret: he is a closet sweet addict, hiding himself away in the lavatory to guzzle whole bags of confectionery. Starusch projects this humiliating image onto the TV screen (the interjection 'Da!' in the following description refers to the image on the screen):

'Sie!' sagte ich, 'Sie wollen mir Hemmungen, womöglich Potenzschwierig-keiten einreden und hocken—Da!—auf dem Klo, sückeln glanzäugig Sahnebonbons, mampfen geil cremegefülltes Konfekt, sabbern Zucker-guß, sind außer sich, weil das Tütchen leer ist und greifen—Da!—sogleich nach der Orgie zum mitgeführten Aqua-Pik-Gerät, um die Spuren der übersüßen Schweinerei mit pulsierenden Wasserstößen zu vertreiben— Sie wollen Arzt sein?'. Als mein Zahnarzt versuchte, den Exzeß auf der Toilette als wissenschaftliche Erprobung des Aqua-Pik-Gerätes zu erklären, kicherte sogar seine Sprechstundenhilfe. (243)

In his fantasy then, Starusch exposes his dentist's bad faith (preaching the dangers of dental decay in public, while secretly indulging his own sweet tooth) and thereby calls into question his professional credibility. He also diagnoses the dentist's binges as a kind of surrogate sexual experience, a form of masturbation. And finally, he portrays the dentist as a man who, unable to admit graciously to his failings, feebly attempts to deny them, a ploy which merely serves to humiliate him further in front of his employee.

Several points can be made about this imaginary scene. First, this is clearly another revenge fantasy, triggered by the dentist's humiliation of Starusch (his reference to Starusch's impotence).[37] This need for revenge is the reflex of a deep insecurity, and points to Starusch's fundamental inability simply to 'be himself' regardless of how others see him or treat him. Secondly, the particular scenario which Starusch selects for his dentist's fall from grace is significant: he chooses to undermine the dentist's professional credibility because, as I have shown, he has doubts about his *own* professional credibility. He worries that he is unfit to be a teacher because of precisely the kind of double standards which he attributes to the dentist: he has violent fantasies, but is bound, as a teacher, to express a fundamental opposition to violence. The dentist's Achilles' heel is therefore a disguised version of Starusch's Achilles' heel, and Starusch's contempt for the dentist's weakness is an expression of his *self*-contempt. Should the reader fail to recognize the mechanism whereby Starusch attributes to his dentist faults of which he is aware in himself, Grass foregrounds it in the passage which follows. Here, the dentist turns the tables on Starusch, claiming to have caught his sweet tooth from his patient and forcing Starusch to admit that he gobbled two bars of chocolate in five minutes when his relationship with Scherbaum was under strain. This suggests that Starusch has chosen sweet-binges as a suitable vice to ascribe to his dentist not just because it is a damning fault in a member of the dental profession, but because he himself is familiar with the addiction and with its capacity to act as a substitute

---

[37] Peter Graves treats the dentist as an autonomous human being (rather than as Starusch's creation), writing of this scene: 'Even the dentist, that apparent epitome of cool reason, has been shown up as a man of irreconcilable inconsistencies: for all his preaching of moderation [. . .], he used to slip out of his surgery several times an hour to indulge in [. . .] a veritable orgy of caries-producing sweet-eating!' (Peter J. Graves, 'Günter Grass's *Die Blechtrommel* and *örtlich betäubt*: The Pain of Polarities', *FMLS* 9 (1973), 132–42 (141)).

for emotional fulfilment. This episode shows clearly how Starusch's imaginings backfire on him: they appear to allow him to take revenge on others, but they may just as easily take revenge on him, placing him on the defensive when he thought he was on the attack.

Clearly, Grass invites us to see the fantasies in a negative light. While Starusch may see his fantasies as a convenient way of solving life's problems without ever having to move from his chair, they offer no more than temporary gratification and, most importantly, allow him to avoid confronting and dealing with the underlying causes of his unhappiness. Starusch's fictional murders, for instance, which are designed to gratify a desire for revenge, fail to bring him any lasting relief from his rancorous feelings towards his fiancée, so that he seems condemned to invent variations on the murder indefinitely, beyond the end of the novel. After relating the final murder fantasy, in which Linde and her children meet their death in a swimming pool when a bogus lifeguard turns up the power on the wave machine, Starusch is only 'teilweise befriedigt' and 'ein wenig enttäuscht' (263). Moreover, after another murder, in which he shoots his fiancée dead, Starusch wishes he could bring her back to life. He pictures her on the television screen lying on a bier: 'meine arme Verlobte, die dreimal erschossen aufgebahrt lag [. . .]. (Wachküssen wollen! Wachküssen wollen!)' (78). The response in brackets seems to be evoked in the first place by association with the children's television programme which is being broadcast at that moment and which evidently puts Starusch in mind of the fairy-tale of Sleeping Beauty, but it also expresses Starusch's desire to 'resurrect' Linde, even though he himself has killed her. In this way, the revenge fantasies merely displace Starusch's real anxiety, which is the trauma of losing his fiancée.

In a similar way, the virility fantasy which Starusch invents in order to reassure himself of his sexual powers merely distracts attention from a more fundamental problem: his inability to relate to women as individuals with emotional needs. Even in the fantasy itself it is clear that for Starusch women are interchangeable, reduced to their sexual function. He can tell us practically nothing about the individual personalities of the housewives (though he remembers making one young woman cry when he laughed at her diary, 'das er [. . .] "Zum Brüllen komisch" fand' (89), thus showing contempt for this expression of her individuality). Indeed, he can only distinguish the women with the help of material prompts: one woman always had coffee beans, one owned a typewriter, one kept a budgerigar etc. In the following quotation, Starusch describes the occupants of the third floor of his tenement block: 'Dort sagten zwei unterschiedlich verbrauchte Frauen in verschieden gemusterten Morgenröcken: "Kommen Sie ruhig rein, junger Mann"' (89). Although the words 'unterschiedlich' and 'verschieden' superficially suggest a distinction between the two women, they draw attention, paradoxically, to the interchangeability and lack of individuality of these two women, who are important to Starusch only for the sexual function they serve.[38]

Finally, in the same way that virility fantasies are never going to cure Starusch of his maladjusted relationship to women, so his dreams about sympathetic listeners and admiring students cannot hope to cure another basic disorder: his lack of wholeness or self-reliance, which results in a need to find confirmation of his own worth and his own being through other people.[39]

It would be wrong, however, to give the impression that Grass means us to condemn Starusch outright: as in all his works Grass does not allow his readers any such comfortable feeling of moral superiority. What preserves Starusch from our contempt is partly the fact that in some of his arguments at least he has right on his side (for instance when he demonstrates the pointlessness of revolution to Scherbaum), but also the fact that he has a measure of self-knowledge and directs some of his irony against himself. For if Starusch

---

[38] For a fuller analysis of Starusch's inability to relate to women on an emotional level, see Pickar, 'Starusch im Felde mit den Frauen'. Pickar notes that Starusch never uses the word 'love' in the context of his relationships (271), treats women as objects (272), considers sexual desire to be 'unbedeutende Frauensache' (273), disparages women as innately adulterous, while boasting about his own infidelities (274), and vents his feelings of powerlessness in the face of female emotions and sexuality through real and imagined violence against women (274–7).

[39] John Reddick also notes of Starusch that 'as a result of initial failure, he has lost his wholeness and centredness of identity, and hence, too, his ability to be and act as it were "organically"' (Reddick, 'Action and Impotence', 567).

allows the dentist of his imaginings to psychoanalyse him, it is surely because he understands something of his own neuroses, and if he imagines himself repeatedly in situations which make him look ridiculous, it is, after all, his choice to do so.

5. Popular Culture and Protest Culture

The ironic dimension to Starusch's narrative provides one of several points of comparison with Frisch's *Gantenbein*, for not only do both Starusch and the *Buch-Ich* choose to expose their own folly, despite exercising ultimate control over their narratives,[40] both men also attempt to use their fantasies as a means of escaping their own inadequacies; and both find that their fictions turn against them, confronting them with aspects of their personality which they would rather repress. However, whereas Frisch is concerned only peripherally with current political affairs, Grass's novel is, first and foremost, a reckoning with the student protest movement of the late 1960s. Moreover, he also uses *örtlich betäubt* to explore the role of popular culture in contemporary society. As the following analysis will show, Starusch's fictions play an important part in Grass's presentation of these two inter-linked themes.[41]

Starusch comes into contact with popular culture partly through his visits to the dentist (he watches television in the surgery and reads magazines in the waiting-room) and partly through his school class (who readily express their popular tastes in their conversations and in their playground games). In this way, Grass is able to work into the novel examples of all the major mass media of the time—TV, cinema, advertising, posters, magazines and newspapers, comic books, and popular music—as well as a broad range of popular genres and forms which make use of these media: detective fiction,

---

[40] See pp. 81–2 above for my comments on this aspect of *Gantenbein*.
[41] For a fuller analysis of this aspect of the text, see: Chloe E. M. Paver, 'Lois Lane, Donald Duck and Joan Baez: Popular Culture and Protest Culture in Günter Grass's *örtlich betäubt*', *GLL* 50 (1997), 53–64.

adventure stories, science fiction, spy thrillers, romantic fiction, quiz shows, pin-ups, children's stories, sex-scandals, serialized (auto)biography, and protest songs. Starusch's attitude to all these popular forms is portrayed as deeply ambiguous. He publicly scorns the popular press, for instance, but reads it avidly in private;[42] and although he views popular culture from a sufficient intellectual distance to be able to parody it,[43] his fantasies (which, as I mentioned earlier, borrow extensively from popular genres) nevertheless suggest an unhealthy fascination with it. Indeed, he becomes so alarmed by his increasing addiction to popular journalism that he pleads with the dentist not to be forced to return to the waiting-room, with its stock of *Quick, Stern, Neue,* and *Bunte.* In attributing this fear to 'die Furcht vor Ihrer Flucht in immer neue Fiktionen' (109), the dentist points to the source of Starusch's fascination with popular culture: his desire for vicarious or surrogate experience. As we have already seen, Starusch is an armchair murderer, a man who is dynamic, assertive, and vengeful, but only in his imagination. Popular culture provides ideal material for his fantasies because, Grass suggests, it works in exactly the same way, offering the vicarious gratification of emotional needs and allowing people to experience fear, revenge, excitement, success, even sex, at second hand. The quiz show, to take just one example, allows the viewer to take vicarious pleasure in the success of the winners, and in Starusch's fantasy quiz show (110–13) this effect is heightened by according the victory to his darling, Scherbaum.

All this may seem a long way from the student protest movement of the late 1960s, which I claimed was at the

[42] When Scherbaum shows him the serialized memoirs of a Nazi youth leader in a popular magazine, Starusch is condescending, despite the fact that he has read the memoirs himself: 'Ich tat, als hätte ich nicht Folge um Folge gelesen: "Auch diese Lektüre wird ihre Liebhaber finden"' (183).

[43] For example, Starusch's parodic depiction of the quiz show betrays a keen observation of the genre (the compère is adept at keeping contestants' answers brief; she uses 'geschickt verbindende Worte' to lead from one item to the next; and she keeps up a bland and cheerful patter throughout, despite the irregular behaviour of one of the contestants); yet the subject of the quiz (military strategy) and the academic pedantry of its contestants (a characteristic they clearly inherit from Starusch) are deliberately and comically out of keeping with a piece of light entertainment.

heart of Grass's novel, but Grass points to important connections between popular culture and protest culture.
For instance, he uses the protest song, a genre which was
very much in vogue during the late 1960s, to explore the
meeting-point between the two cultures. In an attempt to
channel Scherbaum's anger into less aggressive activities,
Starusch suggests that his pupil write protest songs like those
of Joan Baez, or Pete Seeger and Lee Hays's 'If I had a
hammer'; but Scherbaum, who has already tried his hand at
writing political songs, reacts contemptuously to the suggestion, for he knows from experience that protest songs
merely appeal to the emotions, and offer a substitute for
action rather than inspiring action. He tells Starusch: 'Das
ist doch zum Einlullen. . . . Das bewegt doch nichts. Damit
kann man, wenn's gut geht, Geld verdienen. Drückt doch
nur auf die Tränendrüsen' (164). In the same way, Vero's
decision to replace the poster of Bob Dylan which adorns
her bedroom wall with one of Che Guevara signals that
the South American revolutionary has become just another
desirable (and highly marketable) pop icon who feeds teen-
age girls' fantasies about male hero-figures. Finally, one of
the factors which persuades Scherbaum to abandon his dog-
burning plan is the realization that this 'Happening' (like
the Roman circus with which the dentist compares it)[44] will
be a piece of popular entertainment, offering onlookers
an exciting spectacle without convincing them of the need
to intervene in political events. Grass suggests, then, that
protest culture is no different from other forms of popular
culture, not simply because it uses popular forms to dis-
seminate its messages, but because it, too, gratifies emotional
desires and offers vicarious experiences.

At the time he was working on *örtlich betäubt*, Grass was
engaged in a public debate with the student protesters of

---

[44] 'Denn was sagte Seneca über Zirkusspiele? "Aber es ist doch Pause?—So soll
man derweile [sic] den Leuten die Kehle durchschneiden, damit wenigstens etwas
geschieht!"—Ein ähnlicher Pausenfüller ist das Feuer: Öffentliche Verbrennungen
schrecken nicht ab, sondern befriedigen Lust' (130). This sentiment was echoed
by Grass in an interview with the journalist Günter Schäble in which he explained:
'Auch Selbstverbrennungen sind keine "vernünftigen" Taten—sie haben vielmehr
verheerende Folgen, weil sie Emotionen befriedigen' ('Die Ideologien haben
versagt', *Werkausgabe*, X. 59–62 (60)).

his home city, Berlin.[45] While expressing sympathy for the students' demands for university reform and applauding their protests against American involvement in Vietnam, he remained critical of the radical student organization, the SDS, which he suspected of using legitimate, democratic protests as a platform for spreading its particularly aggressive brand of revolutionary Marxism. *Örtlich betäubt* can be read, then, as a response to the radical student wing, a warning, not just against Marxism, but against all utopian and extremist movements.[46] Both in his political speeches and in his literary works (perhaps most clearly in his next prose work, *Aus dem Tagebuch einer Schnecke*), Grass offers the reformist programme of the Social Democrats, with its commitment to gradual progress, as a humane alternative to such movements. He readily admits that this is not the glamorous or exciting option. Social Democracy is not the stuff of thrillers or adventure stories, and it is unlikely to produce politicians who can rival Che Guevara as a teenagers' pin-up. Yet for Grass this is precisely where its merit lies: it is because Social Democracy does not gratify our desires that it remains humane. Although Starusch will always derive more satisfaction from fantasies about rampaging bulldozers and burning department stores than from contemplating the mundane practicalities of small-scale political reform, he recognizes nevertheless the need to commit himself to such reform.

Like Johnson, Frisch, Wolf, and Becker, Grass is concerned with the stories which ordinary people tell about themselves and their pasts. Like these authors he sees our desire to reconstruct our past, and our need to fantasize, as fundamental to human nature. Yet he also demonstrates,

---

[45] For details of Grass's encounters with Berlin students, see Heinz Ludwig Arnold and Franz Josef Görtz (eds.), *Günter Grass: Dokumente zur politischen Wirkung* (Munich: Boorberg (Edition Text + Kritik), 1971), 96–108.

[46] Hanspeter Brode has also considered the part played by *örtlich betäubt* in Grass's response to the student protest movement, noting that Grass correctly predicted the speed with which the movement would peter out. He also highlights the difficulty of pinpointing Grass's position in *örtlich betäubt*, given that each of the main characters appears to share Grass's views to some extent, yet each also embodies attitudes which Grass would clearly question (Hanspeter Brode, 'Von Danzig zur Bundesrepublik. Grass' Bücher *örtlich betäubt* und *Aus dem Tagebuch einer Schnecke*', in Arnold, *Günter Grass* (1978), 74–87).

more clearly than all the other authors except perhaps Johnson, the dangers of fantasy. As a witness to the Nazi years, Grass knew what could happen when a perfectly natural human desire for vicarious experience was exploited by an extremist political movement. He was therefore committed to warning contemporary Germans of the very real dangers inherent in allowing extremist political movements to feed their fantasies. Grass freely admits, through Starusch, that the position of one who has seen it all before and knows better is not always a gratifying one and that it may be tainted by envy ('Bist ja nur neidisch, weil die so links und lustig sein dürfen' (190)), but he maintains his position nevertheless.

CONCLUSION

Daß andere [Schriftsteller] genau das Gegenteil tun, beun-
ruhigt mich so wenig wie es mich beruhigt, wenn andere
etwas Ähnliches unternehmen. Zu vergleichen, denke ich, ist
Sache der Kritik. (Frisch, 'Ich schreibe für Leser')

The narrative strategy which is identified in this study as
'overt fictionalizaton' and which enjoyed a particular popularity in German fiction of the 1960s[1] is characterized by a
specific set of stylistic and structural devices: the projection,
variation, and cancellation of fictional possibilities, the foregrounding of choices faced by the narrator (at each of the
'forks' in the narrative), and the use of *Konjunktiv II* and
modal auxiliaries to indicate supposition and possibility.
While it might seem reasonable to assume that such a strategy will destroy the illusion of reality in a novel, it appears
to do so only temporarily, as the reader quickly becomes
immersed in each new fictional episode and experiences it
as real: such is the power of fiction.

My analysis has not focused solely on the formal aspects of
this technique. I have also explored the particular significance of the narrator's fictions and fantasies in five major
post-war novels; and while each of the five authors tackles a
different subject-matter, certain common thematic concerns
emerge. All five authors are interested in the kinds of stories
which ordinary people tell about themselves and their pasts
(rather than in the imaginative visions of outsider figures
such as artists and madmen). All five are concerned with our
tendency to rewrite our past, to create coherent (and usually
self-flattering or reassuring) stories out of the chaotic (and
often disturbing) material of our past life. In Frisch's words:

---

[1] Apart from the five texts studied here, other examples include Peter Bichsel's
Die Jahreszeiten (Darmstadt and Neuwied: Luchterhand, 1967) and Martin Walser's
Das Einhorn (Frankfurt/Main: Suhrkamp, 1966) and *Fiction* (Frankfurt/Main: Suhrkamp, 1970). Petersen identifies similar techniques in Dieter Kühn's *Die Präsidentin*
(1973) and in Peter Härtling's *Hölderlin* (1976).

'Jeder Mensch erfindet sich früher oder später eine Geschichte, die er für sein Leben hält [. . .] oder eine ganze Reihe von Geschichten.'[2] While none of the five authors condemns this tendency outright (each portrays it as something innately human and therefore understandable), Wolf offers—in the narrator of *Christa T.*—a positive alternative to this method of dealing with the past. She invites us to admire her narrator's courage in confronting painful, repressed memories and in admitting to her own past failings; and also to applaud her imaginative transformation of the past, which aims to throw Christa T.'s special qualities into relief, rather than to flatter her own self-image. Although Becker's narrator transforms the past into neatly rounded anecdotes, his persistent focus on human frailty, on 'the unheroic, those who were afraid, who were apathetic, the insignificant, the cowards',[3] means that he does not offer a reassuring picture of the past, but forces his readers to acknowledge and accept human weaknesses. Where he does transform the past for the better (in punishing the sentry or in imagining Herschel Schtamm comforting the deportees), he is driven to do so by a spirit of humanity. In this way both narrators offer positive examples of the power of a morally informed imagination.

In contrast, Johnson and Grass stress the negative aspects of our urge to rewrite the past. Johnson shows that as Achim's private life and public persona begin to diverge he is obliged to erase parts of his past from the official record of his life, leading to a loss of integrity which damages his relationships with others. In *örtlich betäubt*, both Starusch and his fictional invention Ferdinand Krings offer negative examples of an excessively revisionist attitude to the past. While Krings attempts to transform losses on the battlefield into victories, Starusch attempts to transform his own past failures into successes, triumphing over the fiancée who left him by demonizing and murdering her in his fantasies. Like Achim, Starusch suffers a loss of integrity as his public and private personae become estranged. Moreover, Grass shows that in attempting to create a more gratifying identity for

---

[2] *Mein Name sei Gantenbein*, in Frisch, *Werke*, V. 49.
[3] Jurek Becker, 'Resistance in *Jakob der Lügner*', *Seminar*, 19 (1983), 269-73 (271).

himself Starusch becomes addicted to escapist fantasies which prevent him from confronting the sources of his un-happiness and which can lead to political (as well as per-sonal) violence.

Frisch's exploration of the problem of the stories which we tell about ourselves is slightly more complex. Since he believes that we are more than just the sum of our actions (that is, more than just the image which other people have of us), he wants to preserve the individual's right to include their 'Nicht-Taten' in the stories which they tell about their lives. He considers that since every story which we tell about ourselves is in any case a fiction (that is, a selective and often distorted account of our actions which usually shows us in a favourable light), it must be permissible to include in our account of ourselves some of our unrealized possibilities. This would allow us to resist the fixed images which others have of us (and which are based solely on our 'Taten'). In theory then, the fictional actions of Enderlin, Gantenbein, and Svoboda are as much a part of the *Buch-Ich*'s individu-ality as are the actions which he has performed in real life. In practice, however, the *Buch-Ich*'s imaginings are not pre-sented in so positive a light. Like Starusch, he indulges in escapist fantasies which allow him to avoid confronting fun-damental disorders in his personality.

Finally, my analysis suggests a correlation between the power which these narrators exercise over their fictions and their impotence in real life. Becker's narrator, for instance, has suffered years of powerlessness as an inhabitant of the ghetto, ruled by a totalitarian regime. Nevertheless, in his fictions he is able to exercise power over the past, punishing the sentry who plays a trick on Jakob, comforting Jews on their way to the death camps, and shaping the disordered reality of the past into aesthetically satisfying stories. Simi-larly, the narrator of *Nachdenken über Christa T.* is powerless to stop the progress of Christa T.'s illness and, once her friend is dead, powerless to make amends to her for the dismissive attitude which she showed her during her lifetime. Yet in her fictions she is able to transform the past, to create a past in which Christa T. might have lived more happily, strength-ened and encouraged by a sympathetic environment which could have given her the will to live. At the same time, my analysis has shown that the narrators' power is strictly limited. The narrators of both *Mein Name sei Gantenbein* and *örtlich betäubt* attempt to use the power of their imagination to escape their personalities (which they are in reality powerless to change); yet both find that their control over their fictions is a tenuous one, for their fantasies are always liable to turn against them and confront them with unpleasant truths about themselves which they would rather repress.

BIBLIOGRAPHY

The following bibliography lists the works which I found useful in the preparation of this book. None of the individual bibliographies is intended to be comprehensive, but in each case I have recommended sources of further bibliographical information. In addition to these sources, I recommend Heinz Ludwig Arnold (ed.), *Kritisches Lexikon zur deutschsprachigen Gegenwartsliteratur* (Munich: Edition Text und Kritik, 1978–) which contains detailed and periodically updated bibliographies on each of the five authors examined here.

I have treated volumes of the periodical *Text und Kritik* as monographs, because I have found that libraries tend to catalogue and shelve them as such. Some libraries may, however, shelve them as a periodical, in which case the reader should simply extract the volume number and year of publication from my references.

I. NARRATOLOGY AND THE POST-WAR GERMAN NOVEL

ARNOLD, H. L., and T. BUCK (eds.), *Positionen im deutschen Roman der sechziger Jahre* (Munich: Boorberg, 1974).

BARTHES, ROLAND, *Le Degré zéro de l'écriture* (Paris: Editions du Seuil, 1953).

BATT, KURT, *Die Exekution des Erzählers: westdeutsche Romane zwischen 1968 und 1972* (Frankfurt/Main: Fischer, 1974).

BENJAMIN, WALTER, 'Der Erzähler. Betrachtungen zum Werk Nikolai Lesskows', *Orient und Occident. Staat—Gesellschaft—Kirche. Blätter für Theologie und Soziologie*, new series, 3 (1936), 16–33 (repr. in Benjamin, *Gesammelte Schriften*, ed. Rolf Tiedemann and Hermann Schweppenhäuser, 7 vols. (Frankfurt/Main: Suhrkamp, 1974–89), II. 2 (1977), 438–65).

BICHSEL, PETER, *Die Jahreszeiten* (Darmstadt and Neuwied: Luchterhand, 1967)'.

BOA, ELIZABETH, and J. H. REID, *Critical Strategies: German Fiction in the Twentieth Century* (London: Arnold, 1972).

BOTHEROYD, PAUL F., *Ich und Er: First and Third Person Self-Reference and Problems of Identity in Three Contemporary German-Language Novels* (The Hague and Paris: Mouton, 1976).

BROOKE-ROSE, CHRISTINE, *A Rhetoric of the Unreal: Studies in Narrative and Structure, Especially of the Fantastic* (Cambridge: Cambridge University Press, 1981).

BULLIVANT, KEITH (ed.), *The Modern German Novel* (Leamington Spa, Hamburg, and New York: Berg, 1987).

—— (ed.), *After the 'Death of Literature': West German Writing of the 1970s* (Oxford, New York, and Munich: Berg, 1989).

CHAMBERS, ROSS, *Story and Situation: Narrative Seduction and the Power of Fiction* (Minneapolis: University of Minnesota Press, 1984).

D'HAEN, THEO, 'Postmodern Fiction: Form and Function', *Neophilologus*, 71 (1987), 144–53.

DURZAK, MANFRED, *Der deutsche Roman der Gegenwart* (Stuttgart: Kohlhammer, 1971).

EINHORN, BARBARA, *Der Roman in der DDR 1949–1969: Die Gestaltung des Verhältnisses von Individuum und Gesellschaft. Eine Analyse der Erzählstruktur* (Kronberg/Ts.: Scriptor, 1978).

FELLMANN, FERDINAND, 'Poetische Existentialien der Postmoderne', *DVLG* 63 (1989), 751–63.

HAMBURGER, KÄTE, *Die Logik der Dichtung* (Stuttgart: Klett, 1957), rev. edn. 1968 (repr. Munich: dtv, 1987).

HARVEY, DAVID, *The Condition of Postmodernity: An Enquiry into the Origins of Cultural Change* (Oxford: Blackwell, 1989).

HINTON THOMAS, R., and WILFRIED VAN DER WILL, *The German Novel and the Affluent Society* (Manchester: Manchester University Press, 1968).

—— and KEITH BULLIVANT, *Literature in Upheaval: West German Writers and the Challenge of the 1960s* (Manchester: Manchester University Press, 1974).

HOLTHUSEN, HANS EGON, 'Heimweh nach Geschichte. Postmoderne und Posthistoire in der Literatur der Gegenwart', *Merkur*, 38 (1984), 902–17.

HONNETH, AXEL, 'Der Affekt gegen das Allgemeine. Zu Lyotards Konzept der Postmoderne', *Merkur*, 38 (1984), 893–902.

HUYSSEN, ANDREAS, *After the Great Divide: Modernism, Mass Culture and Postmodernism* (London: Macmillan, 1988).

INGARDEN, ROMAN, *The Literary Work of Art* (Evanston, Ill.: Northwestern University Press, 1973).

JEFFERSON, ANN, *The nouveau roman and the Poetics of Fiction* (Cambridge: Cambridge University Press, 1980).

KLATT, GUDRUN, 'Moderne und Postmoderne im Streit zwischen Jean-François Lyotard und Jürgen Habermas', *WB* 35 (1989), 271–92.

KOSKELLA, GRETEL A., *Die Krise des deutschen Romans: 1960–1970* (Frankfurt/Main: Fischer, 1986).

KURZ, PAUL K., 'Die Verkomplizierung des Erzählens im heutigen Roman', *Welt und Wort*, 22 (1967), 118–19.

LÄMMERT, EBERHARD, *Bauformen des Erzählens* (Stuttgart: Metzler, 1955).

—— et al. (eds.), *Romantheorie. Dokumentation ihrer Geschichte in Deutschland seit 1880* (Königstein/Ts.: Athenäum, 1984).

LODGE, DAVID, *The Modes of Modern Writing: Metaphor, Metonymy and the Typology of Modern Literature* (London: Arnold, 1977).

MCHALE, BRIAN, *Postmodernist Fiction* (London: Methuen, 1987) (repr. London: Routledge, 1989).

MANN, THOMAS, *Bekenntnisse des Hochstaplers Felix Krull* (Frankfurt/Main: Fischer, 1954).

NEUHAUS, VOLKER, *Typen multiperspektivischen Erzählens* (Cologne: Böhlau, 1971).

PETERSEN, JÜRGEN H., 'Die Preisgabe des Erzählten als Fiktion. Zur Wesensbestimmung modernen Erzählens am Beispiel des deutschen Romans der sechziger und siebziger Jahre', *Zeitschrift für Kulturaustausch*, 34 (1984), 112–19.

REID, J. H., *Writing Without Taboos: The New East German Literature* (New York, Oxford, and Munich: Berg, 1990).

SCHMID-BORTENSCHLAGER, SIGRID, *Konstruktive Literatur. Gesellschaftliche Relevanz und literarische Tradition experimenteller Prosa-Großformen im deutschen, englischen und französischen Sprachraum nach 1945* (Bonn: Bouvier, 1985).

SCHOBER, WOLFGANG HEINZ, *Erzähltechniken in Romanen. Eine Untersuchung erzähltechnischer Probleme in zeitgenössischen deutschen Romanen* (Wiesbaden: Athenaion, 1975).

SCHOLL, JOACHIM, *In der Gemeinschaft des Erzählers. Studien zur Restitution des Epischen im deutschen Gegenwartsroman* (Heidelberg: Winter, 1990).

SCHRAMKE, JÜRGEN, *Zur Theorie des modernen Romans* (Munich: Beck, 1974).

STANZEL, FRANZ K., *Typische Formen des Romans* (Göttingen: Vandenhoeck & Ruprecht, 1964).

—— *Theorie des Erzählens* (Göttingen: Vandenhoeck & Ruprecht, 1979), 4th edn. 1989.

TATE, DENNIS, *The East German Novel: Identity, Community, Continuity* (Bath: Bath University Press, 1984).

VESTER, HEINZ-GÜNTER, 'Konjunktur der Konjekturen. Postmodernität bei Pynchon, Eco, Strauß', *L80*, no.34 (1985), 11–28.

WALSER, MARTIN, *Das Einhorn* (Frankfurt/Main: Suhrkamp, 1966).

—— *Fiction* (Frankfurt/Main: Suhrkamp, 1970).

WAUGH, PATRICIA, *Metafiction: The Theory and Practice of Self-Conscious Fiction* (London: Methuen, 1984).

WELLAUER, CAROLYN ANN, 'The Postwar German Novel of Speculations' (unpublished doctoral diss., University of Wisconsin, 1976).

ZIOLKOWSKI, THEODORE, 'Der Blick von der Irrenanstalt: Verrückung der Perspektive in der modernen deutschen Prosa', *Neophilologus*, 51 (1967), 42–54.

2. UWE JOHNSON: *DAS DRITTE BUCH ÜBER ACHIM*

PRIMARY SOURCES

Literary Works

Mutmaßungen über Jakob (Frankfurt/Main: Suhrkamp, 1959).

Das dritte Buch über Achim (Frankfurt/Main: Suhrkamp, 1961).

Karsch, und andere Prosa (Frankfurt/Main: Suhrkamp, 1964).

Zwei Ansichten (Frankfurt/Main: Suhrkamp, 1965).

Jahrestage. Aus dem Leben von Gesine Cresspahl, 4 vols. (Frankfurt/Main: Suhrkamp, 1970–83).

'Skizze eines Verunglückten', in Siegfried Unseld (ed.), *Begegnungen. Eine Festschrift für Max Frisch zum siebzigsten Geburtstag* (Frankfurt/Main: Suhrkamp, 1981), 69–107.

Essays and Speeches

'Berliner Stadtbahn', *Merkur*, 15 (1961), 722–33 (repr. in Johnson, *Berliner Sachen. Aufsätze* (Frankfurt/Main: Suhrkamp, 1975), 7–21; extracts repr. in Eberhard Lämmert *et al.* (eds.), *Romantheorie. Dokumentation ihrer Geschichte in Deutschland seit 1880* (Königstein/Ts.: Athenäum, 1984), 334–7).

[Büchner Prize acceptance speech, 1971], in *Büchner-Preis-Reden 1951–71* (Stuttgart: Reclam, 1972), 217–40.

Begleitumstände. Frankfurter Vorlesungen (Frankfurt/Main: Suhrkamp, 1980).

'Vorschläge zur Prüfung eines Romans', in Eberhard Lämmert *et al.* (eds.), *Romantheorie. Dokumentation ihrer Geschichte in Deutschland seit 1880* (Königstein/Ts.: Athenäum, 1984), 398–403.

Interviews

BIENEK, HORST, [interview with Johnson], *FH* 17 (1962), 33–42 (repr. in Bienek, *Werkstattgespräche mit Schriftstellern* (Munich: Hanser, 1962), 85–98, and in Fahlke, 194–207; extracts repr. in Gerlach and Richter, *Uwe Johnson*, 143–6).

DURZAK, MANFRED, 'Dieser langsame Weg zu einer größeren Genauigkeit. Gespräch mit Uwe Johnson', in Durzak, *Gespräche über den Roman. Formbestimmungen und Analysen* (Frankfurt/Main: Suhrkamp, 1976), 428–60.

FAHLKE, EBERHARD (ed.), *'Ich überlege mir die Geschichte . . . '. Uwe Johnson im Gespräch* (Frankfurt/Main: Suhrkamp, 1988).

NEUSÜSS, ARNHELM, 'Über die Schwierigkeiten beim Schreiben der Wahrheit. Gespräch mit Uwe Johnson', *Konkret*, 8 (1962), 18–19 (repr. in Gerlach and Richter, *Uwe Johnson*, 39–48; and in Fahlke, 184–93).

POST-ADAMS, REE, 'Antworten von Uwe Johnson. Ein Gespräch mit dem Autor', *German Quarterly*, 50 (1977), 241–7 (repr. in Fahlke, 273–80).

SCHWARZ, WILHELM JOHANNES, 'Gespräche mit Uwe Johnson', in Schwarz, *Der Erzähler Uwe Johnson*, 86–98 (repr. in Fahlke, 234–47).

SECONDARY LITERATURE

ARNOLD, HEINZ LUDWIG (ed.), *Uwe Johnson*, Text und Kritik, 65/66 (Munich: Edition Text und Kritik, 1980).

BAUMGART, REINHARD, *Das dritte Buch über Achim*, NDH (1962), 146–8 (repr. in Fellinger, *Über Uwe Johnson*, 97–102).

—— (ed.), *Über Uwe Johnson* (Frankfurt/Main: Suhrkamp, 1970).

BOTHEROYD, PAUL F., *Ich und Er: First and Third Person Self-Reference and Problems of Identity in Three Contemporary German-Language Novels* (The Hague and Paris: Mouton, 1976), 62–94.

BOULBY, MARK, *Uwe Johnson* (New York: Ungar, 1974), 37–65.

BURKHARD, JÜRG, *Uwe Johnsons Bild der DDR-Gesellschaft. 'Das dritte Buch über Achim'. Romaninterpretation* (Bonn: Bouvier, 1988).

BUTLER, GEOFFREY P., '"Mr Karsch" at Twenty-One. Some Comments on *The Third Book About Achim* and its Source', *Internationales Uwe-Johnson-Forum*, 1 (1989), 114–21.

COCK, MARY E., 'Uwe Johnson: An Interpretation of Two Novels', *MLR* 69 (1974), 348–58.

DILLER, EDWARD, 'Uwe Johnson's Karsch: Language as a Reflection of the two Germanies', *MDU* 60 (1968), 35–9.

DURZAK, MANFRED, 'Die Unbeschreibbarkeit des Vorgeschriebenen: *Das Dritte Buch über Achim*', in Durzak, *Der deutsche Roman der Gegenwart* (Stuttgart and Berlin: Kohlhammer, 1971), 195–212.

FELLINGER, RAIMUND (ed.), *Über Uwe Johnson* (Frankfurt/Main: Suhrkamp, 1992).

FICKERT, KURT, *Neither Left nor Right: The Politics of Individualism in Uwe Johnson's Work* (New York: Peter Lang, 1987), 55–73.

—— 'The Reunification Theme in Johnson's *Das dritte Buch über Achim*', *German Studies Review*, 16 (1993), 225–33.

FRIES, ULRICH, 'Überlegungen zu Johnsons zweitem Buch. Politischer Hintergrund und epische Verarbeitung', *Johnson-Jahrbuch*, 2 (1995), 206–29.

FUJIMOTO, ATSUO, 'Verfremdungselemente in Uwe Johnsons Roman *Das dritte Buch über Achim*', *Internationales Uwe-Johnson-Forum*, 1 (1989), 122–33.

GERLACH, RAINER, and MATTHIAS RICHTER (eds.), *Uwe Johnson* (Frankfurt/Main: Suhrkamp, 1984).

GOOD, COLIN H., 'Uwe Johnson's Treatment of the Narrative in *Mutmaßungen über Jakob*', *GLL* 24 (1971), 358–70.

JENS, WALTER, 'Johnson auf der Schwelle der Meisterschaft', *Die Zeit*, 6 October 1961 (repr. in Baumgart, *Über Uwe Johnson*, 108–14; and in Gerlach and Richter, *Uwe Johnson*, 147–51).

MAATJE, FRANK C., 'Die Projektion eines räumlichen Gegensatzes in einen zeitlichen in Uwe Johnsons Roman *Das dritte Buch über Achim*', in Maatje, *Der Doppelroman: Eine literatursystematische Studie über duplikative Erzählstrukturen* (Groningen: Wolters, 1964), 92–7.

MIGNER, KARL, 'Uwe Johnson, *Das dritte Buch über Achim*. Methodische Hinweise zu seiner Erarbeitung', *Der Deutschunterricht*, 16/2 (1964), 17–25.

OPALKA, HUBERTUS, 'Erzählstruktur als phänomenologisch gedeutete Handlungsstruktur, dargestellt an *Das dritte Buch über Achim*', in Manfred Jurgensen (ed.), *Johnson. Ansichten. Einsichten. Aussichten* (Berne: Francke, 1989), 21–40.

PESTALOZZI, KARL, 'Achim alias Täve Schur. Uwe Johnsons zweiter Roman und seine Vorlage', *Sprache im technischen Zeitalter* (1962-3), 479–86 (repr. in Gerlach and Richter, *Uwe Johnson*, 152–63).

PIWITT, HERMANN PETER, 'Chronik und Protokoll. Uwe Johnson, *Das dritte Buch über Achim*', *Sprache im technischen Zeitalter* (1961-2), 83–6.

POST-ADAMS, REE, *Uwe Johnson. Darstellungsproblematik als Romanthema in 'Mutmaßungen über Jakob' und 'Das dritte Buch über Achim'* (Bonn: Bouvier, 1977) (extracts from the chapter on *Achim* repr. as 'Explizite Erzählreflexion: *Das dritte Buch über Achim*', in Gerlach and Richter, *Uwe Johnson*, 165–79).

REICH-RANICKI, MARCEL, 'Registrator Johnson', in Reich-Ranicki, *Deutsche Literatur in West und Ost. Prosa seit 1945* (Munich: Piper, 1963), 231–46 (repr. in Fellinger *Über Uwe Johnson*, 103–15).

RIEDEL, INGRID, 'Johnsons Darstellungsmittel und der Kubismus', in Baumgart, *Über Uwe Johnson*, 59–74.

RIORDAN, COLIN, *The Ethics of Narration. Uwe Johnson's Novels from 'Ingrid Babendererde' to 'Jahrestage'*, Bithell Series of Dissertations, 14 (London: Modern Humanities Research Association, 1989), 3–62.

SCHMITZ, WALTER, *Uwe Johnson*, Autorenbücher, 43 (Munich: Beck, 1984), 49–66.

SCHOBER, WOLFGANG HEINZ, *Erzähltechniken in Romanen. Eine Untersuchung erzähltechnischer Probleme in zeitgenössischen deutschen Romanen* (Wiesbaden: Athenaion, 1975), 119–23.

SCHOLL, JOACHIM, 'Wie entsteht Literatur? *Das dritte Buch über Achim*', in Scholl, *In der Gemeinschaft des Erzählers. Studien zur Restitution des Epischen im deutschen Gegenwartsroman* (Heidelberg: Winter, 1990), 125–37.

SCHWARZ, WILHELM JOHANNES, *Der Erzähler Uwe Johnson* (Berne and Munich: Francke, 1970).

STREHLOW, WOLFGANG, 'Uwe Johnsons Prosa, gelesen in Zeiten des Umbruchs. Am Beispiel des Romans *Das dritte Buch über Achim*', in Carsten

Gansel and Jürgen Grambow (eds.), *Biographie ist unwiderruflich. Materialien des Kolloquiums zum Werk Uwe Johnsons im Dezember 1990 in Neubrandenburg* (Frankfurt/Main, Berlin and Berne: Peter Lang, 1992), 97–106.

—— *Ästhetik des Widerspruchs. Versuche über Uwe Johnsons dialektische Schreibweise* (Berlin: Akademie, 1993), 179–228.

ULLRICH, GISELA, *Identität und Rolle: Probleme des Erzählens bei Johnson, Walser, Frisch und Fichte* (Stuttgart: Klett, 1977), 16–32 (repr. in Fellinger, *Über Uwe Johnson*, 116–38).

WATT, RODERICK H., 'Uwe Johnson's Use of Documentary Material and Style in *Das dritte Buch über Achim*', *FMLS* 13 (1977), 240–52.

Wiegenstein, Roland, 'Die Grenze des Uwe Johnson', *FH* 20 (1965), 795–7.

VAN DER WILL, WILFRIED, 'Approaches to Reality through Narrative Perspectives in Johnson's Prose', in Keith Bullivant (ed.), *The Modern German Novel* (Leamington Spa, Hamburg, and New York: Berg, 1987), 171–95.

WÜNDERICH, ERICH, *Uwe Johnson* (Berlin: Colloquium, 1973), 28–41.

FURTHER BIBLIOGRAPHICAL INFORMATION

RIEDEL, NICOLAI, *Uwe Johnson Bibliographie 1959–1980. Band 1: Das schriftstellerische Werk und seine Rezeption in literaturwissenschaftlicher Forschung und feuilletonistischer Kritik in der Bundesrepublik Deutschland* (Bonn: Bouvier, 1981). For index to works on *Achim* see 281–2.

—— *Uwe Johnson Bibliographie 1959–1977. Band 2: Das schriftstellerische Werk in fremdsprachigen Textausgaben und seine internationale Rezeption in literaturwissenschaftlicher Forschung und Zeitungskritik* (Bonn: Bouvier, 1978). For index to works on *Achim* see 104–5.

—— 'Kommentierte Auswahlbibliographie 1959–1979', in Arnold, *Uwe Johnson*, 120–6.

RIORDAN, *The Ethics of Narration*, 236–42.

3. MAX FRISCH: *MEIN NAME SEI GANTENBEIN*

PRIMARY SOURCES

Complete Works

Gesammelte Werke in zeitlicher Folge, ed. Hans Mayer in collaboration with Walter Schmitz, 6 vols. (Frankfurt/Main: Suhrkamp, 1976). Hereafter referred to as *Werke*.

Literary works

Tagebuch 1946–1949 (Zurich: Atlantis, 1947).
Stiller (Frankfurt/Main: Suhrkamp, 1954).
Homo Faber. Ein Bericht (Frankfurt/Main: Suhrkamp, 1957).
Mein Name sei Gantenbein (Frankfurt/Main: Suhrkamp, 1964) (repr. in *Werke*, V. 5–320). English translation: *A Wilderness of Mirrors*, trans. Michael Bullock (London: Methuen, 1965).
Biografie. Ein Spiel (Frankfurt: Suhrkamp, 1967) (premièred 1 February 1968, Zurich Schauspielhaus).
Tagebuch 1966–1971 (Frankfurt: Suhrkamp, 1972).
Montauk (Frankfurt/Main: Suhrkamp, 1975).
Blaubart (Frankfurt/Main: Suhrkamp, 1982).

Essays and Letters

'Unsere Gier nach Geschichten', *Weltwoche*, 4 November 1960 (repr. in *Werke*, IV. 263).
'Ich schreibe für Leser: Antworten auf vorgestellte Fragen', *Dichten und Trachten*, 24 (1964), 7–23 (repr. in *Werke*, V. 323–34).
Dramaturgisches: Ein Briefwechsel mit Walter Höllerer (Berlin, FRG: Literarisches Colloquium, 1969).

Interviews

ARNOLD, HEINZ LUDWIG, 'Gespräch mit Max Frisch', in Arnold, *Gespräche mit Schriftstellern. Max Frisch, Günter Grass, Wolfgang Koeppen, Max von der Grün, Günter Wallraff* (Munich: Beck, 1975), 9–73.
BIENEK, HORST, [interview with Frisch], in Bienek, *Werkstattgespräche mit Schriftstellern* (Munich: Hanser, 1962), 21–32.

SECONDARY LITERATURE

ARNOLD, HEINZ LUDWIG, 'Möglichkeiten nicht möglicher Existenzen: Max Frischs Roman *Mein Name sei Gantenbein*', *Eckart-Jahrbuch* (1964-5), 298–305 (repr. in Arnold, *Brauchen wir noch die Literatur? Zur literarischen Situation in der Bundesrepublik* (Düsseldorf: Bertelsmann, 1972), 138–42).
—— (ed.), *Max Frisch*, Text und Kritik, 47/8, (Munich: Edition Text und Kritik, 1975), 2nd rev. edn. 1976.
BAUMGART, REINHARD, 'Othello als Hamlet', *Der Spiegel*, 2 September 1964 (repr. in Beckermann, *Über Max Frisch*, 192–7).
BECKERMANN, THOMAS (ed.), *Über Max Frisch* (Frankfurt/Main: Suhrkamp, 1971).
BIER, JEAN PAUL, 'Ein Beitrag zur Deutung von Max Frischs letztem Roman *Mein Name sei Gantenbein*', *RLV* 33 (1967), 607–14.
BIRMELE, JUTTA, 'Anmerkungen zu Max Frischs Roman *Mein Name sei*

Gantenbein', *MDU* 60 (1968), 167–73 (repr. in Schau, *Max Frisch. Beiträge zur Wirkungsgeschichte*, 107–12).

BODINE, JAY F., and GERHARD F. PROBST (eds.), *Perspectives on Max Frisch* (Lexington, Ky.: University of Kentucky Press, 1982).

BOTHEROYD, PAUL, *Ich und Er: First and Third-Person Self-Reference and Problems of Identity in Three Contemporary German-Language Novels* (The Hague and Paris: Mouton, 1976), 95–122.

BUTLER, MICHAEL, *The Novels of Max Frisch* (London: Wolff, 1976), 121–50.

CAUVIN, MARIUS, 'Max Frisch, l'absolu et le nouveau roman', *EG* 22 (1967), 93–8 (repr. in Schau, *Max Frisch. Beiträge zur Wirkungsgeschichte*, 113–18; and as 'Max Frisch, das Absolute und der *Nouveau roman*', trans. Kitty Ausländer, in Schmitz, *Über Max Frisch II*, 335–44).

COCK, MARY E., '"Countries of the Mind": Max Frisch's Narrative Technique', *MLR* 65 (1970), 820–8.

CUNLIFFE, W. GORDON, 'Die Kunst, ohne Geschichte abzuschwimmen. Existenzialistisches Strukturprinzip in *Stiller*, *Homo Faber* und *Mein Name sei Gantenbein'*, in Knapp, *Max Frisch. Aspekte des Prosawerks*, 103–22.

FARNER, KONRAD, 'Mein Name sei Frisch', *SF* 18 (1966), 273–8.

GOCKEL, HEINZ, *Max Frisch. Gantenbein: das offen-artistische Erzählen* (Bonn: Bouvier, 1976).

HANHART, TILDY, *Max Frisch: Zufall, Rolle und literarische Form. Interpretationen zu seinem neueren Werk* (Kronberg/Ts.: Scriptor, 1976), 27–56.

HARTUNG, RUDOLF, 'Max Frisch, Mein Name sei Gantenbein', *NR* 75 (1964), 682–6.

HEIDENREICH, SYBILLE, *Max Frisch. 'Mein Name sei Gantenbein', 'Montauk', 'Stiller'. Untersuchungen und Anmerkungen* (Hollfeld: Beyer, 1976), 75–102.

HILLEN, GERD, 'Autor und Öffentlichkeit in existentieller Sicht. Ein Kommentar zu Max Frischs *Mein Name sei Gantenbein'*, *CG* 20 (1987), 338–56.

HOLTHUSEN, HANS EGON, 'Ein Mann von fünfzig Jahren', *Merkur*, 18 (1964), 1073–7 (repr. in Schau, *Max Frisch. Beiträge zur Wirkungsgeschichte*, 121–5).

HORN, PETER, '"Keine Zukunft . . . keine Wiederholung . . . keine Geschichte". Das spontane, akausale Ereignis und die Diskontinuität des erkennenden und moralischen Ichs in Max Frischs *Mein Name sei Gantenbein'*, in Heinz Rupp and Hans-Gert Roloff (eds.), *Akten des VI. internationalen Germanisten-Kongresses, Basel 1980*, 4 vols. (Berne: Peter Lang, 1980), IV. 180–5.

JURGENSEN, MANFRED, *Max Frisch. Die Romane* (Berne: Francke, 1972), 177–230 (this chapter repr. in Schau, *Max Frisch. Beiträge zur Wirkungsgeschichte*, 126–61).

KNAPP, GERHARD P. (ed.), *Studien zum Werk Max Frischs*, 2 vols. (Berne,

Frankfurt/Main and Las Vegas: Peter Lang, 1978–9), I: *Max Frisch. Aspekte des Prosawerks* (1978).

KRAFT, MARTIN, *Studien zur Thematik von Max Frischs Roman 'Mein Name sei Gantenbein'* (Berne: Herbert Lang, 1969).

KURZ, PAUL KONRAD, '*Mein Name sei Gantenbein*', *Stimmen der Zeit* (1964-5), 57–61.

LUBICH, F. A., 'Todeserfahrung und Lebensentwurf in Max Frischs *Mein Name sei Gantenbein*', *Seminar*, 25 (1989), 147–66.

—— *Max Frisch, 'Stiller', 'Homo Faber' und 'Mein Name sei Gantenbein'* (Munich: Fink, 1990), 82–111.

LÜTHI, HANS JÜRG, *Max Frisch: 'Du sollst dir kein Bildnis machen'* (Munich: Francke, 1981), 76–88.

MANTHEY, JÜRGEN, 'Prosa des Bedenkens', *FH* 20 (1965), 279–82.

MARCHAND, WOLF R., 'Max Frisch, *Mein Name sei Gantenbein*', *ZDP* 87 (1968), 510–35 (repr. in Beckermann, *Über Max Frisch*, 205–34).

MAYER, HANS, 'Mögliche Ansichten über Herrn Gantenbein. Anmerkungen zu Max Frischs neuem Roman', *Die Zeit*, 18 September 1964 (repr. in Schmitz, *Über Max Frisch II*, 314–24).

MERRIFIELD, DORIS FULDA, 'Max Frischs *Mein Name sei Gantenbein*: Versuch einer Strukturanalyse', *MDU* 60 (1968), 155–66 (repr. in Schau, *Max Frisch. Beiträge zur Wirkungsgeschichte*, 162–71).

MILANOWSKA, HALINA, 'Der Erzählstandpunkt als Mittel zur Bestimmung des Erzählers im Roman *Stiller* von Max Frisch', *Studia Germanica Posnaniensia*, 1 (1971), 91–103.

PETERSEN, JÜRGEN H., 'Wirklichkeit, Möglichkeit und Fiktion in Max Frischs Roman *Mein Name sei Gantenbein*', in Knapp, *Max Frisch. Aspekte des Prosawerks*, 131–56.

—— *Max Frisch* (Stuttgart: Metzler, 1978), 140–50 (rev. edn. 1989, 130–40).

POSER, HANS, '*Mein Name sei Gantenbein* oder die Parabel von der ästhetischen Existenz', *Literatur für Leser* (1979), 74–9.

PROBST, GERHARD F., 'Three Levels of Image Making in Frisch's *Mein Name sei Gantenbein*', in Bodine and Probst, *Perspectives on Max Frisch*, 154–65.

PULHAM, MICHAEL, 'A Critical Study of Five Novels by Max Frisch' (unpublished doctoral thesis, University of Oxford, 1975), 219–97.

REICH-RANICKI, MARCEL, 'Plädoyer für Max Frisch. Zu dem Roman *Mein Name sei Gantenbein* und Hans Mayers Kritik', *Die Zeit*, 2 October 1964 (repr. in Reich-Ranicki, *Literatur der kleinen Schritte. Deutsche Schriftsteller heute* (Munich: Piper, 1967), 79–89; and in Schmitz, *Über Max Frisch II*, 325–34).

RESCHKE, CLAUS, *Life as a Man: Contemporary Male–Female Relationships in the Novels of Max Frisch* (New York: Peter Lang, 1990), 191–266.

SCHAU, ALBRECHT (ed.), *Max Frisch. Beiträge zur Wirkungsgeschichte* (Freiburg im Breisgau: Becksmann, 1971).

SCHMITZ, WALTER (ed.), *Über Max Frisch II* (Frankfurt/Main: Suhrkamp, 1976).

—— *Max Frisch: Das Spätwerk (1962–1982)*. *Eine Einführung* (Tübingen: Francke, 1985), 31–66.

SCHOBER, OTTO, 'Max Frisch—*Mein Name sei Gantenbein*. Spiegelungen des Rollenverhaltens im Roman', in Manfred Brauneck (ed.), *Der deutsche Roman im 20. Jahrhundert: Analysen und Materialien zur Theorie und Soziologie des Romans*, 2 vols. (Bamberg: Buchners, 1976), II. 74–96.

SCHOBER, WOLFGANG HEINZ, *Erzähltechniken in Romanen: Eine Untersuchung erzähltheoretischer Probleme in zeitgenössischen deutschen Romanen* (Wiesbaden: Athenaion, 1975), 99–102.

SCHUCHMANN, MANFRED, *Der Autor als Zeitgenosse*. *Gesellschaftliche Aspekte in Max Frischs Werk* (Frankfurt/Main: Peter Lang, 1979), 217–26.

STAUFFACHER, WERNER, 'Langage et mystère. A propos des derniers romans de Max Frisch', *EG* 20 (1965), 331–45.

—— 'Gantenbein—une nouvelle forme romanesque? (Réponse à M. Cauvin)', *EG* 22 (1967), 592–3 (repr. in Schau, *Max Frisch. Beiträge zur Wirkungsgeschichte*, 119–20).

TOMAN, LORE, 'Bachmanns *Malina* und Frischs *Gantenbein*: zwei Seiten des gleichen Lebens', *LK* 12 (1977), 274–8.

ULLRICH, GISELA, *Identität und Rolle: Probleme des Erzählens bei Johnson, Walser, Frisch und Fichte* (Stuttgart: Klett, 1977), 51–63.

VORMWEG, HEINRICH, 'Max Frisch oder Alles wie nicht geschehen', in Vormweg, *Die Wörter und die Welt*. *Über neue Literatur* (Neuwied and Berlin: Luchterhand, 1968), 80–6.

WEISSTEIN, ULRICH, *Max Frisch*, Twayne's World Authors Series, 21 (New York: Twayne, 1967), 78–89.

WHITE, ALFRED D., 'Reality and Imagination in *Mein Name sei Gantenbein*', *OGS* 18–19 (1989–90), 150–64.

WOLF, CHRISTA, 'Max Frisch, beim Wiederlesen oder: Vom Schreiben in Ich-Form', in Arnold, *Max Frisch*, 7–12 (repr. in Wolf, *Die Dimension des Autors. Essays und Aufsätze. Reden und Gespräche 1959–1985* (Darmstadt and Neuwied: Luchterhand, 1987), 166–74; and in Wolf, *Lesen und Schreiben. Neue Sammlung. Essays, Aufsätze, Reden* (Darmstadt and Neuwied: Luchterhand, 1980), 200–8; and in Schmitz, *Über Max Frisch II*, 11–18).

FURTHER BIBLIOGRAPHICAL INFORMATION

RAMER, ULRICH, *Max Frisch. Gesamtbibliografie* (Frankfurt/Main: Fischer, 1993).

4. CHRISTA WOLF: *NACHDENKEN ÜBER CHRISTA T.*

PRIMARY SOURCES

Literary Works

Der geteilte Himmel (Halle/Saale: Mitteldeutscher Verlag, 1963).
Nachdenken über Christa T. (Halle/Saale: Mitteldeutscher Verlag, 1968) (repr. Sammlung Luchterhand, 31 (Darmstadt: Luchterhand, 1971)). English translation: *The Quest for Christa T.*, trans. Christopher Middleton (London: Hutchinson, 1971; repr. London: Virago, 1982).
Unter den Linden. Drei unwahrscheinliche Geschichten (Berlin and Weimar: Aufbau, 1974).
Kindheitsmuster (Darmstadt and Neuwied: Luchterhand, 1977).
Kein Ort. Nirgends (Darmstadt and Neuwied: Luchterhand, 1979).
Kassandra (Darmstadt and Neuwied: Luchterhand, 1983).
Störfall. Nachrichten eines Tages (Darmstadt and Neuwied: Luchterhand, 1987).
Was bleibt (Berlin and Weimar: Aufbau, 1990).
Medea. Stimmen (Darmstadt and Neuwied: Luchterhand, 1996).

Essays and Letters

Lesen und Schreiben. Aufsätze und Prosastücke (Darmstadt and Neuwied: Luchterhand, 1972), rev. edn. *Lesen und Schreiben. Neue Sammlung. Essays, Aufsätze, Reden* (Darmstadt and Neuwied: Luchterhand, 1980).
Die Dimension des Autors. Essays und Aufsätze, Reden und Gespräche 1959–1985 (Berlin: Aufbau, 1986), repr. Darmstadt and Neuwied: Luchterhand, 1987.
Reimann, Brigitte and Christa Wolf, *Sei gegrüßt und lebe. Eine Freundschaft in Briefen. 1964–1973*, ed. Angela Drescher (Berlin and Weimar: Aufbau, 1993).

Interviews

'Auf mir bestehen. Christa Wolf im Gespräch mit Günter Gaus', *NDL* 41/5 (May 1993), 20–40.
Hörnigk, Therese, 'Gespräch mit Christa Wolf', in Hörnigk, *Christa Wolf*, 7–41.
Kaufmann, Hans, 'Gespräch mit Christa Wolf', *WB* 20/6 (1974), 90–112 (extracts repr. in Behn, *Wirkungsgeschichte von Christa Wolfs 'Nachdenken über Christa T.'*, 126–30; repr. as 'Die Dimension des Autors. Gespräch mit Hans Kaufmann', in Wolf, *Lesen und Schreiben. Neue Sammlung*, 68–99; and as 'Subjektive Authentizität. Gespräch mit Hans Kaufmann' in Wolf, *Die Dimension des Autors*, 773–805).

SECONDARY LITERATURE

ARNOLD, HEINZ LUDWIG (ed.), *Christa Wolf,* Text und Kritik, 46 (Munich: Edition Text und Kritik, 1975) (3rd rev. edn. Munich: Edition Text und Kritik, 1985).

BEHN, MANFRED (ed.), *Wirkungsgeschichte von Christa Wolfs 'Nachdenken über Christa T.'* (Königstein/Ts.: Athenäum, 1978).

BOA, ELIZABETH, 'Unnatural Causes: Modes of Death in Christa Wolf's *Nachdenken über Christa T.* and Ingeborg Bachmann's *Malina*', in Arthur Williams, Stuart Parkes, and Roland Smith (eds.), *German Literature at a Time of Change 1989–1990: German Unity and German Identity in Literary Perspective* (Berne: Peter Lang, 1991), 145–54.

BRETT, DORIS, '"Tacit Knowledge" in *Der geteilte Himmel* and *Nachdenken über Christa T.*', *CG* 17 (1984), 257–64.

BUEHLER, GEORGE, *The Death of Socialist Realism in the Novels of Christa Wolf* (Frankfurt/Main: Peter Lang, 1984), 132–52.

CICORA, MARY A., 'Language, Identity and the Woman in *Nachdenken über Christa T.*: A Post-Structuralist Approach', *GR* 57 (1982), 16–22.

DRESCHER, ANGELA (ed.), *Dokumentation zu Christa Wolf 'Nachdenken über Christa T.'* (Hamburg: Luchterhand, 1991).

DURZAK, MANFRED, 'Selbstverwirklichung und Selbsterkundung: *Nachdenken über Christa T.*', in Durzak, *Der deutsche Roman der Gegenwart* (Stuttgart: Kohlhammer, 1971), 263–73.

EINHORN, BARBARA, *Der Roman in der DDR 1949–1969: Die Gestaltung des Verhältnisses von Individuum und Gesellschaft. Eine Analyse der Erzählstruktur* (Kronberg/Ts.: Scriptor, 1978), 452–78.

ERZERGAILIS, INTA, *Woman Writers. The Divided Self. Analysis of Novels by Christa Wolf, Ingeborg Bachmann, Doris Lessing and others* (Bonn: Bouvier, 1982).

GREIF, HANS-JÜRGEN, *Christa Wolf. 'Wie sind wir so geworden, wie wir heute sind?'* (Berne: Peter Lang, 1978), 61–78.

GREINER, BERNHARD, '"Sentimentaler Stoff und fantastische Form": Zur Erneuerung frühromantischer Tradition im Roman der DDR. (Christa Wolf, Fritz Rudolf Fries, Johannes Bobrowski)', *ABNG* 11–12 (1981), 249–328 (esp. 260–74).

—— 'Die Schwierigkeit, "ich" zu sagen: Christa Wolfs psychologische Orientierung des Erzählens', *DVLG* 55 (1981), 323–42.

HAASE, HORST, 'Nachdenken über ein Buch', *NDL* 17/4 (April 1969), 174–85 (extracts repr. in Behn, *Wirkungsgeschichte von Christa Wolfs 'Nachdenken über Christa T.'*, 40–51; and in Drescher, *Dokumentation zu Christa Wolf 'Nachdenken über Christa T.'*, 79–85).

HILZINGER, SONJA, *Kassandra. Über Christa Wolf* (Frankfurt/Main: Haag und Herchen, 1982), 30–7.

—— *Christa Wolf* (Stuttgart: Metzler, 1986), 32–47.

HÖRNIGK, THERESE, 'Ein Buch des Erinnerns, das zum Nachdenken anregte. Christa Wolfs *Nachdenken über Christa T.*', in Inge Münz-Koenen (ed.), *Werke und Wirkungen: DDR-Literatur in der Diskussion* (Leipzig: Reclam, 1987), 168–213.

—— *Christa Wolf* (Göttingen: Steidl, 1989), 115–32.

JACKMANN, GRAHAM, '"Wann, wenn nicht jetzt?": Conceptions of Time and History in Christa Wolf's *Was bleibt* and *Nachdenken über Christa T.*', *GLL* 45 (1992), 358–75.

JURGENSEN, MANFRED, '*Nachdenken über Christa T.*', in Jurgensen, *Deutsche Frauenautoren der Gegenwart: Bachmann, Reinig, Wolf, Wohmann, Struck, Leutenegger, Schwaiger* (Berne: Francke, 1983), 88–95.

KÄHLER, HERMANN, 'Christa Wolfs Elegie', *SF* 21 (1969), 251–61 (extracts repr. in Behn, *Wirkungsgeschichte von Christa Wolfs 'Nachdenken über Christa T.*', 29–37; and in Drescher, *Dokumentation zu Christa Wolf 'Nachdenken über Christa T.*', 67–71).

KAISER, HERBERT, 'Christa Wolf: *Nachdenken über Christa T.*. Erzählen als Modell geschichtlichen Interpretierens', *Literatur für Leser*, 3 (1978), 200–13.

KÖHN, LOTHAR, 'Christa Wolf: *Nachdenken über Christa T.* (1963)', in Paul Michael Lützeler (ed.), *Deutsche Romane des 20. Jahrhunderts. Neue Interpretationen* (Königstein/Ts: Athenäum, 1983), 340–55.

KUHN, ANNA K., 'Ich-Erweiterung und Ich-Aufspaltung. Überlegungen zu Max Frischs *Mein Name sei Gantenbein* und Christa Wolfs *Nachdenken über Christa T.*', in Albrecht Schöne (ed.), *Kontroversen, alte und neue. Akten des VII. internationalen Germanisten-Kongresses. Göttingen 1985*, 11 vols. (Tübingen: Niemeyer, 1986), VI: *Frauensprache-Frauenliteratur?/ Für und Wider einer Psychoanalyse literarischer Werke.* ed. Inge Stephan and Carl Pietzcker, 87–91.

—— *Christa Wolf's Utopian Vision: From Marxism to Feminism* (Cambridge: Cambridge University Press, 1988).

LEWIS, ALISON, '"Foiling the Censor": Reading and Transference as Feminist Strategies in the Works of Christa Wolf, Irmtraud Morgner, and Christa Moog', *German Quarterly*, 66 (1993), 372–86.

LOVE, MYRA, 'Christa Wolf and Feminism: Breaking the Patriarchal Connection', *NGC* 6/16 (1979), 31–53.

MAUSER, WOLFRAM, 'Subjektivität—Chance oder Verirrung? Zu Christa Wolfs *Nachdenken über Christa T.*', *Sprachkunst*, 12 (1981), 171–85.

—— (ed.), *Erinnerte Zukunft: 11 Studien zum Werk Christa Wolfs* (Würzburg: Königshausen & Neumann, 1985).

—— and HELMTRUD MAUSER, *Christa Wolf: 'Nachdenken über Christa T.'* (Munich: Fink, 1987).

MAYER, HANS, 'Christa Wolf. *Nachdenken über Christa T.*', *NR* 81 (1970), 180–6 (extracts repr. in Behn, *Wirkungsgeschichte von Christa Wolfs 'Nachdenken über Christa T.*', 89–95).

MICHAELIS, ROLF, 'Der doppelte Himmel. Christa Wolfs zweites Buch *Nach-denken über Christa T.* Der umstrittene Roman aus der DDR', *FAZ*, 28 May 1969 (extracts repr. in Behn, *Wirkungsgeschichte von Christa Wolfs 'Nachdenken über Christa T.'*, 65–9; and in Drescher, *Dokumentation zu Christa Wolf 'Nachdenken über Christa T.'*, 108–11).

MOHR, HEINRICH, 'Produktive Sehnsucht: Struktur, Thematik und politische Relevanz von Christa Wolfs *Nachdenken über Christa T.'*, *Basis*, 2 (1971), 191–233 (extracts repr. in Behn, *Wirkungsgeschichte von Christa Wolfs 'Nachdenken über Christa T.'*, 102–20; repr. in full in Manfred Brauneck (ed.), *Der deutsche Roman im 20. Jahrhundert. Analysen und Materialien zur Theorie und Soziologie des Romans*, 2 vols. (Bamberg: Buchners, 1976), II. 145–64).

NOLTE, JOST, 'Die schmerzhaften Erfahrungen der Christa T.', in Nolte, *Grenzgänge. Berichte über Literatur* (Vienna: Europaverlag, 1972), 176–81.

PAUL, GEORGINA, 'The Return of the Political Unconscious: Re-reading Christa Wolf's *Nachdenken über Christa T.'*, paper delivered to the Conference of University Teachers of German, September 1996.

RADDATZ, FRITZ J., 'Mein Name sei Tonio K.', *Der Spiegel*, 2 June 1969 (extracts repr. in Behn, *Wirkungsgeschichte von Christa Wolfs 'Nachdenken über Christa T.'*, 73–6; and in Drescher, *Dokumentation zu Christa Wolf 'Nachdenken über Christa T.'*, 121–3).

REICH-RANICKI, MARCEL, 'Christa Wolfs unruhige Elegie', *Die Zeit*, 23 May 1969 (repr. in Reich-Ranicki, *Zur Literatur der DDR* (Munich: Piper, 1974), 114–21; and in a rev. edn.: Reich-Ranicki, *Ohne Rabatt. Über Literatur aus der DDR* (Stuttgart: Deutsche Verlags-Anstalt, 1991), 174–81; extracts repr. in Behn, *Wirkungsgeschichte von Christa Wolfs 'Nach-denken über Christa T.'*, 59–64; and in Drescher, *Dokumentation zu Christa Wolf 'Nachdenken über Christa T.'*, 104–7).

RENOLDNER, KLEMENS, *Utopie und Geschichtsbewußtsein: Versuche zur Poetik Christa Wolfs* (Stuttgart: Akademischer Verlag, 1981), 83–104.

SACHS, HEINZ, 'Verleger sein heißt ideologisch kämpfen', *Neues Deutschland*, 14 May 1969 (extracts repr. in Behn, *Wirkungsgeschichte von Christa Wolfs 'Nachdenken über Christa T.'*, 54–6; and in Drescher, *Dokumentation zu Christa Wolf 'Nachdenken über Christa T.'*, 99–101).

SANDER, VOLKMAR, 'Erinnerungen an die Zukunft: Christa Wolfs *Nachdenken über Christa T.'*, in Ralph Ley *et al.* (eds.), *Perspectives and Personalities: Studies in Modern German Literature. Honoring Claude Hill* (Heidelberg: Winter, 1978), 320–9.

SAUER, KLAUS (ed.), *Christa Wolf. Materialienbuch* (Darmstadt: Luchterhand, 1979; rev. edn. 1983).

SCHMITZ-BURGARD, SYLVIA, 'Psychoanalyse eines Mythos. *Nachdenken über Christa T.'*, *MDU* 79 (1987), 463–77.

SCHULER, BIRGITTA, *Phantastische Authentizität. Wirklichkeit im Werk Christa Wolfs* (Frankfurt/Main: Peter Lang, 1988), 85–119.

SCHUSTER, KARL, 'Christa Wolf: *Nachdenken über Christa T.*. Rezeptionsprobleme mit einem DDR-Roman', in Jakob Lehmann (ed.), *Deutsche Romane von Grimmelshausen bis Walser. Interpretationen für den Literaturunterricht* (Königstein/Ts.: Scriptor, 1982), 469–87.

SEVIN, DIETER, 'The Plea for Artistic Freedom in Christa Wolf's "Lesen und Schreiben" and *Nachdenken über Christa T.*: Essay and Fiction as Mutually Supportive Genre Forms', in Margy Gerber *et al.* (eds.), *Studies in GDR Culture and Society II: Proceedings of the 7th International Symposium on the German Democratic Republic* (Washington: University Press of America, 1982), 45–58.

—— '*Der geteilte Himmel*', '*Nachdenken über Christa T.*' (Munich: Oldenbourg, 1982).

SMITH, COLIN E., *Tradition, Art and Society: Christa Wolf's Prose* (Essen: Verlag Die Blaue Eule, 1987), 63–125.

STEPHAN, ALEXANDER, *Christa Wolf*, Autorenbücher, 4 (Munich: Beck, 1976), 59–92 (3rd rev. edn. Munich: Beck, 1987).

—— *Christa Wolf*, Forschungsberichte zur DDR-Literatur, 1 (Amsterdam: Rodopi, 1980), 38–47.

SWIATLOWSKI, ZBIGNIEW, '*Nachdenken über Christa T.* von Christa Wolf. Versuch einer literaturgeschichtlichen Standortbestimmung', *Germanica Wratislaviensia*, 32 (1978), 13–26.

TATE, DENNIS, *The East German Novel: Identity, Community, Continuity* (Bath: Bath University Press, 1984), 140–76.

THOMASSEN, CHRISTA, *Der lange Weg zu uns selbst. Christa Wolfs Roman 'Nachdenken über Christa T.' als Erfahrungs- und Handlungsmuster* (Kronberg/Ts: Scriptor, 1977).

VON SALISCH, MARION, *Zwischen Selbstaufgabe und Selbstverwirklichung. Zum Problem der Persönlichkeitsstruktur im Werk Christa Wolfs* (Stuttgart: Klett, 1975), 33–59.

WELLAUER, CAROLYN ANN, 'The Postwar German Novel of Speculations' (unpublished doctoral diss., University of Wisconsin, 1976), 218–70.

WERTH, WOLFGANG, 'Nachricht aus einem stillen Deutschland', *Der Monat*, 21 (1969), 90–4.

WIEGENSTEIN, ROLAND, 'Verweigerung der Zustimmung', *Merkur*, 23 (1969), 779–82 (extracts repr. in Behn, *Wirkungsgeschichte von Christa Wolfs 'Nachdenken über Christa T.*', 77–80).

ZEHM, Günter, 'Nachdenken über Christa W.', *Die Welt*, 27 March 1969 (extracts repr. in Behn, *Wirkungsgeschichte von Christa Wolfs 'Nachdenken über Christa T.*', 38–9; and in Drescher, *Dokumentation zu Christa Wolf 'Nachdenken über Christa T.*', 75–7).

FURTHER BIBLIOGRAPHICAL INFORMATION

BEHN, *Wirkungsgeschichte von Christa Wolfs 'Nachdenken über Christa T.'*, 187–91. (NB: this bibliography does not contain references to those reviews etc. which Behn has reprinted in his *Wirkungsgeschichte*, and for which references can be found in the text itself.)

GEIST, ROSEMARIE, and MARITTA ROST, 'Auswahlbibliographie', in Angela Drescher (ed.), *Christa Wolf. Ein Arbeitsbuch: Studien—Dokumente—Bibliographie* (Berlin and Weimar: Aufbau, 1989), 461–587, esp. 521–32 (repr. Frankfurt/Main: Luchterhand, 1990, 417–541, esp. 475–86).

HILZINGER, *Christa Wolf*, 148–87, esp. 161–4.

STEPHAN, ALEXANDER, in Arnold, *Christa Wolf*, 3rd rev. edn., 113–33, esp. 125–7.

—— 'Schrifttumsverzeichnis' in Stephan, *Christa Wolf* (1980), 83–139, esp. 119–26.

5. JUREK BECKER: *JAKOB DER LÜGNER*

PRIMARY SOURCES

Literary Works

Jakob der Lügner (Berlin, GDR: Aufbau, 1969); repr. Bibliothek Suhrkamp, 510 (Frankfurt/Main: Suhrkamp, 1976). English translation: *Jacob the Liar*, trans. Melvin Kornfeld (New York: Harcourt Brace Jovanovich, 1975).

Irreführung der Behörden (Rostock: Hinstorff, 1973).

Der Boxer (Rostock: Hinstorff, 1976).

Schlaflose Tage (Frankfurt/Main: Suhrkamp, 1978).

Aller Welt Freund (Frankfurt/Main: Suhrkamp, 1982).

Bronsteins Kinder (Frankfurt/Main: Suhrkamp, 1986).

Amanda herzlos (Frankfurt/Main: Suhrkamp, 1992).

Essays and Lectures

'Wäre ich hinterher klüger? Mein Judentum', *FAZ*, 13 May 1978, supplement: *Bilder und Zeiten*, 4 (repr. as 'Mein Judentum' in Heidelberger-Leonard, *Jurek Becker*, 15–24).

Warnung vor dem Schriftsteller. Drei Vorlesungen in Frankfurt (Frankfurt/Main: Suhrkamp, 1990).

Interviews

'Resistance in *Jakob der Lügner*', *Seminar*, 19 (1983), 269–73.

'Answering Questions about *Jakob der Lügner*', *Seminar*, 19 (1983), 288–92.

'"Das Vorstellbare gefällt mir immer besser als das Bekannte": Gespräch mit Marianna Birnbaum (1988)', in Heidelberger-Leonard, *Jurek Becker*, 89–107.

ARNOLD, HEINZ LUDWIG, 'Gespräch mit Jurek Becker', in Arnold, *Jurek Becker*, 4–14.

GEISLER, WOLFGANG, and PETER E. KALB, 'Ich will Ihnen dazu eine kleine Geschichte erzählen', in Peter E. Kalb and Wolfgang Geisler (eds.), *Einmischung: Schriftsteller über Schule, Gesellschaft, Literatur* (Weinheim and Basel: Beltz, 1983), 56–66.

SECONDARY LITERATURE

ARNOLD, HEINZ LUDWIG (ed.), *Jurek Becker*, Text und Kritik, 116 (Munich: Edition Text und Kritik, 1992).

BAUM, GREGORY, '*Jakob der Lügner* in Christian Perspective', *Seminar*, 19 (1983), 285–8.

BROWN, RUSSELL E., 'Radios and Trees: A Note to Jurek Beckers Ghetto Fiction', *Germanic Notes*, 19 (1988), 22–4.

BUSSMANN, RUDOLF, 'Die Ohnmacht der Betroffenen', *Drehpunkt*, 4 (1972), 39–41.

DORMAN, MICHAEL, 'Deceit and Self-Deception: An Introduction to the Works of Jurek Becker', *ML* 61 (1980), 28–37 (esp. 28–30).

HAGE, VOLKER, 'Die Wahrheit über Jakob Heym: Über Meinungen, Lügen und das schwierige Geschäft des Erzählens. Eine Lobrede auf den Schriftsteller Jurek Becker', *Die Zeit*, 15 March 1991, 73 (repr. in Heidelberger-Leonard, *Jurek Becker*, 125–32).

HALVERSEN, RACHEL J., 'Jurek Becker's *Jakob der Lügner*: Narrative Strategies of a Witness' Witness', *MDU* 85 (1993), 453–63.

HEIDELBERGER-LEONARD, IRENE, 'Schreiben im Schatten der Shoah. Überlegungen zu Jurek Beckers *Jakob der Lügner*, *Der Boxer* und *Bronsteins Kinder*', in Arnold, *Jurek Becker*, 19–29 (esp. 19–23).

—— (ed.), *Jurek Becker* (Frankfurt/Main: Suhrkamp, 1992).

HERBURGER, GÜNTER, 'Ein Radio im Getto', *Der Spiegel*, 28 September 1970, 209.

JOHNSON, SUSAN M., *The Works of Jurek Becker: A Thematic Analysis* (New York: Peter Lang, 1988).

JOHO, WOLFGANG, 'Lüge aus Barmherzigkeit', *NDL* 17/12 (December 1969), 151–3.

KANE, MARTIN, 'Tales and the Telling: The Novels of Jurek Becker', in Kane (ed.), *Socialism and the Literary Imagination: Essays on East German Writers* (New York and Oxford: Berg, 1991), 163–78

KARNICK, MANFRED, 'Die Geschichte von Jakob und Jakobs Geschichten', in Heidelberger-Leonard, *Jurek Becker*, 207–21.

KRUMBHOLZ, MARTIN, 'Standorte, Standpunkte: Erzählerpositionen in den Romanen Jurek Beckers', in Arnold, *Jurek Becker*, 44–50.

LAUCKNER, NANCY A., 'The Treatment of Holocaust Themes in GDR Fiction from the Late 1960s to the Mid-1970s: A Survey', in Margy Gerber *et al.* (eds.), *Studies in GDR Culture and Society: Proceedings of the Sixth International Symposium on the German Democratic Republic* (Washington: University Press of America, 1981), 141–54.

LESLEY, ARTHUR M., 'Jacob as Liar in Jurek Becker's *Jakob der Lügner*', *Seminar*, 19 (1983), 273–9.

LUKENS, NANCY, 'Schelm im Ghetto: Jurek Beckers Roman *Jakob der Lügner*', *ABNG* 20 (1985–6), 199–218.

MICHAELIS, ROLF, 'Der andere Hiob. *Jakob der Lügner*. Der moralische Roman aus den mörderischen Jahren von dem Ost-Berliner Jurek Becker', *FAZ*, 30 March 1971, supplement: *Literaturblatt*, 2.

NÄGELE, RAINER, 'Discourses about Absent Trees: Fiction, Lie, and Reality in Jurek Becker's *Jakob der Lügner*', *Seminar*, 19 (1983), 280–4.

PRÉVOST, CLAUDE, 'Vérité du mensonge et mensonge de la vérité: sur deux romans de Jurek Becker', in Prévost, *Littératures du dépaysement* (Paris: Les éditeurs français réunies, 1979), 94–103.

RADDATZ, FRITZ, 'Eine neue sozialistische Literatur entsteht. Jurek Becker, Brigitte Reimann, Christa Wolf, Manfred Bieler, Fritz Rudolf Fries', in Raddatz, *Traditionen und Tendenzen. Materialien zur Literatur der DDR* (Frankfurt/Main: Suhrkamp, 1972), 372–400 (esp. 372–4).

REICH-RANICKI, MARCEL, 'Das Prinzip Radio', *Die Zeit*, 20 November 1970, 36 (repr. as 'Roman vom Getto: Jurek Becker, *Jakob der Lügner*', in Reich-Ranicki, *Zur Literatur der DDR* (Munich: Piper, 1974), 145–8; and in a rev. edn.: Reich-Ranicki, *Ohne Rabatt. Über Literatur aus der DDR* (Stuttgart: Deutsche Verlags-Anstalt, 1991), 251–4; and in Heidelberger Leonard, *Jurek Becker*, 133–6).

SCHMIEDT, HELMUT, 'Das unterhaltsame Ghetto. Die Dimension des Raumes in Jurek Beckers *Jakob der Lügner*', in Arnold, *Jurek Becker*, 19–29.

WANIEK, ERDMANN, '"Aber warum verbieten sie uns die Bäume?" Frage und Antwort in Beckers *Jakob der Lügner*', *Seminar*, 29 (1993), 279–93.

WETZEL, HEINZ, 'Four Questions about Jurek Becker's *Jakob der Lügner*: an Introduction', *Seminar*, 19 (1983), 265–9.

—— '"Unvergleichlich gelungener"—aber "einfach zu schön"? Zur ethischen und ästhetischen Motivation des Erzählens in Jurek Beckers Roman *Jakob der Lügner*', in Albrecht Schöne (ed.), *Kontroversen, alte und neue. Akten des VII. Internationalen Germanisten-Kongresses, Göttingen, 1985*, 11 vols. (Tübingen: Niemeyer, 1986), VII. 107–14.

—— 'Fiktive und authentische Nachrichten in Jurek Beckers *Jakob der Lügner* und *Aller Welt Freund*', in Roland Jost and Hansgeorg Schmidt-

Bergmann (eds.), *Im Dialog mit der Moderne. Zur deutschsprachigen Literatur von der Gründerzeit bis zur Gegenwart* (Frankfurt/Main: Athenäum, 1986), 439–51.

—— 'Holocaust und Literatur. Die Perspektive Jurek Beckers', *CG* 21 (1988), 70–6.

WHITE, I. A., and J. J., 'Wahrheit und Lüge in Jurek Beckers Roman *Jakob der Lügner*', *ABNG* 7 (1978), 207–31.

WIECZOREK, JOHN P., 'Irreführung durch Erzählperspektive?: The East German Novels of Jurek Becker', *MLR* 85 (1990), 640–52.

ZIMMERMANN, WERNER, 'Jurek Becker: *Jakob der Lügner*', in Zimmermann, *Deutsche Prosadichtungen des 20. Jahrhunderts: Interpretationen*, 3 vols. (Düsseldorf: Schwann, 1966–88), III (1988), 10–39. NB: the first 2 volumes were published under the title *Deutsche Prosadichtungen unseres Jahrhunderts*.

FURTHER BIBLIOGRAPHICAL INFORMATION

RIEDEL, NICOLAI, 'Internationale Jurek-Becker-Bibliographie (1969–1992)', in Heidelberger-Leonard, *Jurek Becker*, 349–80 (esp. 363–5). A slightly abridged version of Riedel's bibliography appears in Arnold, *Jurek Becker*, 87–97 (esp. 91–2).

6. GÜNTER GRASS: *ÖRTLICH BETÄUBT*

PRIMARY SOURCES

Complete Works

Werkausgabe in zehn Bänden, ed. Volker Neuhaus (Darmstadt and Neuwied: Luchterhand, 1987), hereafter abbreviated to *Werkausgabe*. This edition contains all works up to and including *Die Rättin*.

Literary Works

Die Blechtrommel (Darmstadt and Neuwied: Luchterhand, 1959).

Katz und Maus (Darmstadt and Neuwied: Luchterhand, 1961).

Hundejahre (Darmstadt and Neuwied: Luchterhand, 1963).

'Zorn Ärger Wut', in Günter Grass, *Ausgefragt* (Neuwied and Berlin, Luchterhand, 1967), 57–68 (repr. in *Werkausgabe*, I. 182–90).

örtlich betäubt (Darmstadt and Neuwied: Luchterhand, 1969) (repr. in *Werkausgabe*, IV. 6–264). English translation: *Local Anaesthetic*, trans. Ralph Manheim (New York: Harcourt, Brace and World, 1970; repr. Harmondsworth: Penguin, 1973).

Davor. Ein Stück in 13 Szenen, *Theater heute* (April 1969), 41–54 (repr. in *Werkausgabe*, VIII. 479–555). Premièred at the Schiller-Theater in

Berlin in February 1969. English translation: *Max: A Play*, trans. A. Leslie Willson and Ralph Manheim (New York: Harcourt Brace Jovanovich, 1972).

Aus dem Tagebuch einer Schnecke (Darmstadt and Neuwied: Luchterhand, 1972).

Der Butt (Darmstadt and Neuwied: Luchterhand, 1977).

Das Treffen in Telgte. Eine Erzählung und dreiundvierzig Gedichte aus dem Barock (Darmstadt and Neuwied: Luchterhand, 1979).

Kopfgeburten oder Die Deutschen sterben aus (Darmstadt and Neuwied: Luchterhand, 1980).

Die Rättin (Darmstadt and Neuwied: Luchterhand, 1986).

Unkenrufe (Göttingen: Steidl, 1992).

Ein weites Feld (Göttingen: Steidl, 1996).

Essays

Über das Selbstverständliche. Politische Schriften (Neuwied and Berlin: Luchterhand, 1968).

Über meinen Lehrer Döblin und andere Vorträge (Berlin, FRG: Literarisches Colloquium, 1968). Of particular use was: 'Über meinen Lehrer Döblin', 7–26 (first pub. in *Akzente*, 14 (1967), 290–309; repr. in *Werkausgabe*, IX. 236–55).

'Zu örtlich betäubt', ad lectores, 9 (1969), 6 (repr. in *Werkausgabe*, IX. 410).

ARNOLD, HEINZ LUDWIG, and FRANZ JOSEF GÖRTZ (eds.), *Günter Grass: Dokumente zur politischen Wirkung* (Munich: Boorberg (Edition Text und Kritik), 1971). This volume contains a selection of Grass's political writings from 1961 to 1971, and also documents their reception.

Aufsätze zur Literatur (Neuwied: Luchterhand, 1980).

Interviews

ARNOLD, HEINZ LUDWIG, 'Gespräche mit Günter Grass', in Arnold, *Günter Grass* (1969), 1–39.

—— 'Gespräch mit Günter Grass', in Arnold, *Gespräche mit Schriftstellern. Max Frisch, Günter Grass, Wolfgang Koeppen, Max von der Grün, Günter Wallraff* (Munich: Beck, 1975), 74–108.

BUCERIUS, GERD, 'Wogegen sie kämpfen, das wissen sie. Impulse und Irrtümer bei den jungen Revolutionären in Berlin', *Die Zeit*, 15 March 1968 (repr. in Arnold and Görtz, *Günter Grass: Dokumente zur politischen Wirkung*, 100–4).

CEPL-KAUFMANN, GERTRUDE, 'Gespräch mit Günter Grass', in Cepl-Kaufmann, *Günter Grass*, 295–305.

KLUNKER, HEINZ, 'Ich und meine Rollen. Wirklichkeit und Roman, Literatur und Politik—ein Gespräch', *Deutsches Allgemeines Sonntagsblatt*, 12 October 1969 (repr. in *Werkausgabe*, X. 81–7).

RISCHBIETER, HENNING, 'Gespräch mit Günter Grass', *Theater heute* (April

1969), 30–4 (repr. as 'Die Krise des Berufes, der sich Theaterkritik nennt' in *Werkausgabe*, X. 63–73).

Schäble, Günter, 'Die Ideologien haben versagt. Interview der Stuttgarter Zeitung mit Günter Grass', *Stuttgarter Zeitung*, 18 February 1969 (repr. in *Werkausgabe*, X. 59–62).

SECONDARY LITERATURE

Arnold, Heinz Ludwig, 'Die intellektuelle Betäubung des Günter Grass. Zu seinem Roman *örtlich betäubt*', in Arnold, *Günter Grass*, Text und Kritik, 4/4a (Munich: Edition Text und Kritik, 1969), 72–6.

—— *Günter Grass*, Text und Kritik, 1/1a, 5th edn. (Munich: Edition Text und Kritik, 1978).

Brode, Hanspeter, 'Von Danzig zur Bundesrepublik. Grass' Bücher *örtlich betäubt* und *Aus dem Tagebuch einer Schnecke*', in Arnold, *Günter Grass* (1978), 74–87 (repr. in Brode, *Günter Grass*, Autorenbücher, 17 (Munich: Beck, 1979), 149–65).

Bruce, James C., 'The Motif of Failure and the Act of Narrating in Günter Grass's *örtlich betäubt*', *MFS* 17 (1971), 45–60 (repr. in Patrick O'Neill (ed.), *Critical Essays on Günter Grass* (Boston: Hall, 1987), 144–59).

Cepl-Kaufmann, Gertrude, *Günter Grass: Eine Analyse des Gesamtwerks unter dem Aspekt von Literatur und Politik* (Kronberg/Ts.: Scriptor, 1975).

Durzak, Manfred, 'Abschied von der Kleinbürgerwelt. Der neue Roman von Günter Grass', *Basis*, 1 (1970), 224–37 (repr. in Durzak, *Der deutsche Roman der Gegenwart* (Stuttgart: Kohlhammer, 1971), 150–2).

Enright, Dennis J., 'Always New Pains: Günter Grass's *Local Anaesthetic*', in Enright, *Man is an Onion: Reviews and Essays* (London: Chatto & Windus, 1972), 96–102 (first pub. *New York Review of Books*, 4 June 1970, 20–3).

Friedrichsmeyer, Erhard, 'The Dogmatism of Pain: *Local Anaesthetic*', *Dimension* (1970), special issue, 36–49 (repr. in A. Leslie Wilson (ed.), *A Günter Grass Symposium* (Austin, Tex., and London: University of Texas Press, 1971), 32–45).

Gerstenberg, Renate, 'Struktur und Integrationsmöglichkeiten von *örtlich betäubt*', in Gerstenberg, *Zur Erzähltechnik von Günter Grass* (Heidelberg: Winter, 1980), 87–119.

Glaser, Hermann, 'Wer ist örtlich betäubt?', *Tribüne*, 8 (1969), 3382–6.

Graves, Peter J., 'Günter Grass's *Die Blechtrommel* and *örtlich betäubt*: The Pain of Polarities', *FMLS* 9 (1973), 132–42.

Hollington, Michael, *Günter Grass: The Writer in a Pluralist Society* (London: Boyars, 1980), 122–35, 136–47.

Jurgensen, Manfred, *Über Günter Grass* (Berne: Francke, 1974), 172–8.

Kurz, Paul Konrad, 'Das verunsicherte Wappentier. Zu *Davor* und *örtlich betäubt* von Günter Grass', *Stimmen der Zeit* (1969), 374–89 (repr. in

KURZ, *Über moderne Literatur*, 3 vols. (Frankfurt/Main: Knecht, 1967–72), III (1972), 89–112).

MASON, ANN L., *The Skeptical Muse: A Study of Günter Grass' Conception of the Artist* (Berne: Herbert Lang, 1974), 86–128.

NEUHAUS, VOLKER, *Günter Grass*, Sammlung Metzler, 179 (Stuttgart: Metzler, 1979), 106–17 (a revised version of this chapter appears as '"Was sich ablagert". Nachwort zu *örtlich betäubt*' in *Werkausgabe*, IV. 572–81).

PAVER, CHLOE E. M., 'Lois Lane, Donald Duck and Joan Baez: Popular Culture and Protest Culture in Günter Grass's *örtlich betäubt*', *GLL* 50 (1997), 53–64.

PICKAR, GERTRUD BAUER, 'Günter Grass's *örtlich betäubt*: The Fiction of Fact and Fantasy', *GR* 52 (1977), 289–303.

—— 'Spielfreiheit und Selbstbefangenheit: Das Porträt eines Versagers. Zu Günter Grass' *örtlich betäubt*', in Manfred Durzak (ed.), *Zu Günter Grass. Geschichte auf dem poetischen Prüfstand* (Stuttgart: Klett, 1985), 96–114.

—— 'Starusch im Felde mit den Frauen. Zum Frauenbild in Grass' *örtlich betäubt*', *CG* 22 (1989), 260–82.

REDDICK, JOHN, 'Action and Impotence: Günter Grass's *örtlich betäubt*', *MLR* 67 (1972), 563–78.

—— 'Vom Pferdekopf zur Schnecke. Die Prosawerke von Günter Grass zwischen Beinahe-Verzweiflung und zweifelnder Hoffnung', in Heinz Ludwig Arnold and Theo Buck (eds.), *Positionen im deutschen Roman der sechziger Jahre* (Munich: Edition Text und Kritik, 1974), 39–54.

REICH-RANICKI, MARCEL, 'Eine Müdeheldensoße', *Die Zeit*, 29 August 1969 (repr. in Reich-Ranicki, *Lauter Verrisse* (Frankfurt/Main: Ullstein, 1973), 75–81; and in Reich-Ranicki, *Günter Grass. Aufsätze* (Zürich: Ammann, 1992), 91–101).

TABERNER, STUART, 'Feigning the Anaesthetization of Literary Inventiveness: Günter Grass's *örtlich betäubt* and the Public Responsibility of the Politically Engaged Author', *FMLS* 34 (1998), 69–81.

THOMAS, NOEL L., '*Davor* and *örtlich betäubt*: Evolution or Revolution', in Thomas, *The Narrative Works of Günter Grass: A Critical Interpretation* (Amsterdam, Phil.: Benjamins, 1982), 170–209.

WEBER, WERNER, 'Günter Grass, *örtlich betäubt*', *Der Monat*, 21 (1969), 94–8 (repr. in Weber, *Forderungen* (Zürich: Artemis, 1970), 179–85).

ZIOLKOWSKI, THEODORE, 'The Telltale Teeth: Psychodontia to Sociodontia', *PMLAA* 91 (1976), 9–22.

FURTHER BIBLIOGRAPHICAL INFORMATION

GÖRTZ, FRANZ JOSEF, 'Kommentierte Auswahl-Bibliographie', in Arnold, *Günter Grass* (1978), 175–99 (esp. 189–91).

O'NEILL, PATRICK, *Günter Grass. A Bibliography 1955–1975* (Toronto and Buffalo: University of Toronto Press, 1976), 66–70.

7. OTHER SOURCES

FOWLES, JOHN, *The French Lieutenant's Woman* (London: Cape, 1969) (repr. London: Pan, 1992).

GUTTRIDGE, PETER, 'The Long, Ambiguous Journey into the Ark: Peter Guttridge Talks to Thomas Keneally', *Independent*, 19 February 1994, 29.

GYSSLING, WALTER, *Anton Möller und seine Schule. Ein Beitrag zur Geschichte der niederländischen Renaissancemalerei* (Strasbourg: Heitz, 1917).

ULBRICHT, WALTER, *Zur Geschichte der deutschen Arbeiterbewegung: Aus Reden und Aufsätzen*, 10 vols. (Berlin, GDR: Dietz Verlag, 1953–71).

INDEX